Beloved Brother or Slave?

Cascade Library of Pauline Studies

The aim of the series is to advance Pauline theology by publishing monographs that make original scholarly proposals in conversation with existing scholarly debates, and which have the potential to shape future trajectories in research.

As both the title of the series and the list of categories above suggests, it is their contribution to critical discussion of Pauline theology that will be the hallmark of books published in CLPS. However, the nature and scope of Pauline theology is intended to be understood in a somewhat expansive manner, with an openness to the use of methodologies (e.g., social-scientific or post-colonial approaches) that have sometimes been regarded as standing in opposition to theological modes of Pauline interpretation. The criterion by which the suitability of a study for inclusion in the series will be assessed is its theological interest. This judgment will be made on the basis of the potential benefits of a particular approach or methodology for our understanding of Pauline theology rather than on the basis of conformity to preconceived ideas of what constitutes an appropriately theological approach to Pauline interpretation. As such, CLPS will also be open both to studies that are broadly confessional in tone and to those that are more critical of perspectives expressed in the Pauline texts.

Series Editors:
Stephen Chester, Wycliffe College, Toronto
Dorothea H. Bertschmann, Abbey House Palace Green, Durham University

Editorial Board:
John M. G. Barclay, Durham University
Lisa Marie Bowens, Princeton Theological Seminary
Andreas Dettwiler, Université de Genève
Susan Eastman, Duke Divinity School
Beverly Roberts Gaventa, Baylor University
Jonathan Linebaugh, Beeson Divinity School, Samford University
Grant Macaskill, Durham University
Matthew V. Novenson, Princeton Theological Seminary
Volker Rabens, Friedrich Schiller University Jena
Jennifer Strawbridge, University of Oxford

Beloved Brother or Slave?

Rethinking *Koinonia* in Paul's Letter to Philemon

Laurent Okitakatshi

CASCADE Books • Eugene, Oregon

BELOVED BROTHER OR SLAVE?
Rethinking *Koinonia* in Paul's Letter to Philemon

Cascade Library of Pauline Studies

Copyright © 2025 Laurent Okitakatshi. All rights reserved. Except for brief quotations in critical publications or reviews, no part of this book may be reproduced in any manner without prior written permission from the publisher. Write: Permissions, Wipf and Stock Publishers, 199 W. 8th Ave., Suite 3, Eugene, OR 97401.

Cascade Books
An Imprint of Wipf and Stock Publishers
199 W. 8th Ave., Suite 3
Eugene, OR 97401

www.wipfandstock.com

PAPERBACK ISBN: 979-8-3852-1783-0
HARDCOVER ISBN: 979-8-3852-1784-7
EBOOK ISBN: 979-8-3852-1785-4

Cataloguing-in-Publication data:

Names: Okitakatshi, Laurent, author. | Dettwiler, Andreas, foreword.

Title: Beloved brother or slave? : rethinking koinonia in Paul's letter to Philemon / Laurent Okitakatshi ; foreword by Andreas Dettwiler.

Description: Eugene, OR: Cascade Books, 2025. | Cascade Library of Pauline Studies. | Includes bibliographical references.

Identfifiers: ISBN 979-8-3852-1783-0 (paperback). | ISBN 979-8-3852-1784-7 (hardcover). | ISBN 979-8-3852-1785-4 (ebook).

Subjects: Bible. Philemon—Criticism, interpretation, etc. | Bible—New Testament—Criticism, Narrative. | Rome—History—Empire, 30 B.C.–284 A.D. | Lefebvre, Henri, 1901–1991. | Soja, Edward W. | Congo (Democratic Republic). | Christianity—Congo (Democratic Republic). | Congo (Democratic Republic)—History—1997–.

Classification: BS2715.52 O55 2025 (print). | BS2715.52 (epub).

VERSION NUMBER 08/20/25

Unless otherwise noted, Scripture quotations are taken from the New Revised Standard Version Bible © 1989 Division of Christian Education of the National Council of the Churches of Christ in the United States of America. Used by permission. All rights reserved.

Unless otherwise noted, translations of works orignally published in French are mine.

To Reyline Artiaga and Thomas Fleming

Without your love and support, I would have been a PhD dropout.

Thanks for being the giving hands of God's generosity!

Contents

Series Introduction | ix
Foreword by Andreas Dettwiler | xiii
Acknowledgments | xvii
Introduction | xix
Abbreviations | xxv

1. The Letter to Philemon and Its Multivocality | 1
2. Roman Slavery as a Complex Network of Relationships | 46
3. Narrative Dynamics and Spatial Negotiations in Philemon | 71
4. Live What You Believe: *Koinōnia* against the Evil of Dehumanization | 103
5. The Letter to Philemon and the Construction of a *Koinōnia:* Space in the DRC | 132

General Conclusion | 169
Bibliography | 173
Index | 185

Series Introduction

FOR THE APOSTLE PAUL, his own significance rested entirely on his commission as an apostle and his proclamation of the gospel of Christ ("by the grace of God, I am what I am," 1 Cor 15:10). For this reason, the heart of Pauline studies must lie in Paul's exposition of this gospel, which is to say his theology, as it comes to expression in his surviving letters. Here Paul expresses both his deepest convictions about the significance of Jesus Christ and his perspectives on their embodiment in the life of early church communities. The Cascade Library of Pauline Studies (CLPS) will focus squarely on engagement with the theological content of the Pauline letters, along with its impact on human thought and behavior throughout the centuries. The series aims to provide a home for research efforts that produce fresh insight into Paul's theology in its original contexts, its legacies and reception, and its significance today; efforts that therefore possess the potential to shape trajectories in future research.

To stake such a claim for the centrality of Pauline theology within its discipline implies both something about the current state of Pauline studies and also an aspiration for its future. For the discipline is simultaneously marked by impressive vitality and by fragmentation. A wide range of theoretical approaches are employed, and even among those adopting a more traditional approach, the list of different frameworks within which Paul is understood is substantial: the apocalyptic Paul, the covenantal Paul, the Paul of the New Perspective, the Paul of the Old Perspective, Paul within Judaism etc. It is easy for the scholarly discourses which result to feel like separate conversations. Forums are needed within which a shared focus on Paul's theological ideas can stimulate new thinking, promote dialogue, and help to map pathways forward beyond the reassertion of incommensurate conclusions. CLPS aims to provide such a forum.

Series Introduction

Yet an insistence on the centrality of Pauline theology within Pauline studies ought not to mean imposing a forced uniformity or understanding the scope of Pauline theology in a narrow manner. For one thing, engagement with the theological content of Paul's message is impossible without the careful historical work necessary to understand Paul's ideas in their own ancient contexts. The study of Pauline theology cannot be advanced by the erection of artificial divides between theological and historical approaches to interpretation. Neither can our attempts to understand Paul's ideas in their own ancient contexts be detached from the influence upon us of our own historical location as interpreters. We are impacted both by previous traditions of interpreting Paul and by our own social and cultural contexts. They shape our concerns, and they both enable and constrain our understanding of the past. Implicit in even the most historical approaches to the study of Pauline theology are present day questions and horizons. Some theological interpreters simply take account of the impact of historical location upon their task, keeping their focus on Paul in his own time and place. Others instead embrace the constructive task of explicitly recontextualizing Paul's theology for contemporary readers, connecting the historical study of Paul's ideas in varied ways with the Christian tradition today.

There is thus considerable and appropriate diversity within the study of Pauline theology. For this reason, exegetical studies, studies comparing Paul's ideas with those of others in the ancient world, studies exploring Paul's ideas in their canonical contexts, studies of reception history, and studies bringing Paul's theological ideas into dialogue with contemporary theological concerns are all welcome within CLPS. Some of these types of studies may employ analytical tools drawn from the Christian theological tradition. Their methodology will be theological as well as their content. However, engagement with the theological content of Paul's message can also sometimes be served by inter-disciplinary methodologies that have not typically been understood as theological or have even been understood by some of their practitioners as antithetical to theological interpretation. Post-colonial interpretation, the use of various forms of political philosophy that prioritize liberation, and various kinds of feminist interpretation all provide examples of such inter-disciplinary methodologies. Where studies use such methodologies to engage with Paul's theological ideas or to recontextualize them for the contemporary world they too will be welcome within CLPS. It is the kinds of questions asked, the quality of the

Series Introduction

theological reflection offered, and the depth of critical engagement that we intend to be the hallmark of CLPS.

Dorothea H. Bertschmann
Stephen J. Chester
Series Editors

Foreword

IT IS HARDLY SURPRISING that Paul's Letter to Philemon has for a long time lived a shadowy existence within Pauline literature. A brief look at the history of interpretation shows that the letter was more a source of embarrassment and perplexity than of theological inspiration. Numerous interpreters in the early church—Tertullian, John Chrysostom, Theodore of Mopsuestia, and others—endeavored to defend its inclusion in the canon of the New Testament as best they could in view of the brevity and, at least at first glance, the modest theological content of this text. There is no doubt that the emergence of the historical-critical paradigm since the eighteenth century has helped to sharpen our view of this little pearl of Pauline rhetoric. Numerous historical studies have enabled us to better understand the complex phenomenon of slavery in antiquity. We have learned to grasp Paul's sometimes idiosyncratic rhetoric in its contemporary historical context. And finally, we have become accustomed to specifying the context of communication for Paul's letters in order to avoid generalizing their theological affirmations too quickly, but to take them seriously as context-dependent statements. Of course, many detailed questions concerning this, the shortest of Paul's Letters, remain open and are the subject of controversial debate in current research. It also seems to me that many of its contemporary interpreters find it difficult to come to terms with this document. But at least Paul's Philemon has emerged from its shadowy existence and aroused the curiosity of exegetes.

With this important book—a revised version of his PhD dissertation written at the Graduate Theological Union (Berkeley, California) under the supervision of Jean-François Racine—Okitakatsi joins the ranks of those who are eager to give the Letter to Philemon more credit. What distinguishes his study is not only its excellent prose and its outstanding ability to succinctly summarize complex historical and methodological subjects, but also, and perhaps above all, its interest in taking seriously Paul's Letter to Philemon as a text that is also interesting from a theological point of view. I would like to emphasize three points that seem important to me in assessing Laurent Okitakatshi's book.

First, Okitakatshi combines narrative criticism and social-spatial theory for the study of the letter. While elements of narrative criticism have been entering Pauline studies for some time, the author breaks new ground with the inclusion of more recent spatial theories in the field of sociology and philosophy. He rightly emphasizes an understanding of space as the result of social action (space as a network of relationships) rather than as a preexisting, quasi-objective given (space as a container). Here, he essentially draws on the theoretical work of the French philosopher Henri Lefebvre (*La production de l'espace*, first published in 1974), taken up by the American urban geographer and social theorist Edward Soja (notably in *Thirdspace: Journeys to Los Angeles and Other Real-and-Imagined Places*, 1996), distinguishing between perceived space, conceived space, and lived space or third space (in French *espace imaginé*). Okitataktshi's presentation of Lefebvre and Soja is excellent, convincing in form and substance. In particular, he shows the extent to which the work of Soja—a well-known figure in the English-speaking world of the so-called spatial turn—essentially drew on the intuitions of the French researcher. Okitakatshi's use of the analytical tools of narrative criticism, including Gérard Genette, Seymour Chatman, and Paul Ricœur, seems to me to be less original: the author proposes to read the Pauline letter as a narrative, or more precisely, as a discursive text that includes an underlying narrative, or even several narratives; Philemon "is a moment in the story" (73). Nevertheless, it's worth noting that, here too, Okitakatshi demonstrates a remarkable ability to synthesize numerous theoretical approaches, some of them highly complex.

To what extent can elements of social-spatial theories help us better understand Paul's request to Philemon in favor of Onesimus? For Okitakatshi, the concept of *koinōnia*, a Greek term with a wide range of meanings—communion, partnership, fellowship, common gift, etc.—is crucial. The letter intends to create a "*koinōnia*-space," an alternative, subversive space that challenges the power relationships of Roman slavery and invites the reader to conceive an ethos anchored in faith in Christ and favoring mutual appreciation and support within the community of Christ-believers. Somewhat provocatively, the author states that "those who read Phlm only as a note requesting manumission in the Roman sense of the term completely forget the theological aspect of this letter. If his purpose were only to claim

Foreword

Onesimus's freedom by following the process provided by Roman law, Paul would not have written this letter" (131).

Second, Laurent Okitakatshi's concise discussion of slavery in the ancient Roman world is of great value. It is historically nuanced, avoids hasty, anachronistic judgments and shows a very solid knowledge of the specialized literature. Contrary to our modern perception, "Roman slavery was not based on race or on ethnicity" (49). Another significant difference between slavery in ancient Rome and slavery in the New World was that "many slaves in Rome enjoyed the prestige of higher education and a relatively high standing in society" (68). However, the author in no way relativizes the oppressive and dehumanizing character of Roman slavery. Even though the social and juridical institution of Roman slavery is a reality of the past, social practices which disrespect the human right to dignity have by no means disappeared. The author therefore builds a convincing bridge to our present day: "I understand slavery today as an umbrella metaphor for many sforms of exploitation and dehumanization—human trafficking, sexual exploitation, rape in war zones, forced labor, debt bondage, child soldiers, unpaid and underpaid labor, and so forth." (69).

Third, Laurent Okitakatshi, using the hermeneutical category of the "fusion of horizons" of text and modern interpreter, as articulated by Hans-Georg Gadamer, attempts to set up a dialogue between the biblical text and the social and political situation of the Democratic Republic of the Congo, the author's native country. He shows convincingly the questioning power of the biblical text: "Reading the Letter to Philemon contextually is to challenge the predominantly Christian population of the DRC to make effective their *koinōnia* of faith" (133). Within this dialogical, deliberately anachronistic setting across times and cultures, Okitakatshi reaffirms Onesimus— "no longer a slave, but . . . a beloved brother" (Phlm 16)—as a figure who not only passively endures, but also acts and takes initiative—he runs away! Thus, he offers himself as a figure for identification to members of Congolese society: Onesimus, "a subversive and revolutionary character who managed different spaces to gain his dignity and freedom" (153).

In short, this is an original study by a promising Congolese scholar: beautifully written, methodologically creative, and theologically insightful!

Andreas Dettwiler
Professor of New Testament Studies at the University of Geneva
June 2024

Acknowledgments

WRITING TO THE CORINTHIANS, Saint Paul asks, "what do I have that I have not received?" (1 Cor 4:7) The obvious response to Paul's rhetorical question is, nothing. Everything is a gift from God. Like Paul, I am convinced that it is by God's grace and the love and generosity of countless people that the completion of my dissertation that is now published as a book has been possible. Consequently, it is my duty to record here a few words of gratitude.

I would like to express my deepest gratitude and appreciation to Dr. Jean-François Racine for serving both as my mentor throughout my doctoral program and as the coordinator of my dissertation committee. His dedicated support and guidance, his knowledge and teaching experience, and his rigor and candor shaped the scholar that I have become. I extend the same gratitude and appreciation to Dr. Deena Aranoff and Dr. Carlos Noreña, who served as members of my dissertation committee. Their courses and my various conversations with them greatly enriched this project. Through them, I thank the faculty and staff of the Graduate Theological Union community.

I am grateful to Professor Andreas Dettwiler for writing the foreword for this book. As a member of the editorial board for the Cascade Library of Pauline Studies, he critically and rigorously evaluated my manuscript and offered helpful feedback. His remarks improved the quality of the present study. I sincerely thank him, the series editorial board, and the staff at Cascade Books for their guidance throughout the process of writing this book.

Special thanks to my friend Eleanor Wilkinson. She graciously agreed to edit the drafts of this project. An academic work written in a fourth language necessitates considerable pruning. Her thorough editing helped improve the readability, the clarity, and the tone of this book. I also thank Michael Thomson, Matthew Wimer, Stephen Chester, and the editors of the Cascade Library of Pauline Studies series for their collaboration and support throughout the process of publishing this book.

Acknowledgments

I am thankful to Bishop Emeritus Nicolas Djomo of the Diocese of Tshumbe and Archbishop Emeritus Robert Carlson of the Archdiocese of St. Louis, Missouri. Thanks to their friendship, I was granted the opportunity to pursue my studies in the United States of America. Thanks for their love, support, and examples.

My family deserves endless gratitude: my parents, Modeste Okitakatshi and Henriette Sango, for teaching me to respect and promote human dignity; my siblings and nephews (Bijou, Godée, Jules, Eric, Marina, Jean-Marie, André, Gloire, and Laurent), for enduring this long process with me, away from me, always offering support and love. Our family life was my first experience of a *koinōnia*-space.

Sincere thanks to Fr. Nick Glisson and the faithful of Saint Mary Magdalen Parish in Berkeley. You offered an environment of faith, love, and friendship during my three years of residency. Special thanks to the staff, the students, and the entire St. John Henry Newman community at Southeast Missouri State University for their support and patience throughout the redaction of this book. Thank you also to Fr. Allan Saunders and the faithful of St. Mary of the Annunciation Cathedral for their generosity and encouragement.

I owe a debt of gratitude to my brother priests, religious, colleagues, and friends: the Reverend Allen Kirchner, the Reveremd Raphael Okitafumba, the Reverend Patrick Ike Nwokoye, the Reverend Jacob Onyumbe, Sister Mathilde Mboyo, the Heschmeyer family, the Moloney family, Kristine and John Kelley, Tom Hall, Dennis and Kathy Vollink, Florence Wahl, and Antoinette Betshchart. You and all the many friends I cannot name here have taught me the value of friendship and borderless *koinōnia*. Thank you!

Introduction

ADDRESSING PHILEMON AS WELL as the church that meets in Philemon's house, Paul writes: "When I remember you in my prayer, I always thank my God because I hear of your love for all the saints and your faith toward the Lord Jesus. I pray that the *koinōnia* of your faith may become effective when you realize all the good that we may do for Christ" (Phlm 4–6).[1] What was Paul's intention in revealing the content of his prayer for Philemon in a letter he knew would be read publicly? Why was Philemon's *koinōnia* of faith both a matter of praise and an object of concern for Paul? The text does not answer these questions until ten verses later. In v. 16, one finds this radical and earth-shaking request, namely, that Philemon receive Onesimus "no longer as a slave, but more than a slave, a beloved brother . . . in the flesh and in the Lord."

This book stems from the realization that the word "brother" in verse 16 not only explains why Philemon's *koinōnia* of faith was ineffective (v. 6), but also strengthens my claim that a call to an ethic of *koinōnia* is the central message of the letter. Moreover, considering the fact that Phlm 16 is the only place in the New Testament where a slave is directly called a brother,[2] the present book transcends the binary approach to Phlm that has been the modus operandi of Western scholars. Instead of making v. 16 the basis for supporting or opposing the runaway-slave hypothesis, I will argue that the word "brother" in v. 16 completes the idea of *koinōnia* in v. 6 and

---

1. The word κοινωνία is a cognate of the Greek verb κοινωνέω, which means, to have or to do in common with; to have a share of or take part in a thing with another; to have dealings with or intercourse with; to share in an opinion, to agree; to form a community. Following the same semantic logic, the noun κοινωνία means communion, association, partnership, fellowship, participation. As a genitive objective or when modifying a noun in the genitive objective (see Phlm 6), it means communion with, partnership in, participation in. cf. Liddell and Scott, *Greek-English Lexicon*, 440–41.

2. Witherington, *Letters to Philemon, the Colossians, and the Ephesians*, 80.

Introduction

serves as the new identity marker for the community of Christ's disciples. More concretely, I will demonstrate how the kinship language in the letter dictates a reorganization of social space not only in Philemon's household, but also in the domestic space of the Democratic Republic of the Congo (hereafter DRC).³ I submit that kinship is a spatial language that creates an alternative space, a *koinōnia*-space, where kinship replaces the dehumanizing network of social relationships.

It should be clear from the outset that as a Congolese reader, my context will inevitably influence my reading of Phlm.⁴ However, without giving in to eisegesis, my conclusions will denote a fusion of horizons: the letter will illuminate the sociopolitical situation in the DRC and, conversely, some aspects of Congolese society will open new ways of reading the letter. Among other things, the implication of my contextual reading is that the evil of dehumanization that Paul's letter tries to eradicate in the domestic space inhabited by Philemon and his congregation is a pervasive phenomenon in the DRC with profound implications for peace and human well-being.

Although significantly different from the Roman institution known by Paul and his converts, slavery in the DRC is a dehumanizing evil that has taken different shapes and forms. Since the infamous time of slave trade and the dark period of colonization that followed, the DRC has experienced great humiliations. Under the Belgian colonial occupation, and especially the personal fiefdom of King Leopold II, the people of the DRC were victims of a particularly brutal brand of slavery enforced through torture, limb amputation, and murder. To describe this appalling disregard for human dignity, the expression "crimes against humanity" was first used. To be sure, the driving force behind this assault was the extraction of Congo's riches, focused then on rubber and ivory.⁵ Since then, the DRC,

---

3. Throughout its history, the country now known as the Democratic Republic of the Congo has borne various names under various political regimes. Before foreign invasion, the territory was part of the large Kingdom of Kongo. As Leopold II's private colony, it was called the Congo Free State. As a Belgian colony, it became the Belgian Congo. After independence, it was named the Republic of Congo. During president Joseph Mobutu's dictatorship, the Republic of Congo became known as Zaire. Under President Laurent-Désiré Kabila, the country bore the current official name: the Democratic Republic of the Congo. In this book, I will use DRC and Congo interchangeably and regardless of the period of history.

4. To avoid confusing the character Philemon with the name of the letter addressed to him, I will use the abbreviation Phlm when referring to the letter.

5. Ndaywel, *Histoire du Congo*, 123.

Introduction

especially the eastern part, has been a space of permanent conflicts and systemic dehumanization as both neighboring countries and Western powers, in complicity with the Congolese elite, loot Congo's natural resources. This looting of natural resources is also accompanied by the looting of human dignity: many children are forced to carry arms and perform hard labor, countless women are systematically raped, and many civilians are kidnapped for forced labor and sexual exploitation.

Moreover, in a country where the rule of the law is quasi-inexistent, systemic corruption has become the law of the land, and as a consequence, the most vulnerable are the perpetual prey for the merciless powerful Congolese elite. In universities, business, and even churches, women are constantly forced to offer their bodies in exchange for success. Many employees work without pay, or if they are paid at all, their salary hardly takes them beyond sustenance level. These are just a few examples of the many ways human dignity is trampled down in the DRC. Reading Philemon through the prism of narrative criticism and social-spatial theory, I will propose to Congolese Christians an ethic of *koinōnia* as the foundation on which to build a better domestic space, where power serves, unites, and humanizes.

In the light of what precedes, the thesis of this book is that the Letter to Philemon constructs a *koinōnia*-space, a space of radical kinship that challenges both the noxious nucleus of Roman slavery and modern systems of dehumanization in the DRC. To demonstrate this thesis, I organize this book into five chapters.

In the first chapter, I survey the various questions and approaches that have guided the interpretation history of the Letter to Philemon. This survey reveals a dialectical approach to the letter among Pauline exegetes: endorsement of the *fugitivus* hypothesis as set forth by John Chrysostom or its rejection by recent interpreters who identify themselves as marginal readers. To advance the conversation, I posit narrative criticism and social-spatial theory as lenses through which one can interpret Phlm and show the relevance of its message beyond the Western world. By paying attention to a text's rhetoric, setting, characters, and plot, narrative criticism allows a fusion of horizons, a mutual illumination between the text and its reader. By applying insights from social-spatial theory, I shall demonstrate how the Letter to Philemon deconstructs the perceived, conceived, and lived spaces,[6] in order to produce an alternative space, which I call "*koinōnia*-space," a place of radical kinship and human authenticity.

6. Both Lefebvre and Soja speak of "trialectics of spatiality" that comprise three axes:

Introduction

In the second chapter, I situate the Letter to Philemon in its sociohistorical context by exploring the different facets of the institution of Roman slavery in the Early Empire (from the late Republic to the end of the second century CE). Was Rome a slave society? What was the relationship between slavery and Roman social hierarchies? Who could become a slave in the Roman Empire? Was manumission true freedom for Roman slaves? What can we learn from ancient theories of slavery and freedom? These are some of the questions I discuss in this chapter to demonstrate that Roman slavery was not a monolithic institution. Rather, it was a complex network of relationships based on the denial of another person's human dignity. As such, Roman slavery can compare, to some degree, with the various forms of dehumanization in the DRC.

The third chapter is essentially exegetical. Reading the Letter to Philemon as a narrative, I argue that beneath the epistolary discourse lies a story or even stories that undergird it and constitute the theological matrix that constructs a worldview, an alternative space for the followers of Christ. Since the Letter to Philemon tells a story whose plot is played out on the management and negotiation of space, I reconstruct the three spaces that constitute the narrative world of the letter, following Lefebvre's and Soja's model. This reconstruction allows me to attend to narrative dynamics and rhetorical features such as characterization, identification and naming, repetition, and kinship language.

The fourth chapter is a theological synthesis of the exegetical claims set forth in chapter 3. Focusing on Paul's prayer for Philemon in the thanksgiving section (vv. 4–6), I highlight the significant theological themes that situate the Letter to Philemon within the broader structure of Pauline thought. In praying that Philemon's "*koinōnia* of faith" may become effective through the realization of the good to be done for Christ, Paul is being faithful to the general theological and ethical structure that undergirds all his writings, namely, an eschatological structure shaped by the indicative and the imperative. I borrow Victor Paul Furnish's theoretical framework of

---

perceived space, conceived space, and lived space. Soja calls Lefebvre's *perceived space* "first space." This is the physical space, perceptible by the senses. It can be a building, a piece of land, any structure of everyday life that can be demarcated. The *conceived space* or Soja's "second space" is the mental or theoretical space. It is the signified that one sees beyond the sign, the meaning that a building represents, for example. It is a space produced by structures of power. The *lived space* or Soja's "thirdspace," is the social life with its joys and struggles. It is a space where the perceived and the conceived are experienced. Soja, *Thirdspace*, 67, 74–74.

three motifs (eschatological, theological, and christological) to accomplish a twofold goal. On the one hand, I bring to light the neglected theological aspects of the Letter to Philemon and prove that they are consistent with the coherent structure of Paul's thought found in other undisputed letters. On the other hand, I submit that the goal of the Letter to Philemon is a call to an ethic of *koinōnia*. Faith in Christ creates a new identity and an alternative space where all are partners for the building of God's kingdom. In this way, Paul's request to Philemon is a call to an ethic of *koinōnia*, the only one capable of transforming relations of exploitation and inhumanity into authentic, humane, and Christocentric relationships.

The last chapter of this book is the fusion of two horizons: the horizon of the text and the horizon of the Congolese reader. In other words, this chapter is an appropriation of the message of the Letter to Philemon in the context of the DRC. Reading the Letter to Philemon contextually, I challenge the predominantly Christian population of the DRC to make effective their *koinōnia* of faith. To do so, Congolese Christians need to honestly assess the work of evangelization in their land, revisit their collective memory as narrativized in their national anthem, reclaim both cultural and Christian ethical values, and revolutionize their minds for the construction of a *koinōnia*-space, that is, a place of authentic humanity.

Abbreviations

AB	Anchor Bible
AFDL	Alliances des Forces Démocratiques de Libération du Congo
ANTC	Abingdon New Testament Commentaries
BDB	Brown, Francis, et al. *The Brown-Driver-Briggs Hebrew and English Lexicon*. Peabody, MA: Hendrickson, 2005.
BCE	Before the Common Era
Bib	*Biblica*
BMW	Beer, Music, and Women
BN	*Biblische Notizen*
BZNW	Beihefte zur Zeitschrift für die neutestamentliche Wissenschaft
CBQ	*Catholic Biblical Quarterly*
CE	Common Era
CENCO	Conférence Episcopale Nationale du Congo
CENI	Commission Eléctorale Nationale Indépendante
ConcC	Concordia Commentary
DRC	Democratic Republic of the Congo
ETL	*Ephemerides Theologicae Lovanienses*
EvQ	*Evangelical Quarterly*
FF	Foundations and Facets
GBS	Guides to Biblical Scholarship
HTR	*Harvard Theological Review*
ICC	International Critical Commentary
JBL	*Journal of Biblical Literature*
JSNT	*Journal for the Stuy of the New Testament*

Abbreviations

Jub	Jubilees
LHBOTS	The Library of Hebrew Bible/Old Testament Studies
LNTS	The LIbrary of New Testament Studies
LXX	The Septuagint
NA²⁸	*Novum Testamentum Graece*, Nestle-Aland, 28th ed.
NCB	New Century Bible
NICNT	New International Commentary on the New Testament
NTL	New Testament Library
NICNT	New International Commentary on the New Testament
NIDB	*New Interpreter's Dictionary of the Bible*. Edited by Katharine Doob Sakenfeld. 5 vols. Nashville: Abingdon, 2006–2009
NIGTC	New International Greek Testament Commentary
NovTSup	Supplements to Novum Testamentum
NPNF¹	*Nicene and Post-Nicene Fathers*, Series 1
NRSV	New Revised Standard Version
Phlm	Letter to Philemon
PRSt	*Perspectives in Religious Studies*
Pss Sol	Psalms of Solomon
PST	Points Sexuellement Transmissibles
RCD	Rassemblement Congolais pour la Démocratie
SBLDS	Society of Biblical Literature Dissertation Series
SemeiaSt	Semeia Studies
SP	Sacra Pagina
STRev	*Sewanee Theological Review*
SymS	Symposium Series
TBT	*The Bible Today*
UNICEF	United Nations Children's Fund
UNITSHU	Université Notre Dame de Tshumbe
WUNT	Wissenschaftliche Untersuchungen zum Neuen Testament
ZNW	*Zeitschrift für die neutestamentliche Wissenschaft und die Kunde der älteren Kirche*

1

The Letter to Philemon and Its Multivofcality

Patristic Interpretation and Its Legacy

AS ATTESTED BY THE fcanonical order of New Testament books, the Letter to Philemon is the shortest of the Pauline epistles (335 words in the Greek text). The brevity of the letter as well as its subject matter have contributed to its neglect by many interpreters throughout history. Already in the early church, many readers of this epistle were unsympathetic particularly to the subject matter. In comparison with Paul's other letters such as Romans, 1 & 2 Corinthians, Galatians, and so forth, Phlm[1] was judged trivial, superfluous, and theologically insignificant. Many wondered, why care about the fate of a single insignificant slave, long since dead and gone? What did such content matter to those for whom the battle over doctrine, theological heresy, and the creeds was violently raging? Moreover, Phlm seemed to provide little instruction in matters of ecclesiastical discipline. Therefore when no practical use could be found for the letter, some even began to deny that Paul had written it.[2]

Such an attitude vis-à-vis the Letter to Philemon prompted apologetic interpretive activity on the part of the church fathers. The homilies of John Chrysostom, commentaries by Jerome and Theodore of Mopsuestia, and even Augustine's reference to Phlm in his *De Doctrina Christiana* suffice to

---

1. To avoid the confusing the character Philemon with the name of the letter addressed to him, I will be using the abbreviation Phlm when referring to the letter.

2. Williams, "No Longer as a Slave," 18.

show how they devoted their work to a defense of the letter against those who rejected it.³ The interpretation of Phlm in this period did not depart from the ways in which the early church read biblical texts: the focus was on the divine meaning of the texts for readers. Thus, the church fathers interpreted Philemon more figuratively than literally. They saw in this letter Christian virtues to be emulated. To be sure, this interpretation never faded away, even after the Protestant Reformation. In what follows, I shall discuss some figures who promoted this figurative interpretation—namely, John Chrysostom, Jerome, Theodore of Mopsuestia, and Augustine.

John Chrysostom (347–407)[4]

Also known as John of Antioch, John Chrysostom was a patriarch of Constantinople and one of the greatest preachers in the history of Christianity. The power of his homilies was so transformative that his contemporaries called him "Midas in the pulpit" or "Golden-Tongued."[5]

Like his expositions of other biblical books, so Chrysostom's commentary on Philemon is preserved in his homilies. And right in the introduction to his homilies, one can already see the apologetic nature of Chrysostom's exegesis. He puts it quite blatantly:

> But because some say, that it is superfluous that this Epistle should be annexed, since he is making a request about a small matter in behalf of one man, let them learn who make these objections, that they are themselves deserving of very many censures. For it was not only proper that these small Epistles, in behalf of things so necessary, should have been inscribed, but I wish that it were possible to meet with one who could deliver to us the history of the Apostles, not only all they wrote and spoke of but also the rest of their conversation, even what they ate, and when they ate, when they walked, and where they sat, what they did every day, in what parts they were, into what house they entered, and where they lodged—to relate everything with minute exactness, so replete with advantage is all that was done by them. But the greater part, not knowing the benefit that would result thence, proceed to censure it.[6]

3. Decock, "Reception of the Letter to Philemon," 273.

4. Since all the dates here will be CE, I will not be attaching CE in the subsequent usages.

5. Aquilina, *Fathers of the Church*, 177.

6. Schaff, *Chrysostom*, 545.

The Letter to Philemon and Its Multivofcality

Clearly, Chrysostom is concerned with the usefulness of the letter, in argument against those who claim that it was not worth incorporating this letter in the Pauline corpus, since it deals with a small and personal matter. For Chrysostom, small epistles deal with necessary issues, and nothing in the life of a spiritual person, let alone an apostle like Paul, would be useless.[7] As it shall be clear by the end of this section, Chrysostom's defense of the canonicity and usefulness of the letter reflects the fundamental principle of biblical interpretation in the early church after Origen, namely, that the Bible is divinely inspired, and everything was imbued with divine wisdom to lead the soul to greater and greater perfection.[8] To challenge the claim that Phlm is superfluous and trivial, Chrysostom brings out three important matters addressed in Phlm:

> We have this one thing first, that in all things it becomes one to be earnest. For if Paul bestows so much concern upon a runaway, a thief, and a robber, and does not refuse nor is ashamed to send him back with such commendations; much more does it become us not to be negligent in such matters. Secondly that we ought not to abandon the race of slaves, even if they have proceeded to extreme wickedness . . . Thirdly, that we ought not to withdraw slaves from the service of their masters. For if Paul, who had such confidence in Philemon, was unwilling to detain Onesimus, so useful and serviceable to minister to himself, without the consent of his master, much less ought we so to act. For if the servant is so excellent, he ought by all means to continue in that service, and to acknowledge the authority of his master, that he may be the occasion of benefit to all in that house. Why dost thou take the candle from the candlestick to place it in the bushel?[9]

In Chrysostom's interpretation, the good examples of the apostle Paul and the Christian slave owner Philemon, the virtue of humility, and the respect for existing social structures constitute the essential message of the letter. Chrysostom justifies the usefulness of the Letter to Philemon by pointing out Paul's exemplary attitude toward a runaway slave and a robber as well as Philemon's humility and laudable good works toward the members of his community. Based on what Paul says about Philemon in the letter (vv. 4–7), Chrysostom canonized Philemon as an exemplary slave owner, an excellent man who bore witness to the gospel and made his

---

7. Decock, "Reception of the Letter to Philemon," 277.
8. Yarchin, *History of Biblical Interpretation*, 41.
9. Schaff, *Chrysostom*, 546.

house a lodging for the saints. He read the argument of the letter as Paul's recommending a runaway slave, Onesimus, to his good master, that on every account he should forgive him, and receive him as one now regenerated. Developing a paraenesis of the virtues of love, humility of obedience, Chrysostom preached that Christians should be humble and obedient to God, because just as Philemon owed something to Paul (v. 19), we owe everything to God.[10] Thus, Chrysostom assumed that Philemon acquiesced in Paul's exhortation and responded with humility.

Moreover, by identifying himself with his audience—which consisted mainly of upper- and middle-class citizens, most of whom had slaves[11]—Chrysostom baptized the status quo and set forth a characterization of Onesimus that would influence the history of interpretation of the Letter to Philemon, namely, that Onesimus was a *fugitivus* (a runaway slave), a robber, and a thief. For him, the interpretation of Phlm does not allow Christianity to be subversive to the structures established in society. Chrysostom prohibited any attempt to withdraw slaves from their masters without the consent of the masters.

We shall come back to Chrysostom in chapter 3 when reading closely the text of Phlm. For now, suffice it to say that Chrysostom's homilies are the first extant commentary on Phlm, and as such, they constitute an indispensable resource for the study of the letter. As an indefatigable defender of the letter's canonicity and usefulness; as an attentive reader who paid close attention to the grammar, the rhetoric, the culture and even the world behind the text of Phlm, Chrysostom is always a great dialogue partner for anyone interpreting this letter.

Jerome (342–420)

A native of the province of Dalmatia, modern Croatia, Jerome stands out among the church fathers because of his singular literary and intellectual gifts.[12] Editor of the famous Latin Bible, the Vulgate, Jerome remains a legendary interpreter of Scripture. In 386, he settled in Bethlehem where he composed his first exegetical works, namely those on Phlm, Galatians,

---

10. Schaff, *Chrysostom*, 556–57.

11. For a more detailed discussion on the nature of Chrysostom's audience, see Mayer, "Who Came to Hear John Chrysostom Preach?"

12. Aquilina, *Fathers of the Church*, 194.

The Letter to Philemon and Its Multivofcality

Ephesians, and Titus.[13] The order in which Jerome worked on the books of the Bible is significant. Why did he choose to begin his exegetical series with Paul's letters, and especially with the Letter to Philemon?

Alfred Friedl, a specialist of Jerome, tells us that when Jerome settled in Bethlehem, he lectured on the classic authors at the monastic school, while presiding over three convents for women and one for men built by the noble widow Paula and her daughter Eustochium.[14] These two women induced him to write explanations of the Pauline epistles for them. In answer to their request, Jerome composed his exegetical work on the Pauline corpus using Origen's homilies and explanations as the primary source for his interpretation. Consequently, by starting his exegetical work on the Pauline epistles with Phlm, Jerome probably modeled himself on Origen.[15]

Like Chrysostom, Jerome devotes his introductory remarks on Phlm to defending the importance of this short letter. He skillfully pleads in favor of the canonicity of Phlm against those who consider it uninspired. To those who question the Pauline authorship of Phlm because there is nothing in the letter that edifies, Jerome gives an exegetical lesson: the fact that the letter deals with a trivial issue cannot be taken as a criterion in respect of canonicity, since several of the accepted letters contain such passages. The Holy Spirit is not chased away when one occupies oneself with the needs of the body, as if these were sins.[16] For Jerome, "those who reject the letter because of its brevity and simplicity do not understand the power and wisdom hidden in it."[17]

Jerome employs all his philological skills to demonstrate that Phlm is wisdom-filled. In his work of editing the Latin text, Jerome scrutinizes every word and emphasizes the virtues of faith and love as imbedded in the text. To drive home his hermeneutical point, Jerome exclaims: "Quantis gradibus quantisque profectibus apostolicus in altiora sermo se tendit!" ("With which great steps and with which great advances does the apostolic word direct its course towards the heights!")[18] Through a close reading of v.

---

13. Friedl, "St. Jerome's Dissertation on the Letter to Philemon," 289.
14. Friedl, "St. Jerome's Dissertation on the Letter to Philemon," 290.
15. Friedl, "St. Jerome's Dissertation on the Letter to Philemon," 291.
16. Decock, "Reception of the Letter to Philemon," 278.
17. Quoted in Decock, "Reception of the Letter to Philemon," 278.
18. Quoted in Decock, "Reception of the Letter to Philemon," 279 (Latin), 279n29 (English).

14, Jerome demonstrates one of these heights toward which the brief letter directs the reader: Philemon's example of voluntary love.

In the Vulgate, v. 14 reads: *consilio autem tuo nihil volui facere, uti ne velut ex necessitate bonum tuum esset, sed voluntarium* ("but I preferred to do nothing without your consent, in order that your good deed might be voluntary and not something forced" [NRSV]).[19] Highlighting the adjective *voluntarium*, Jerome speaks of love. According to him, Philemon epitomizes the virtue of love, love in the sense of a good done out of voluntary action, not out of necessity. For him, "God could have created humans in such a way that they would not be able to do evil, but then they would be good by necessity, not voluntarily . . . Certainly, nothing can really be called good, except if it is voluntary."[20]

Evidently, Jerome is reading this verse in light of a theology of free will. To do good or evil comes from the choice one makes. Since God's nature is freedom, not necessity, to be like God is to be free to choose to do good. This is what Philemon was called to do. Therefore, all Christians should emulate Philemon and love voluntarily, not out of necessity. Decock perceives in this interpretation Origen's argument against the Gnostics, who wanted to blame the Creator for the evil in the deeds of creatures.[21] Just as Origen would have used Phlm 14 for apologetic and paraenitic reasons, Jerome also used it for the same reasons in his time.

Moreover, just like Chrysostom, Jerome does not question the institution of slavery. According to Frield, Jerome grew up on a wealthy Christian family estate with many slaves and had moved in the best circles of Rome and Constantinople, where slavery was basically accepted and a traditional institution.[22] Consequently, he proposed an allegorical interpretation of the letter, highlighting the virtues of Paul and Philemon, while condemning the disgraceful behavior of the villainous slave, Onesimus. For Jerome, Onesimus's freedom in Christ was of the spiritual order, not societal.

---

19. All English translations of the biblical text come from the NRSV, unless otherwise stated.

20. Quoted in Decock, "Reception of the Letter to Philemon," 280.

21. Decock, "Reception of the Letter to Philemon," 281.

22. Friedl, "St. Jerome's Dissertation on the Letter to Philemon," 313.

Theodore of Mopsuestia (350–428)

A native of Antioch, Theodore of Mopsuestia was undoubtedly one of the most important and famous representatives of the so-called "Antiochene school of exegesis and one of the most prolific theologians of the post-Constantinian church."[23] He wrote a series of commentaries on both the Old Testament and the New Testament. With regard to his commentaries on Paul's letters, John Fitzgerald notes that Theodore wrote them in response to requests from some individuals. Although the Latin translation of Theodore's commentary on Phlm does not preserve the names of any individual, Fitzgerald believes that Theodore wrote it in response to a specific request.[24]

In his commentary on Phlm, Theodore deals with two main issues, namely, the canonicity of the letter and the proper interpretation of vv. 15–16. With regard to the canonicity of the Letter to Philemon, Theodore, like the church fathers, defended the importance of the letter against those who rejected it because of its limited scope. He explains the usefulness of the letter in the following terms:

> It is so that all who are kept in the service of the Church, especially those seen to be in charge of the churches, may know how they must act with those who joined to us in faith, especially when there is a question of matters that seem a personal concern of theirs. Someone would then be able to see the benefit (*utilitatem*) of this especially if he were to look at the behavior of many people in our own times. And now, as people appointed to build up the benefit of others, we want to admonish those joined to us in faith about what ought to agree with that mode of life with which Paul with his most earnest entreaty wants them to agree.[25]

The moral lesson that comes across in Theodore's interpretation is unmistakable: the Letter to Philemon is useful in that it offers examples of faith, love, and humility to his contemporaries. He insists that those who believe in Christ should have a mode of life consonant with Paul's intention in the letter: building up, constructing a community that seeks the benefit of one another.

The second issue that Theodore tackles in his commentary on Phlm is the interpretation of vv. 15–16 (my translation): *This is perhaps the reason*

---

23. Fitzgerald, "Theodore of Mopsuestia on Paul's Letter to Philemon," 333–37.
24. Fitzgerald, "Theodore of Mopsuestia on Paul's Letter to Philemon," 344–35.
25. Quoted in Dahl, "Particularity of the Pauline Epistles," 268.

he was separated from you for a while, so that you might have him back no longer as a slave but more than a slave, a beloved brother—especially to me but also to you, both in the flesh and in the Lord. Against some of his contemporaries who saw in these verses Paul's willingness to abolish slavery, Theodore argued that the apostle Paul was not hinting here at Onesimus's emancipation. Instead, he simply asks the master to pardon his slave because Onesimus's judgment has changed for the better.[26] In "Theodore's view," Fitzgerald writes, "Paul accepted disparities in the social order for two principal reasons—God permitted them, and they did not damage the true religion, namely Christianity."[27] In short, Theodore, like any other interpreter, read the Letter to Philemon in the light of the hermeneutical concerns of his time and drew conclusions that applied to his immediate social context.

Augustine of Hippo (354–430)

Augustine was one of the church's most influential figures in the post-apostolic period. Educated as a Latin rhetorician, he was an accomplished writer whose works on philosophy, theology, ecclesiology, and biblical interpretation continue to inspire and edify both Christians and non-Christians.

Fond of Ambrose's allegorical interpretation of Scripture, Augustine realized that allegory provided a way to acceptably interpret the Bible and grow in Christian virtues. For him, what the Christian reader seeks to understand in Scripture is primarily the doctrines underlying the words of the text. The goal of such understanding, Augustine pointed out, is the increase of the Christian virtues of faith, hope, and charity.[28] It is in this way that Augustine reads the Letter to Philemon.

Unlike other church fathers, Augustine did not write a commentary or a homily on the Letter to Philemon. Instead, he evokes the letter, and especially verse 20, in his discussion of *uti* and *frui*. In his work *On Christian Doctrine* (*Doctrina Christiana*), he discusses the great question whether human beings ought to regard themselves as things to be enjoyed (*frui*), or to be used (*uti*), or both.[29] He argues that only eternal and unchanging things can be enjoyed; other things are to be used. Regarding our fellow

---

26. Fitzgerald, "Theodore of Mopsuestia on Paul's Letter to Philemon," 351.
27. Fitzgerald, "Theodore of Mopsuestia on Paul's Letter to Philemon," 353.
28. Yarchin, *History of Biblical Interpretation*, 61.
29. Decock, "Reception of the Letter to Philemon," 282.

human beings, Augustine says that we are commanded to love them, not to use them. And we love them, not for their own sake, but for God's sake.

In conformity with this line of reasoning, Augustine interprets v. 20 as follows: "And accordingly, Paul says to Philemon, 'Yea, brother, let me have joy of thee in the Lord.' For if he had not added 'in the Lord,' but had only said, 'Let me have joy of thee,' he would have implied that he fixed his hope of happiness upon him, although even in the immediate context to 'enjoy' is used in the sense of to 'use with delight.'"[30] Manifestly, Augustine interprets the Letter to Philemon in the light of his theology of Christian love. God is the ultimate happiness of every human being. Loving a person truly is finding joy in the Lord, the Creator. By receiving Onesimus "no longer as a slave but . . . a beloved brother . . . in the flesh and in the Lord," Philemon would cause Paul and other Christians to rejoice in the Lord, for to love is to participate in the very life of the Triune God.

From Chrysostom to Augustine, one can identify three hermeneutical concerns characteristic of patristic exegesis of the Letter to Philemon. The first hermeneutical concern is the canonicity and the utility of the letter. Against those who rejected it because of its brevity and lack of theological significance, the church fathers demonstrated the importance of Paul's shortest epistle, especially when read through the lenses of canonical and allegorical interpretation.

This first concern is intimately connected to the second concern, namely, the theological and spiritual meaning of the letter. For the early church, the Letter to Philemon is a mine of Christian virtues of faith, hope, and love. Defending the thesis that Onesimus was a runaway slave who deserved punishment, the church fathers sang the praises of Paul and Philemon, offering them to their contemporaries as exemplars of Christian virtue to be emulated.

And such a reading explains their third concern: the legitimation of the slave system and social stability.

Against radical and enthusiastic interpreters who saw in this letter a call to change the social order,[31] the church fathers argued that Paul was

---

30. Augustine, *On Christian Doctrine*, 21.

31. Based on the interpretation of Phlm 15–16, contemporaries of Theodore of Mopsuestia seem to have adopted an egalitarian manner of treating each other, including slaves. Theodore does not precisely identify who these enthusiastic proponents of emancipation were, but his line of reasoning almost surely reflects an ecclesiastical debate that was raging in the early church over whether a slave who converted to Christianity was to be emancipated. As Fitzgerald notes, "in that debate, Onesimus was the key piece of

not subverting social structures, nor was he condoning the running away of slaves from their masters, a common practice in the early church. These three concerns constitute the legacy of the patristic interpretation of the Letter to Philemon until after the Protestant Reformation. But before we discuss the post-Reformation interpretation of the letter, we shall first comment on the legacy of the patristic interpretation among the medieval interpreters and the Reformers.

The interpretation of the Letter to Philemon did not vary much in the medieval period. Ambrosiaster, for instance, celebrates the humility of the apostle Paul, who does not command Philemon, but rather asks that he receive Onesimus. Ambrosiaster also highlights Onesimus's moral progress during the time he was separated from his master.[32] Thomas Aquinas, arguably the greatest theologian of the medieval period, also reads the Letter to Philemon in the light of patristic exegesis. For Aquinas, the letter offers a model of behavior that masters should imitate in their relationship with their slaves.

At the time of the Protestant Reformation, Martin Luther, former Augustinian Catholic priest, followed the christological interpretation of the church fathers. Notwithstanding his rejection of the fourfold sense of Scripture, Luther's literal interpretation of Phlm sounded deeply Augustinian. For him, "this epistle is an adorable chef-d'oeuvre of Christian love."[33] He presents Paul as an example of sacrificial love, because the apostle took upon himself the faults committed by Onesimus. Unequivocally, one hears here echoes of Luther's theology of penal substitution. Luther commends also the example of Paul, who did not abolish slavery, but respected Philemon's property right and returned Onesimus to him.[34]

Demonstrably, Luther—much like the medieval theologians—inherited Patristic exegesis, concerned mainly with canonicity, moral exhortation, and the preservation of the predominant social order. This line of interpretation, although not completely obliterated, will give way to another concern among modern scholars, namely, the world behind the text.

---

apostolic evidence, as can be seen from Apostolic Canons, which comprise the concluding chapter of the Apostolic Constitutions." See Fitzgerald, "Theodore of Mopsuestia on Paul's Letter to Philemon," 351.

32. Marguerat, *La lettre à Philémon et l'Ecclésiologie paulinienne*, 5.
33. Marguerat, *La lettre à Philémon et l'Ecclésiologie paulinienne*, 6.
34. Marguerat, *La lettre à Philémon et l'Ecclésiologie paulinienne*, 6.

The Letter to Philemon and Its Multivofcality

Historical-Critical Approach to Philemon

The first historical analysis of Paul's Letter to Philemon emanates from Hugo Grotius in his *Annotationes in Epistolam ad Philemonem* of 1642. Renowned humanist, historian, and lawyer of Dutch nationality, Grotius made use of his philological skills and knowledge of Roman law to do exegesis.[35] Unlike the church fathers, Grotius is not interested in a dogmatic or moral interpretation of Phlm. Rather, he is concerned with the background of the Pauline epistle, namely, the Roman jurisdiction of the environment Paul and his contemporaries inhabited.

As an expert in Roman law, "Grotius showed that Paul's intervention on Onesimus' behalf was a completely legal step and left untouched the master's rights over the slave."[36] According to Grotius, Paul may not think that the doctrinal teaching of the gospel can make a difference to social status. Grotius is thought to be the first to refer to Pliny the Younger's intercession on behalf of a runaway slave.[37] And since then, almost all commentators of Philemon have used this parallel between Paul's Letter to Philemon and Pliny's letter to Sabinianus, both interceding for runaway slaves.

Subsequent historical-critical interpretation of Phlm followed Grotius's path. Historically, exegetes have attempted to identify the location wherefrom Paul sent his letter. According to John Knox, "the understanding of this letter will hardly increase substantially by knowledge of Paul's actual situation at the time of writing."[38] Phlm's being among the Captivity letters (Colossians, Ephesians, Philippians, and Philemon), many scholars have proposed different hypotheses concerning the place of Paul's incarceration. Three places are discussed: Ephesus, Caesarea, and Rome. More recently, Caesarea, as a place of composition, has fallen out of favor in Pauline scholarship. This is due to lack of clear support for this location.[39] Rather, scholarly opinion is divided between proponents of Ephesus and advocates of Rome, as places of composition.

Among the reasons advanced by those who argue in favor of Rome,[40] I would retain the following two: first, Rome was a favored place of refuge for

---

35. Marguerat, *La lettre à Philémon et l'Ecclésiologie paulinienne*, 6.
36. Barth and Blanke, *Letter to Philemon*, 207.
37. Barth and Blanke, *Letter to Philemon*, 207.
38. Barth and Blanke, *Letter to Philemon*, 122.
39. Nordling, *Philemon*, 6.
40. Grotius, Lightfoot, Cerfaux, Feuillet, Metzger, and so forth.

runaway slaves. "In the crowded city, they hoped to be safe from private and official hunters. Here they could hope to find work and/or a protector. And here existed the rare chance to eventually move up the social ladder as high as the status of the powerful 'emperor slaves.'"[41] Second, Acts 28:16–30 tells us that Paul was relatively free and able to receive visitors in his compound.

The proponents of the Ephesus hypothesis also offer a number of reasons among which I retain only two. First, Ephesus, the capital of the province of Asia Minor, recommends itself thanks to its proximity to Colossae,[42] the place where Philemon lived. As they did not fly or drive during that period, Onesimus would have managed a one-hundred-mile walk rather than a seemingly endless journey to distant Rome. Second, Paul stayed for at least two and a half years in Ephesus. In this city, he established a school that became a mission center for Asia Minor.[43] Thus, after his conversion, Onesimus would have been useful for the mission of evangelization together with Paul's other coworkers in Ephesus.

The historical method tries also to determine the *vorgeschichte*,[44] that is, the circumstances in which Onesimus found asylum next to Paul. If since the time of the church fathers Onesimus was considered a *fugitivus*, that is, a runaway slave, Peter Lampe's hypothesis opened the debate on the subject. In 1985, Lampe challenged the traditional *fugitivus* view by proposing the hypothesis of *amicus domini* (the master's-friend hypothesis.)[45]

Lampe's rationale is that a runaway slave normally would have fled abroad or to a large city, or would have become a member of a group of robbers.[46] Consequently, it is difficult to explain Onesimus's fleeing to Paul if he was a *fugitivus*. Lampe draws insights from Roman legal texts to argue that Onesimus would legally not have been considered a *fugitivus*, because he intended to return to his master. "He had done something wrong, but like other slaves of his time, he went to a third party (in this instance, Paul), whom he wished to intercede on his behalf so that he could return to him."[47] Thus, the Letter to Philemon is not about what Roman law called *fugitivus*, but about a slave who went to seek the intercession of an *amicus domini*.

41. Barth and Blanke, *Letter to Philemon*, 122.
42. Barth and Blanke, *Letter to Philemon*, 125.
43. Barth and Blanke, *Letter to Philemon*, 125.
44. Marguerat, *La lettre à Philémon et l'Ecclésiologie paulinienne*, 7.
45. Lampe, "Keine Sklavenflucht des Onesimus."
46. Tolmie, "Tendencies in the Research on the Letter to Philemon," 3.
47. Tolmie, "Tendencies in the Research on the Letter to Philemon," 3.

Another important contribution to the historical-critical approach to Phlm is Norman Petersen's *Rediscovering Paul: Philemon and the Sociology of Paul's Narrative* (1982). Petersen combines literary, sociological, and theological approaches to contrast social relationships as determined by Greco-Roman society with the symbolic world constructed by Paul. Considering the sociology of the narrative world, Petersen raises a distinction between worldly roles (master and slave) and churchly roles (fellow worker and partner); he also specifies Paul's roles in relation to Philemon and Onesimus (as a prisoner and a father).[48] The structures of the Roman world are challenged by the antistructural church relations, and this antistructural church is saturated with family metaphors. For instance, Onesimus is sent back to Philemon, no longer as a slave, but as a beloved brother (v. 16).

Petersen focuses on the interaction between sociological data and the reshaping of ecclesial relations. He believes that the only possible response that Philemon had to give to Paul's request was to grant Onesimus's manumission. Petersen writes, "Because they are in Christ, Onesimus cannot be both Philemon's slave and his brother, and Philemon cannot be both Onesimus' master and his brother."[49]

As can be seen, from Grotius to Petersen, the Letter to Philemon was interpreted mainly on the basis of the world behind its text. In other words, the historical-critical approach has been concerned mostly with the sociopolitical context that created the text. In the next section, I shall discuss another approach that has focused not on the world behind the text, but on the world in front of the text.

A Pragmatic Approach to Philemon

The current research on Philemon has made v. 16 the hermeneutical key for understanding the whole letter. The verse reads, "οὐκέτι ὡς δοῦλον ἀλλ᾽ ὑπὲρ δοῦλον, ἀδελφὸν ἀγαπητόν, μάλιστα ἐμοί, πόσῳ δὲ μᾶλλον σοὶ καὶ ἐν σαρκὶ καὶ ἐν κυρίῳ (Phlm 16 NA[28]), *no longer as a slave but more than a slave, a beloved brother—especially to me but how much more to you, both in the flesh and in the Lord* (Phlm 16 my translation).

Many recent interpreters acknowledge the shattering and revolutionary effects of this verse on Paul's first audience. Reading the letter sociorhetorically, Ben Witherington III affirms that "Phlm. 16 is the only place in

48. Tolmie, "Tendencies in the Research on the Letter to Philemon," 17.
49. Petersen, *Rediscovering Paul*, 269.

the New Testament that a slave is directly called a brother, and this fact must be allowed to have its full force."[50] Interpreting the same verse more pragmatically, N. T. Wright writes: "Those who have read this letter without seeing the profound, and profoundly revolutionary theology it contains should ponder the social and cultural earthquake which Paul is attempting to precipitate—or rather, which he believes has already been precipitated by God's action in the Messiah."[51] Marcus Barth and Helmut Blanke also agree that v. 16 is the core and highlight of Phlm. "Here, finally, Paul clearly formulates what he expects his friend Philemon to do. This verse and the next offer a vision on the social change in mind."[52]

The pragmatic interpretation of Phlm had already begun with John Barber Lightfoot in 1875. Contrary to the traditional reading of his time, Lightfoot interpreted Phlm as a prefiguration of modern emancipation from slavery. He admits that Paul never speaks explicitly of Onesimus's emancipation, but only implicitly: "It is a remarkable fact that St. Paul in this epistle stops short of any positive injunction. The word 'emancipation' seems to be trembling on his lips, and yet he does not once utter it . . . In fact he tells him to do very much more than emancipate the slave, but this one thing he does not directly enjoin."[53]

For Lightfoot, Paul does not directly command Philemon to manumit Onesimus; he expects Philemon to go beyond simple emancipation. Hence, Lightfoot does not see Paul attacking the institution of slavery up front, but ruining it from within by substituting for the master-slave connection a relation of Christian brotherhood, which excludes any form of domination.

With the advent of newer approaches called "readings from the margins,"[54] Lightfoot's pragmatic and revolutionary interpretation of Phlm became tremendously valuable. For African American, postcolonial, and feminist readers of the letter, the center of attention is no longer the virtuous Philemon but the marginal and defenseless Onesimus.[55] By

---

50. Witherington, *Letters to Philemon, the Colossians, and the Ephesians*, 80.
51. Wright, *Paul and the Faithfulness of God*, 9.
52. Barth and Blanke, *Letter to Philemon*, 410.
53. Lightfoot, *St. Paul's Epistles to the Colossians and to Philemon*, 21.
54. These newer approaches (postcolonial interpretation, African American interpretation, feminist interpretation, and so forth) do not represent particular methods. Rather, they are reading strategies that seek to answer certain questions from the perspective of specific readers. They are contextualized and contextualizing readings, a kind of reader-response approach to the biblical text.
55. Williams, "No Longer as a Slave," 43.

making Onesimus the center of their interpretation, marginal readers challenge the long-standing *fugitivus* hypothesis that has dominated Phlm's history of interpretation.

From John Chrysostom's sermonic musings to recent commentaries on Philemon, the story behind this letter has been that Onesimus was the slave of a Christian leader named Philemon. Useless and unprofitable as he had become, Onesimus wronged his master, most probably by robbing him, and ran away. Finding refuge with Paul who was in prison, Onesimus became very helpful to the apostle and eventually became a Christian. Paul sent him back to his master with a letter in which he was asking Philemon to forgive Onesimus instead of punishing him and to accept him as a brother. This majority opinion has been seriously called into question. In what follows, I propose to discuss some insights that have expanded the boundaries of interpretation.

Already in 1935, John Knox ingeniously challenged the *fugitivus* hypothesis. He argued that Onesimus was the slave, not of Philemon but of Archippus, based on his interpretation of Phlm 2, and Col 4:17. According to Knox, Philemon lived in Laodicea and was the overseer of the churches in the Lycus Valley. Onesimus and Tychicus were to stay over at his house, on their way to Colossae with the letter. The goal of the letter was to persuade Philemon to use his influence on Archippus so that Onesimus would be sent back to Paul to support him in his ministry. Knox is convinced that the letter achieved its goal, because Onesimus later became the bishop of Ephesus, and eventually the collector of Paul's letters.[56] Radical and controversial as it was, Knox's interpretation did not have much grounding in the text and, consequently, failed to convince many people.

As if Knox's interpretation was not radical enough, Allan D. Callahan proposed a reading that is perhaps the most subversive in the interpretation history of Phlm. For him, the story behind this short letter is not about a Christian master and his slave. Rather, it is a story of estrangement between two Christian brothers, Onesimus and Philemon.[57] Unlike other interpreters, Callahan refused to believe that Onesimus was a slave at all. Rather, he argued that Onesimus was Philemon's blood brother. He interpreted the term δοῦλος (slave) in v. 16 figuratively. The most important word for him is ὡς (as), which indicates a virtual not actual sense of the word δοῦλος, following

---

56. Knox, *Philemon among the Letters of Paul*, 67–70.
57. Callahan, *Embassy of Onesimus*, ix.

the same pattern found in other Pauline letters (Rom 1:1; Phil 1:1; Titus 1:1).[58] Thus, according to Callahan, Paul was asking Philemon to stop treating his own brother like a slave, but as he truly is, a beloved brother both in the flesh and in the Lord. Obviously, Callahan's interpretation can hardly convince, because of a lack of textual and historical evidence for his position.

Craig de Vos rejects manumission as the main concern of the letter. For him, the Letter to Philemon identifies a much deeper problem. It exposes the effects of problematic relational patterns in Greco-Roman households. One of these patterns is what de Vos calls "stereotyped slave personality." He explains:

> In support of this we find a stereotyped slave personality, commonly held and espoused by the elite, that slaves were by definition lazy, negligent, willful, cowardly, and criminals. There is a similar stereotyped slave persona found in the caricature of slaves in Greek comedy, a caricature that could only work if there was some basis in reality. So, for example, Menander portrays slaves as scheming and deceitful, negligent and insolent.[59]

For de Vos, Paul was not seeking Onesimus's manumission as this would not have changed much about his situation in profoundly stereotyped society. Rather, Paul was trying to change Philemon's worldview, because structure change happens only when people change their mentality and perception.

In his article, "Paul's Letter to Philemon: An Appeal Above and Beyond the Law," Robert Van Dyke wonders why Onesimus was not converted while in Philemon's household. He writes: "The question that screams at me is: How did they have a practicing Christian household, doing what they were supposed to be doing and teaching, and living into the faith, while neglecting to spend the effort to convert their servants? Why did Paul have to convert Onesimus?"[60] Answering this question in the light of Paul's prayer in verse 6, Van Dyke concludes that Paul was challenging Philemon and the entire church community to make their faith effective.

Espousing Van Dyke's position, Lewis Brogdon proposed what he calls "exclusionary *koinōnia* interpretation." For him, the central issue of the letter was the failure of Philemon and Christian congregation to include "outsiders" in some sense. Reading intertextually, Brogdon concludes that selective sharing of fellowship was a problem Paul had encountered before

---

58. Callahan, *Embassy of Onesimus*, 44.
59. DeVos, "Once a Slave, Always a Slave?" 95.
60. Van Dyke, "Paul's Letter to Philemon," 391.

with Peter, Barnabas, certain men associated with James, and even in the church at Corinth.[61] Thus, Paul was urging Philemon to make his house a place of *koinōnia* for all, including the marginalized.

Departing from the mainstream interpretation (Phlm as a cover letter on behalf of a runaway slave), Sabine Bieberstein has proposed a feminist reading of the Letter to Philemon. She starts with an observation: "Like many other New Testament texts, Paul's letter to Philemon is connected with a long history of Christian guilt. As with the household codes, Philemon too has been misused in order to stabilize systems of domination that despise human beings, and to keep slaves enslaved."[62]

Against such an infamous use of the letter, Bieberstein proposes a feminist approach that rests on four basic principles: first, modern readers must abandon the perspective of the history written by Christian victors, making visible the history of injustice and offering a critical reflection on this history. Second, one must make a distinction between this *Wirkungsgeschichte* (reception history) and the analysis of Phlm's function in the context of classical slavery, which in turn is to be seen within the patriarchal system of domination. In this way, the struggle for survival of men, women, and children is seen within the dominant system of the Pax Romana. Third, this change of perspective allows one to see how the case of the slave Onesimus is one of those extremes in which reality is revealed, and the truth becomes visible and known. For no matter what the precise facts of the affair of the slave Onesimus may be, his reality as rendered in the Letter to Philemon brings about a rupture in the normal reality of slavery. Fourth, a feminist analysis of Phlm finds it exceptionally significant that a woman, Apphia, is summoned as witness precisely in this 'test case' of liberating praxis, something unique in the Pauline corpus.[63] Thus, for Bieberstein, a feminist reading of the letter allows one to approach history from the perspective of the victim, not the victor, the oppressor. And she also emphasizes the role of Apphia in the implementation of the new relationship that Paul is trying to establish between Philemon and Onesimus.

One more exegete I wish to add in this overview is Joseph Marchal. In his article "The Usefulness of Onesimus," Marchal raises awareness of the sexual use of slaves in antiquity as neglected yet invaluable background

---

61. Brogdon, *Companion to Philemon*, 4.
62. Bieberstein, "Disrupting the Normal Reality of Slavery," 105.
63. Bieberstein, "Disrupting the Normal Reality of Slavery," 105–6.

to the rhetoric of Paul's Letter to Philemon.[64] Interpreting the word χρῆσις (as utility, usefulness, or sexual intercourse) in the light of ancient sources (Horace, Seneca, Herodas, and so forth), Marchal argues that Paul's discussion of the utility of Onesimus in his Letter to Philemon is a rhetorical choice that places the letter within the imperial gendered system.[65] For Marchal, "Onesimus's name reflects his own placement within this imperially gendered slave system, since it contains a constellation of characteristics sought by owners in their slaves": economic benefit, social prestige and honor, sexual pleasure. "The slave exists not for his or her own benefit, profit, or pleasure but for the enjoyable use of the master, and Paul's description of Onesimus in terms of his utility . . . reinforces the status quo of this erotically kyriarchal system."[66]

Marchal's thesis is problematic and frankly unconvincing if one interprets the word χρῆσις in the light of the immediate context provided by the text. Both the word κοινωνία and the motif ἐν Χριστῷ do not allow Marchal's conclusion that both Paul and Philemon were negotiating the use of Onesimus to assuage their sexual urges. Despite the fact that Marchal's article opens a new way of reading Phlm that departs from mainstream interpretation, I remain unconvinced by his conclusions.

In sum, from the patristic period to the twenty-first century, history has witnessed a multivocal interpretation of Paul's short Letter to Philemon. The brief survey of literature I have presented above shows a significant variation in terms of approaches. It also reveals that the study of this letter resembles a football match where two teams of mainly Western scholars kick the letter in all kinds of directions like a ball to determine the most plausible, if not the accurate, interpretation. The first team is made up of scholars who embrace the *fugitivus* hypothesis, whereas the second team is composed of marginal readers who reject the *fugitivus* hypothesis and re-center their interpretation on the marginalized slave Onesimus. Although some postcolonial interpreters from non-Western countries have been recently interested in the study of the Letter to Philemon, it should be acknowledged that the study of this letter has been shaped by readers in societies where the slave system was legally established. In the next section of this chapter, I will add my voice to the conversation about *how* to read

---

64. Marchal, "Usefulness of Onesimus."
65. Marchal, "Usefulness of Onesimus," 751.
66. Marchal, "Usefulness of Onesimus," 760.

Paul's Letter to Philemon so that the message of this first-century text may reach a broader audience, including the people of the DRC.

Narrative Criticism and Social-Spatial Theory: A Fresh Interdisciplinary Framework for the Study of Paul's Letter to Philemon

Much like a scribe trained for the kingdom of heaven, whom Jesus likens to a householder that brings out of his treasure what is new and what is old (Matt 13:52), I propose a fresh framework for the study of Phlm. I posit a combination of narrative criticism and social-spatial theory—both lenses through which one can interpret Phlm and show the relevance of its message beyond the Western world. I submit that Paul is a storyteller and a space producer. He narrates space and spatializes narrative in order to produce an alternative world, a *thirdspace*,[67] where Jesus is Lord and believers live the authentic *koinōnia* of brothers and sisters. To this end, I shall first review scholarship on both spatial theory and narrative theory. Then, I will discuss the use of narrative criticism in the study of Paul's Letters, before demonstrating how the combination of both spatial theory and narrative criticism constitutes a fresh framework for the study of Paul's Letter Philemon.

Narrative Theory

For several years now, interest in narrative has increased across a variety of academic disciplines. From its turning point with structuralist theories in France in the 1960s to postmodern approaches, narrative theory has dominated a wide range of disciplinary fields and research contexts. It has been overwhelmingly concerned with historical, political, and ethical questions. At the same time, it has moved from its initial home in literary studies to take in examination of other media (including film, music, and painting) and other nonliterary fields such as law and medicine.[68] In this section, I present an overview of the two main divisions of narrative theory, namely, the formalist approach (structuralism and poststructuralism) and the pragmatic approach, generated by the self-conscious and self-critical nature of

---

67. I borrow these expressions ("an-Other," "thirdspace") from Soja, *Thirdspace*.
68. Phelan and Rabinowitz, *Companion to Narrative Theory*, 1.

much narrative theory.[69] For the sake of brevity, I shall single out a few names, representatives of each side, to understand the development of the discipline of narratology.

Formalist Narrative Theory

It is generally agreed among literary critics that narratology reached its peak with the French structuralists Roland Barthes, Claude Bremond, Gérard Genette, and Tzvetan Todorov. Building their research projects on Ferdinand de Saussure's structuralism, these authors developed what came to be termed "structuralist narratology." In the words of Monika Fludernik, "structuralism, based on Ferdinand de Saussure's linguistic insights into the language as a system (*langue*) irrespective of speakers' faulty performances in their *parole*, set the parameters for early literary structuralism of which narratology was one important offshoot."[70] Put simply, structuralist narratologists followed de Saussure's preference of *langue* (system) over *parole* (different language components), and distinguished between narrative as a system and narrative as a message.

This "formalist narrative theory" built on German, Russian, and Anglo-Saxon formalism. For instance, the domain of narrative poetics witnessed the rise of the morphological model in Germany, a model later furthered by Russian formalists. Central to this model is "the distinction between the *disposition* (logical arrangement) and *composition* (artistic arrangement) of the structural elements contained within narratives."[71] Russian formalists widened the scope of this approach and invented stylistic models to encompass the widest possible range of prose forms, including the full gamut of narrative genres. David Herman concludes that "this widened investigation focus was a decisive development in the history of modern-day narrative theory."[72] As we shall see below, the formalists prepared the ground for an interdisciplinary approach to narrative.

Before discussing some key figures of Formalist Narrative Theory, I wish to mention another important foundation for narratology, especially for Anglo-Saxon narrative theory. In his 1884 essay on "The Art of Fiction," Henry James set the tone for narrative fiction. Like Russian formalists after

69. Phelan and Rabinowitz, *Companion to Narrative Theory*, 2.
70. Fludernik, "Histories of Narrative Theory (II)," 38.
71. Herman, "Histories of Narrative Theory (I)," 23.
72. Herman, "Histories of Narrative Theory (I)," 24.

him, James sees literary work as a living organism. A novel, he wrote, "is a living thing, all one and continuous, like every other organism, and in proportion as it lives will it be found, I think, that in each of the parts there is something of each of the other parts."[73] James went on to ask, "What is character but the determination of incident? What is incident but the illustration of character?" Clearly, James saw narrative fictions as verbal structures higher and greater than the sum of their components. More than Russian formalists, he emphasized the interdependence, the imbrication of the system (*langue*, narrative), and the different parts of narrative (*parole*, narrative components). His insights proved instrumental in the narratology developed by French structuralists.

Gérard Genette

A renowned French structuralist and a prominent theorist of narratology from its classical phase, Gérard Genette is internationally acknowledged as an authoritative voice in literary studies. While Genette's narratological oeuvre fits into German and Russian formalism as well as Saussurean linguistics, it also marks a shift or a renewal of narratogical studies. Chief among his works, Genette's 1980 *Discours du récit* (*Narrative Discourse*) has shaped many approaches to narrative across academic disciplines. For the purpose of this chapter, I propose to highlight some key insights from this pivotal magnum opus that continue to influence narratological studies.

Concepts, even the most familiar in a language, necessitate a definition, a contextualization, to spare users the danger of confusion and ambiguity. So Genette proposes a tripartite definition of the term "narrative." First, "narrative" is *un énoncé narratif* (a narrative statement), the oral or written discourse that tells or relates an event or a series of events.[74] Second, "narrative" designates the succession of events, real or fictitious, that are the subject of the discourse, and their diverse relations of sequence, opposition, and repetition.[75] Third, "narrative" refers to an event: no longer the recounted event, but the one consisting in the act of narrating itself.[76] The three meanings that Genette ascribes to "narrative" have helped many narratologists rethink the rich semantics behind their discipline as well as

---

73. James, "Art of Fiction," 506.
74. Genette, *Discours du récit*, 1381.
75. Genette, *Discours du récit*, 1381.
76. Genette, *Discours du récit*, 1381.

its fields of application. Thus, Genette helps literary critics discern the relations between discourse (narrative statement), story, and narration when engaging any particular text (oral or written).

Genette's *Narrative Discourse* is praiseworthy for emphasizing the temporality of narrative. This temporality is clearly seen in the distinction Genette makes between order, duration (tempo), and frequency.[77] For him, there is a temporal duality embedded in every narrative, be it oral or written. Hence, he proposes that relations between the time of the story and the time of narrative be studied in order to determine connection between order, duration, and frequency. Genette provided key terms that became household words for literary criticism: *analepsis* (the narrator recounts an event that took place earlier than the present point in the main story), *metalepsis* (the narrator anticipates events that will occur after the main story ends), *pause*, *scene*, *summary*, *ellipsis*, and *repetition*.

Genette also established concepts such *homodiegetic*, *heterodiegetic*, *intradiegetic*, *extradiegetic*, and *focalization*. Playing with the root term *diegetic* (from Greek *diēgesis*, "story"), Genette makes a distinction between person and level in a story. A narrative is *homodiegetic* if the narrator is part of the story, *heterodiegetic* if the narrator is not part of the story, *intradiegetic* if the events narrated are inside the story level, and *extradiegetic* if events narrated are outside the story level.[78] With the concept of focalization, Genette makes a distinction between "who speaks" (the narrator) and "who sees":[79] In other words, focalization highlights the double-narrative dimension of "telling" and "showing." Such focalization can be internal or external to the story.[80]

Genette's narratological oeuvre has been indispensable for literary studies, especially at this moment when narrative is studied from different angles across a panoply of disciplines. It is, however, important to notice that despite his innovations, Genette could not escape the binarism and typology of structuralist narratology. As Fludernik remarks, Genette's typology of narrative forms (1980) sports a panoply of binary oppositions: homodiegetic versus heterodiegetic; extradiegetic versus intradiegetic; *focalisation interne* versus *focalisation externe*, and so forth.[81] Such a binary typology assumes that texts are stable, ready for readers to extract meaning,

77. Genette, *Discours du récit*, 1537.
78. Genette, *Discours du récit*, 5580.
79. Fludernik, "Histories of Narrative Theory (II)," 40.
80. Genette, *Discours du récit*, 4492.
81. Fludernik, "Histories of Narrative Theory (II)," 38.

and that no external factor is allowed in the interpretation. This view would not go unchallenged, as we shall see in the following pages.

Seymour Chatman

A second prominent figure of classical narratology is Seymour Chatman, an American film and literary critic, and professor emeritus of rhetoric at the University of California, Berkeley. His 1978 *Story and Discourse* has been a standard textbook of narratology study in the United States and beyond. I shall briefly present here some of his insights into narrative theory.

In the preface of his book, Chatman asks: What is narrative in itself? He notices that literary critics tend to think too exclusively of the verbal medium, even though they consume stories daily through films, comic strips, paintings, sculptures, dance movements, and music. For him, limiting narrative to the verbal is a narrow understanding of narrative. All artifacts, whether verbal or not, have in common some substractum.[82] Put differently, Chatman extends the definition of narrative beyond the usual verbal form to include a variety of narrative media, especially film. Following other structuralists such as Barthes, Todorov, and Genette, Chatman posits what he calls "a what" and "a way." The "what" of narrative he calls "story," and the "way" he calls "discourse."[83]

As can be seen, Chatman and Genette define narrative in similar terms. "Story is the content of the narrative expression, while discourse is the form of that expression."[84] More than Genette, though, Chatman focuses on narrative form in its diversity. The material manifestations of narrative discourse take the shape of words, drawings, or whatever. Hence, a medium—language, music, stone, paint and canvas, or whatever—actualizes the narrative, makes it into a real object like a book, a musical composition, a statue, or a painting. But the reader must unearth the virtual narrative by penetrating its medial surface.[85]

Fludernik suggests that Chatman's *Coming to Terms: The Rhetoric of Narrative in Fiction and Film* significantly expanded his concept of narrativity. He integrated narrative with other text types like argument and

---

82. Chatman, *Story and Discourse*, 9.
83. Chatman, *Story and Discourse*, 9.
84. Chatman, *Story and Discourse*, 23.
85. Chatman, *Story and Discourse*, 27.

description.[86] As we shall see below, this integration opened narrative theory to an interdisciplinary approach.

Paul Ricoeur

Paul Ricoeur ranks as one of the most significant theorists of hermeneutics and narrative in the twentieth century. He is a bridge between structuralist narratology and postmodern narratology. Working within the tradition of hermeneutic phenomenology, Ricoeur proposes a theory of the narrative text that challenges both structuralist and poststructuralist approaches. In his famous 1985 *Temps et récit*, volume 3: *Le temps raconté*, he contrasts fiction and historical narrative. He neither separates nor collapses historical and fictional narrative. Rather, he interweaves them, creating a linkage between the past and the present, the cosmic time and the lived time.[87]

Ricoeur's effort to reconcile history and narrative has provided literary critics with important notions about "the world behind the text," "the world of the text," and "the world before the text" or "the world of the reader." These combined worlds functioning simultaneously is what Ricoeur calls "triple mimesis."[88] Mimesis 1 is the precomprehension or reception of the world of action that is necessary for the production of a narrative; mimesis 2 is the creation of the plot or the narrative itself; and mimesis 3 is the intersection of the world of the text and the world of the reader. Thus, there is an intrinsic connection between a prefigured time, a refigured time, and a configured time. As stated above, Ricoeur's theory links together structuralist and postmodern narrative approaches in a remarkable way. He goes beyond the structuralist understanding of narrative text as stable and self-sufficient, and at the same time, he challenges the postmodern tendency to ignore the world behind the text or even the world of the text itself, focusing mostly on sthe world of the reader.

Pragmatic or Contextual Narratology

The study of narrative has not been static. From German and Russian formalism to contemporary approaches, narrative has undergone refinements

---

86. Fludernik, "Histories of Narrative Theory (II)," 42.
87. Ricoeur, *Le temps raconté*, 147.
88. Ricoeur, *Le temps raconté*, 9.

and developments. The field has moved from structuralist and Saussurean narratology to a more pragmatic, contextual, ideological, globalized, and interdisciplinary narratology. According to Fludernik, two sources are responsible for the emergence of this contextual and pragmatic narratology. On the one hand, there is the revival of Henry James's tradition as developed in *The Art of the Novel*, a tradition that found its apogée in Wayne Booth's studies of irony in the *The Rhetoric of Fiction*. On the other hand, there is the pragmatic revolution in linguistics which displaced linguistic structuralism and generative grammar and reintroduced semantics, context-orientation, and textual issues to the study of language.[89]

The pragmatic approach to narrative goes beyond its role of creating expression and representation. Narrative appears to be an essential component of human thought, communication, and interaction. As Constance Devereaux and Martin Griffin put it, narrative serves as an analytical framework for understanding a wide spectrum of human activities.[90] In other words, narrative emerges from culture and, at the same time, determines culture. Narrative forms identity and policy and informs the network of human interactions. Hence narratological research has been expanded by newer theoretical disciplines such as feminist criticism, postcolonial criticism, New Historicism, cultural studies, and spatial studies.

Common to these newer approaches is what Fludernik calls a symptomatic reading of texts. For her, "critical discussion of texts and genres attempts to locate textual strategies that signal unconscious or repressed psychological or ideological 'drives' which the critic uncovers, 'reading against the grain' of the text."[91] Put differently, most newer approaches to narrative are reader-oriented in nature, emphasizing more what Ricoeur calls the world before the text.

In addition to the prominence of the reader's role in pragmatic narratology, one should also note the concern for a forgotten component of narrative, namely, space. As we have seen with Genette, Chatman, Ricoeur, and other structuralist narratologists, temporality has dominated discussions of narrative poetics at the expense of space. This is due, in part, to a misconception of space among literary theorists. As a response to such neglect, authors such as Michel de Certeau, Frank Moretti, and Susan Friedman, have argued that space and temporality are intimately connected. Friedman

---

89. Fludernik, "Histories of Narrative Theory (II)," 44.
90. Devereaux and Griffin, *Narrative, Identity, and the Map of Cultural Policy*, 1.
91. Fludernik, "Histories of Narrative Theory (II)," 45.

explains this connection: "Space restored to its full partnership with time as a generative force for narrative allows for reading strategies focused on dialogic interplay of space and time as mediating co-constituents of human thought and experience."[92] More than the static, flat background to as story, space is active, mobile, and indispensable in the creation of narrative. To fully appreciate this notion of space and its impact in literary studies, I shall now discuss the second component of my methodological framework: namely, spatial theory.

Spatial Theory

Most spatial theorists associate Michel Foucault with a paradigm shift in spatial studies. In his 1967 lecture titled "Of Other Spaces," Foucault claims that "the great obsession of the nineteenth century was, as we know, history ... The present epoch will perhaps be above all the epoch of space. We are in the epoch of simultaneity: we are in the epoch of juxtaposition, the epoch of near and far, of the side-by-side, of the dispersed."[93] Although he was not a professional geographer, Foucault's work placed space in the center of scholarly debates and posited it as the basis for human history. He bravely contested the traditional notion of linear time, asserting that concepts of time have been understood in various ways, under varying historical circumstances.

Distancing himself from thinkers like Heidegger and Nietzsche, Foucault critiqued what he referred to as the project of total history (*histoire globale*): one that seeks to reconstitute the overall form of civilization, the principle of society, the significance common to all the phenomena of a period.[94] This nineteenth-century view of history was anathema to Foucault. For him, nothing was fundamental and indistinctly applicable to all the periods of history. In fact, he attributes all the inequalities of modernity to such hegemonic narratives. Hence, through his teasing out of how space works in history, tracing the spatial configurations that expose how power and knowledge operate in countless (mal)treatments of the unloved, Foucault threw into relief many of the more questionable contours of the present.[95]

---

92. Friedman, "Spatial Poetics and Roy's *The God of Small Things*," 195.
93. Foucault, "Of Other Spaces," 22.
94. Foucault, *L'archéologie du savoir*, 17–18.
95. Philo, "Michel Foucault," 124.

Even though Foucault's concern for space was not new,[96] his relational conception of space called attention to the reinterpreted notions of utopia and heterotopia. Utopia (an unreal place) and heterotopia (both a real and a mythic place) are designations of sites that exist in relation to all other sites, but in such a way as to bring under suspicion, to neutralize, or to invert the ensemble of relations they happen to designate. This so-called paradigm shift subsequently influenced postmodern studies. In what follows, I discuss two prominent figures of spatial theory, namely, Henri Lefebvre and Edward Soja, and conclude by showing the importance of combining both narrative theory and spatial theory in the study of Scripture and especially of Paul's letters.

Henri Lefebvre

An existentialist philosopher and French sociologist of urban and rural life, Henri Lefebvre was an influential thinker whose work on space goes beyond twentieth-century philosophical musings. Shaped by what he lived through, Lefebvre's work on space emerged from the modernization of everyday life, the industrialization of the economy and the suburbanization of cities in France. He witnessed the destruction of the rural life of the traditional peasant. He was profoundly affected by the post–World War II malaise of the French populace, who felt alienated from the new industrialized forms of work and the bureaucratic institutions of civil society.[97]

These alienating postwar conditions of everyday life in France formed the core of Lefebvre's humanism and spatial thought. Between 1947 and 1988, he published four volumes on *La vie quotidienne et sa critique* (*Cristique of Everyday Life*).[98] As a Marxist, Lefebvre presented in this work a materialist critique of the *quotidienneté* (everydayness or banality) as a soul-destroying feature of modernity, social interaction and the material environment.[99] Against the boring *métro-boulot-dodo* (subway-work-sleep) of the suburban commuter, Lefebvre proposed that attention be paid to all

---

96. We find such concern already in the work of Georg Simmel, who, as early as 1903, pointed out that, rather than as a natural and pre-given container of society, space should be understood as socially produced, constructed, segmented, and given meaning. Simmel, *On Individuality and Social Forms*, 2004 (Original in German in 1903).

97. Shields, "Henri Lefebvre," 208.

98. Lefebvre, *La critique de la vie quotidienne*.

99. Lefebvre, *La critique de la vie quotidienne*.

"moments" of revelation, emotional clarity, and self-presence as the basis for becoming *l'homme total* (a more fulfilled person).

Lefebvre's initial work on space was concerned with life in the suburbs and in urban environments. He extended his critique of household, domestic life to neighborhoods and urban life. Explaining Lefebvre's understanding of "the urban," Rob Shields writes: "The urban is not a certain population, a geographic size, or a collection of buildings. Nor is it a node, a transshipment point or a centre of production. It is all these together, and thus any definition must research for the essential quality of all these aspects."[100] Put differently, Lefebvre understands the urban space as both a container and a network of relationships as well as the gathering and distribution of goods and information. Given the social centrality of the city, Lefebvre argues that everyone has the right to the city, that is, to the urban space, to the site of social interaction and exchange.

Lefebvre's concern with suburban and urban spaces was seminal to his famous 1974 volume *La production de l'espace* (*The Production of Space*). This book marked the second phase of Lefebvre's analysis of space. Expanding his field of application, Lefebvre deals here with social space as a national and planetary expression of modes of production. Moreover, as Shields puts it, "Lefebvre moved his analysis of space from the old synchronic order of discourses on space to the manner in which understandings of geographical space, landscape and property are cultural and thereby have a history of change."[101] Simply put, Lefebvre thought of space in a dynamic and dialectical way. Contrary to historicist views of space, he understood space not as static, void, passive, or nonsensical, but as an ensemble of relations. Such a fresh understanding of space is conveyed in the book's title: *The Production of Space*. In other words, space is a social product, a phenomenon incessantly produced, grasped, and transformed through complex interactions of human activities, experiences, and cognitive ideations.[102]

Lefebvre's Marxist and socialist ideas of space are not my interest here. Rather, it is his methodological approach that is key. In the foreword to *La production de l'espace*, Remi Hess explains Lefebvre's methodology as follows:

> *The Production of Space* is therefore one of Henri Lefebvre's great books, a pivotal book in his entire body of work. It is the product of a method: the regressive-progressive method. Lefebvre starts

---

100. Shields, "Henri Lefebvre," 208.
101. Shields, "Henri Lefebvre," 210.
102. Lefebvre, *La production de l'espace*, 35.

from an analysis of the present. To understand current contradictions, he goes back into the past with a query: when did these contradictions arise? He returns to the present, then sketches out the potentialities that may be realized in the future. He then makes a forecast.[103]

Lefebvre's approach to space draws on many disciplines: sociology, history, geography, and philosophy, to name a few. Aware that the present social situation did not come out of a vacuum, Lefebvre investigates the history of its production. He then offers an alternative vision of things, the possibility of a new equilibrium, an alternative space that is more just and accessible to all. In the light of this regressive-progressive and interdisciplinary methodology, one is well prepared to understand what Lefebvre calls the *triplicité de l'espace*[104] (the triplicity of space).

Lefebvre's triplicity of space or *dialectique de la triplicité* (dialectic of triplicitity) comprises the following three axes: *l'espace perçu* (perceived space), *l'espace conçu* (conceived space), and *l'espace vécu* (lived space). *L'espace perçu* is the everydayness of social life. Lefebvre defines it as the *pratique spatiale*, the *quotidienneté de la vie*, the ensemble of popular activities and blends of human interactions.[105] *L'espace conçu* or *les représentations de l'espace* (representations of space) is the space of scholars, urban planners, cartographers, and technocrats. It is the dominant mode of production, the dominant space of society, a system of verbal signs ideologically elaborated by intellectuals, professionals, and other people of power.[106] Finally, *l'espace vécu* (lived space) or *les espaces de représentation* (the space of the imagination), which has been kept alive by artists and philosophers,[107] offers an alternative space, challenging the dominant space imposed on society by powerful people. As Rob Shields puts it, "this third space not only transcends but has the power to refigure the balance of popular perceived space and official conceived space."[108]

Clearly, Lefebvre's multidimensional approach to space challenged the conventional understanding of space. Space is not an immobile background to history and narrative. For Lefebvre, space is politically, economically,

---

103. Lefebvre, *La production de l'espace*, xvi.
104. Lefebvre, *La production de l'espace*, 49.
105. Lefebvre, *La production de l'espace*, 48.
106. Lefebvre, *La production de l'espace*, 49.
107. Lefebvre, *La production de l'espace*, 49.
108. Shields, "Henri Lefebvre," 210.

and ideologically produced by every society. Narratives produce spaces just as spaces produce narratives. Lefebvre's *l'homme total* (complete or total human being) is the one who lives in all three spaces and proposes an alternative space, where all could live with dignity and equal opportunities. Postmodern thinkers such as Edward Soja and others took Lefebvre's triple dialectic to the next level.

Edward Soja

American urban geographer and social theorist Edward Soja is one of the proponents of the so-called spatial turn in the postmodern era. Building on Lefebvre's *La production de l'espace*, Soja claims that we must be insistently aware of how space can be made to hide consequences from us, how relations of power and discipline are inscribed into the apparently innocent spatiality of social life, and how human geographies become filled with politics and ideology.[109] Soja views Lefebvre's fresh perspectives on space as a spatial turn, a shifting moment from a historicist understanding of space to a focus on its materiality and ideological background.

In his *Postmodern Geographies*, Soja departs from a *durée*-oriented geography and narrative toward a human geography. He puts it quite clearly: "My aim is to spatialize the historical narrative, to attach to *durée* an enduring critical human geography."[110] Using Soja's theoretical framework, one is able to approach narrative as a map, a geography of simultaneous relations and meanings that are tied together by a spatial rather than a temporal logic. For Soja, spatiality is fundamentally constitutive of social life. Critical social theory needs to take space seriously if it is to make sense of society.

Elaborating further his vision on space and place in postmodernity, Soja wrote another influential book in 1996: *Thirdspace: Journeys to Los Angeles and Other Real-And-Imagined Places*. At the heart of this book lies the notion of a *trialectics of being*, a refined theoretical framework that Soja uses to understand spatiality. The insight of this notion, as explained by Alan Latham, is that the ontology of being can only be interpreted by examining the interlocking of spatiality, historicality, and sociality.[111] Soja argues that every life, every event, every activity we engage in is usually unquestionably assumed to have a pertinent and revealing historical and social

---

109. Soja, *Postmodern Geographies*, 6.
110. Soja, *Thirdspace*, 1.
111. Latham, "Edward Soja," 272.

dimension. Hence, one should be aware of the simultaneity and interwoven complexity of the social, the historical, and the spatial, their inseparability and interdependence.[112]

Anyone familiar with Lefebvre's *La production de l'espace* understands where Soja is developing his theoretical framework from. He refers to Lefebvre's central argument that the ontological, epistemological, and theoretical balancing of spatiality, historicality, and sociality are all-embracing dimensions of human life (*l'homme total*). From Lefebvre's metaphilosophy that goes beyond Hegel and Marx's dualism, Soja presents his method as a critical "thirding-as-othering." As a result of this critical thirding, Soja uses the term "trialectics," to describe not just a triple dialectic but also a mode of dialectical reasoning that is more inherently spatial than the conventional, temporally defined dialectics of Hegel and Marx.[113] Soja revisits Lefebvre's perceived space, conceived space, and lived space to define thirdspace as "an-Other way of understanding and acting to change the spatiality of human life, a distinct mode of critical spatial awareness that is appropriate to the new scope and significance being brought about in the rebalanced trialectics of spatiality-historicality-sociality."[114] Simply put, thirdspace is a new way of thinking, an alternative spatial imagination, a *thirding* that goes beyond mental and material spaces.

On the surface, Soja's theoretical framework does not seem different from Lefebvre's. However, put in a postmodern context, it is clear that the concept of thirdspace represents an important step toward making spatial theory a transdisciplinary approach. In his analysis of Soja's work, Latham observes that while Lefebvre maintains his privileged position, Soja is keen to demonstrate the openness of his postmodern/thirdspace project. The discussion of postcolonial and feminist writers like bell hooks, Homi Bhabha, Edward Said, Gayatri Spivak, and Cornel West attests to this openness.[115] Soja shows how hooks and West have reopened the exploration of thirdspace by discussing new politics of identity and difference that enhance the human dignity of black Americans.

For instance, bell hooks suggests that the production of space is simultaneously contextual and hegemonic, echoing here both Lefebvre's *La production de l'espace* and Soja's *Thirdspace*. She proposes, then, to see the

---

112. Soja, *Thirdspace*, 2–3.
113. Soja, *Thirdspace*, 10.
114. Soja, *Thirdspace*, 10.
115. Lutham, "Edward Soja," 272.

margin as a space of radical openness. Rather than a site of deprivation, marginality is a space of radical possibility, a space of resistance. It offers one the possibility of radical perspective from which to see and create, from which to imagine alternatives, new worlds.[116] With hooks, one can see how spatial theory has evolved from a modernist understanding of space to a more plural, nonconventional, postmodern approach to space. By spatializing narratives, events, identities, and cultures, thinkers across disciplines have demonstrated the necessity to imagine new ways of thinking about space and place.

Soja's critical spatial theory does not go unchallenged. Among the geographers, Soja's theory and its interdisciplinary distinctiveness has been received with some degree of suspicion and skepticism. Clive Barnett, a reviewer of Soja's *Thirdspace*, categorizes Soja's work as self-indulgence and an undisciplined form of contemporary academic celebrity rather than a contribution to the theorization of time and space.[117] For Barnett, Soja, like many Anglo-American geographers, seeks to elevate geography to cultural studies with all the confusion that such a move can entail.

While Barnett's critique seems to me normal resistance in the face of new and audacious ideas, his assessment of Soja's concept of thirdspace is worth considering. He notes that Soja's thirdspace becomes banal and meaningless when it encompasses everything and nothing. Barnett goes on to quote Soja's definition of thirdspace: "Everything comes together in Thirdspace: subjectivity and objectivity, the abstract and the concrete, the real and the imagined, the knowable and the unimaginable, the repetitive and the differential structure and agency, mind and body, consciousness and unconsciousness, the disciplined and the transdisciplinary, everyday life and unending history."[118]

That everything comes together in thirdspace made Barnett wonder whether Elvis might still be alive in thirdspace! I concur with Barnett that Soja's concept of thirdspace is confusing and perhaps daunting. However, I still find it useful as a theoretical framework, without rehearsing Soja's confusion and vagueness. Sharing the view of another geographer and exegete, Matthew Sleeman, I argue that thirdspace remains a productive exegetical lens, especially when used alongside other approaches such as

---

116. McKittrick, "bell hooks," 191.
117. Barnett, Review of *Thirdspace*, 529.
118. Soja, *Thirdspace*, 56–57.

narrative criticism.[119] Unlike Soja's all-encompassing spatiality, the apostle Paul's letters, especially the one to Philemon, produce a thirdspace that is inherently theological and irrevocably embedded within the dynamics of the unfolding biblical narrative, beginning with Israel and culminating in Jesus. Before illustrating the interconnectedness between narrative and space, a theoretical discussion is in order.

Narratology and Spatial Theory in Literary Studies

The preceding discussion and evaluation of both narrative theory and spatial theory prepares the ground for the central claim of this section, namely, the necessity to apply narratology and spatial theory to literary studies, and more specifically to the study of Paul's Letter to Philemon. Both theories have opened new ways of understanding the world. Narrative theory has gone from a purely structuralist and dualist understanding of narrative to a more pragmatic, world-before-the-text, reader-concerned, and contextual narratology. In the same way, geography has gained fresh perspectives since what people like Edward Soja and Fredric Jameson have termed the "spatial turn" of the late twentieth century. This spatial turn has been the awareness that space is not a neutral, immobile background of history, but rather a product of society. Space and place have material dimensions, both societal and cultural, that make them important for theoretical and methodological purposes.

As has been stated above, this chapter aims to bridge narratology and spatial theory for literary studies. Narratology and its broad concern for storytelling cannot ignore space and place without lapsing into mere historicism. By the same token, spatial theory would be mere physical geography if it were to lose sight that space is the medium in which narrative is deployed, or even that space is produced by past and present narratives. Hence, I draw substantially from *Narrating Space, Spatializing Narrative: Where Narrative Theory and Geography Meet*[120] in order to argue that by bridging narrative and space, one can gain both deeper understanding of human spatial experience and greater insight into narrative forms—and spatial experience and narrative forms are certainly embedded in biblical texts. Toward that end, I shall underline the importance of understanding the metaphors of "space as a container" and "space as a network of

---

119. Sleeman, "Lukan Narrative Spatiality in Transition," 152.
120. Ryan et al., *Narrating Space, Spatializing Narrative*.

relationships," explain how space can be a universal feature of plot, show that space functions also as a particular feature of plot, and explore the tensions between emotional and strategic space in narrative.

Isaac Newton and Gottfried Leibniz have provided future generations with two important metaphors for speaking of space: space as a container and space as a network of relationship. Regarding Newton's cosmology, Mary Jane Rubenstein writes: "Newton [argued] that absolute space is an inert, extended background through which objects may or may not move. Similarly, he insisted that 'absolute time' flows universally and inexorably, 'without regard to anything external.'"[121] Contesting Newton's absolute view of space and time, Leibniz argued that these terms were but descriptions of relations between objects. Space and time have no independent existence; they are purely relative to each other and to the matter within them.[122]

The container metaphor, as explained by George Lakoff and Mark Johnson, views space as a bounded surface with an in-out orientation. They put it quite eloquently:

> We are physical beings, bounded and set off from the rest of the world by the surface of our skins, and we experience the rest of the world as outside us. Each one of us is a container, with a bounding surface and in-out orientation. We project our own in-out orientation onto other physical objects that are bounded by surfaces. Thus we also view them as containers with an inside and an outside.[123]

Lakoff and Johnson's explanation of the container metaphor implies also that there is a relationship between individual containers. Despite the boundaries imposed, the subject is prone to relating to another subject, another container. This calls forth a second metaphor for space, namely, space as a network of relationship. As a network of relationship, space is a dynamic system of relations that allows movement, and that is often actively created by the subject.[124]

Every instance of storytelling involves interplay between space as a container and space as a network. It is in negotiating the tension between containers within a network of social interactions that the narrator helps the reader come to grips with the narrative's plot. Thus if narrative and space are to be combined in the study of literary texts, it is important that

---

121. Quoted in Ryan, *Narrating Space, Spatializing Narrative*, 19.
122. Ryan, *Narrating Space, Spatializing Narrative*, 19.
123. Lakoff and Johnson, *Metaphors We Live By*, 29.
124. Ryan, *Narrating Space, Spatializing Narrative*, 19.

the interpreter pay attention to narrative space as both a container and a network of social relationships.

Central to storytelling is plot. Every reader seeks to understand the events being narrated. The negotiation of narrative space as both container and network informs the logic of the story's plot. Hence, it is important for the reader to know the role of space in understanding the narrative's plot. The role of space plays on two different levels: universal and particular. On the general level, space can be regarded as an indispensable element of plot, the medium-independent cognitive structure that defines narrativity.[125] This cognitive structure underlying narrative texts is called by Jurij Lotman "the topographical concept of boundary."[126] The topographical concept of boundary, he argues, structures story worlds into differentiated zones obeying different rules. Consequently, a plotted text is a text where boundaries are crossed. Lotman puts it more plainly: "the movement of the plot, the event, is the crossing of that forbidden border which the plotless structure establishes . . . A plot can always be reduced to a basic episode—the crossing of the basic topological border in the plot's spatial structure."[127]

Once crossed, the boundaries that generate a plot become conceptual pairs: "high-low," "left-right," "near-far," or "open-closed." Lotman argues that the contrast "high-low" can, for instance, stand for good versus evil, far versus near, movement versus. immobility, freedom versus slavery, culture versus nature, or harmony versus strife.[128] Such spatial concepts inform the patterns of individual writers as they narrate stories. Therefore, a reader of literary texts should attend to the crossing of spatial boundaries as it determines the underlying plot of a narrative on a general level.

In addition to building a universal model of plot, spatial concepts can also constitute the particular features of plot. In all societies, space is produced and thematically organized. One recalls here Lefebvre's thesis that space is a product of society. In storytelling, this lived experience of space is conveyed and narrated under several themes. Architecturally, as well as plot-functionally, narrative space can be described in terms of partitions, both natural and cultural, that organize it into thematically relevant subspaces like walls, hallways, and political or economic boundaries.[129] Narra-

---

125. Ryan, *Narrating Space, Spatializing Narrative*, 35.
126. Ryan, *Narrating Space, Spatializing Narrative*, 35.
127. Ryan, *Narrating Space, Spatializing Narrative*, 35.
128. Ryan, *Narrating Space, Spatializing Narrative*, 35.
129. Ryan, *Narrating Space, Spatializing Narrative*, 38.

tives can confirm or challenge the lived spaces as they create a story world plotted with various spatial themes. In other words, lived experience can generate different social and cultural themes that reveal the different facets of a narrative's plot. The reader should determine the role of space in revealing the plot, both on a universal level and on a particular level.

Combining narrative and space in literary studies entails also having an awareness of the two contrasting relations that play major roles in shaping narrative content: the emotional relation and strategic relation. "In the emotional relation, spatial objects matter for what experiences they afford, for what aesthetic feelings they inspire, and for what memories they bring to mind."[130] Emotional space is linked to stories and memories that spatial object inspire, an emotion that can be negative or positive feeling. Put differently, emotional relations to space are projection of affective relations to people, it is all the values that bind one person to a space: love, family, ancestry, work, memory, and so forth. For example, in the Letter to Philemon, Onesimus had an emotional relation to Philemon's household that may have become negative. From the text, the reader may deduce that Philemon's house became for Onesimus a space of marginality, oppression, and unfriendly treatment—all of which led him to find refuge with Paul.

The second relation to space is strategic. While emotional space typically takes the form of an appealing or a frightening place, strategic space can be symbolized by the metaphor of a chessboard. "The squares on a chessboard have no intrinsic emotional value for the player; they only matter because of the actions that they allow to be perfored. For instance, you want to move your rook to a certain square because by doing so you can capture one of your opponent's pieces."[131] In other words, a strategic relation to space takes the form of keen attention to space, purposeful planning of space, or calculated negotiation of space that serves the interest of a subject or a group of subjects (individuals).

Two examples can help us illustrate the notion of strategic space. The first example is the so-called Scramble for Africa;[132] here is an instance of a strategic relation to space. Westerners gathered in Berlin in 1885 to divide

130. Ryan, *Narrating Space, Spatializing Narrative*, 39.

131. Ryan, *Narrating Space, Spatializing Narrative*, 39.

132. The "Scramble for Africa," also known as the Partition of Africa at the Berlin Conference and the Conquest of Africa, was the invasion, occupation, division, and colonization of African territory by European powers between 1881 and 1914. The outcome of the Berlin Conference was that Europeans marked out their "spheres of influence." See Grant, *Africa*, 81.

up the African continent for imperialist and colonialist purposes. They marked boundaries that served their interests, imposing both a space and a narrative that would define Africa for subsequent generations. The second example is Paul's Letter to Philemon: The Roman Empire has produced a hierarchical space, where slaves occupy the bottom of the social ladder. With Onesimus, one sees how the slave moves strategically between the spaces created by the Roman Empire in order to save his own life and define his own identity.

These examples suggest that in the interpretation of texts, it is important to understand the contrast between the emotional and the strategic relations characters have to space because such relations advance the plot and convey the meaning that could go beyond the implied reader. Approaching the Bible as literature, biblical scholars have used narrative theory to interpret biblical texts. However, few studies have included insights from spatial theory to provide fresh readings of the New Testament. In the following section, I discuss the use of narrative method in biblical studies, focusing mostly on Paul's letters. I shall argue that Paul's letters can be read as stories, and that narrative criticism and spatial theory should be combined for a better understanding of Paul's correspondence.

A Narrative Approach to Paul

"Paul is a man of the proposition, the argument and the dialogue, not a man of the parable or story."[133] This statement by J. Christiaan Beker constituted the view of the Pauline corpus by New Testament scholars in the post-Enlightenment era. Pauline literature was considered immune from narrative criticism for the simple reason that Paul wrote letters, not narratives.[134] Such a view has been revised as many Pauline interpreters have shown interest in narrative features of Paul's thought and discourse. In this section, I hope to add my voice to the voices of others who propose to study Paul's letters using narrative criticism. But more than just applying to Paul's corpus narrative criticism as it is used in biblical studies, I propose the intersection of narrative approaches and spatial theory for the study of Paul's letters, and I take Phlm as a case study. Before this, however, I shall first explain the genesis and the application of narrative theory in biblical studies.

---

133. Beker, *Paul the Apostle*, 353.
134. Longenecker, "Narrative Interest in the Study of Paul," 3.

Beloved Brother or Slave?

Narrative Analysis and Biblical Studies

The very nature of human beings is to tell stories. As Daniel Marguerat and Yvan Bourquin put it, "Since time immemorial, the human being, male and female, tells stories."[135] The purposes of storytelling are various and variegated. We tell stories to instruct, to communicate, to testify, to console, to entertain, and because it is natural for humans to tell stories, including people of faith. What we call the Bible is a story or stories about God and his people. Beginning with Israel and culminating in Jesus and his followers, believers throughout generations have told and retold the story of God's covenant with his people.

Acknowledging that the Bible is a story or that it tells stories is to affirm that the Bible is literature. Because the biblical text is literature, the domain of secular literature and the domain of biblical exegesis have always been in fruitful dialogue. In his acclaimed work from 1953, *Mimesis: The Representation of Reality in Western Literature*,[136] Erich Auerbach, the German Jewish literary critic, argued that biblical narrative can be studied according to the canons of general literary criticism.

Comparing a scene in Homer's *Odyssey* and the story of the binding of Isaac in Gen 22, Auerbach points out that Homer's epic, like any other traditional oral constructions, sets everything in the flat foreground, with nothing happening in the background. In contrast, Genesis constructs a narrative fraught with background, in which dialogue and action arise from movements occurring within characters, movements the narrator does not directly describe.[137] "Thus, an untold story unfolds simultaneously with the one told, three-dimensionality is constructed, and readers are drawn into the gripping mystery of the human and divine depths."[138] Hence, even before classical narratology, Auerbach had already approached the Bible through the lenses of narrative criticism.

Auerbach is not the only literary critic to approach biblical stories through literary lenses. Narrative analysis, like other literary approaches to scriptures, arose from a dissatisfaction many people felt with the historical-critical method. Instead of merely unearthing the biblical world, the world behind the text, many literary critics shifted attention to the world of the

---

135. Marguerat and Bourquin, *La Bible se raconte*, 5.
136. Auerbach, *Mimesis*.
137. Auerbach, *Mimesis*, 11–12.
138. Tull, "Narrative Criticism and Narrative Hermeneutics," 38.

text. It is in this context that Robert Alter is considered a pioneer of narrative criticism as applied to biblical studies. In his groundbreaking 1981 book, *The Art of Biblical Narrative*, Alter describes how the authors of the Bible used innovative literary styles and devices (including parallelism, contrastive dialogue, and narrative tempo) to tell one of the most revolutionary stories of all time: the revelation of a single God. Answering the question, What role does literary art play in the shaping biblical narrative? Alter answers: "a crucial one, I shall argue, finely modulated from moment to moment determining in most cases the minute choice of words and repeated details, the pace of narration, the small movements of dialogue, and a whole network of ramified interconnections in the text."[139] Masterfully, Alter shows that the Bible writers reshaped not only history but also the art of storytelling itself.

It goes without saying that Alter is not the first to ask how the Bible tells stories. However, as Marguerat notes, he is the first to review systematically the features of biblical narration.[140] His work is the first application of narrative analysis to the study of biblical literature. This application, one should notice, was particularly concerned with the Hebrew Bible. Alter himself acknowledges that New Testament narratives were written in a different language, at a later time, and, by and large, according to different literary assumptions. He humbly admits his lack of linguistic and scholarly competence to deal with the New Testament.[141]

One year after Alter, in 1982, David Rhoads and Donald Michie published the first study that focused on the New Testament and that expounded systematically a biblical book in its entirety. In *Mark as Story: An Introduction to the Narrative of a Gospel*, Rhoads and Michie introduce readers to the rhetorical and narrative skill that makes Mark so arresting and compelling a story. Drawing their inspiration from narratologists whose ideas we have surveyed, they increased our appreciation for the Gospels, and for Mark in particular, in new ways—as narratives originally created in an oral culture for oral performance. Rhoads, it should be noted in passing, coined the term "narrative criticism."[142]

---

139. Alter, *Art of Biblical Narrative*, 1.

140. Marguerat and Bourquin, *Pour lire les récits bibliques*, 13. All English translations are mine.

141. Alter, *Art of Biblical Narrative*, 86.

142. Marguerat and Bourquin, *Pour lire les récits bibliques*, 15.

Many other New Testament interpreters embraced narrative criticism and published extensively on the subject.[143] *What Is Narrative Criticism?*[144] by Mark Allan Powell and *Narrative Criticism of the New Testament: An Introduction*[145] by James L. Resseguie, come to mind. Although these textbooks mention the New Testament in their titles, they don't see all the books of the New Testament as containing narratives, and consequently not all can be interpreted through the lenses of narrative analysis. Chief among such texts are the letters of Saint Paul. Powell, for example, makes it clear that "in the New Testament, the four Gospels and Acts qualify as narratives. The epistles probably not."[146] Notice Powell's hesitation concerning the epistles. He is certainly aware of Norman R. Petersen's suggestion that Paul's letters can be interpreted through narrative analysis as they contain stories.[147] I think Petersen is right. Paul's letters do tell stories and thus call for narrative criticism. Coupling narrative criticism and spatial theory for the study of the Letter to Philemon, I shall demonstrate how Paul narrated space and spatialized narratives in his pastoral work.

Narrative Criticism and Paul's Letters

Paul's letters, as we said earlier, have been immune from narrative analysis just because they are letters, not stories. As Ben Witherington III provocatively puts it, "approaching Paul's thought from the point of view of narrative, one could argue, is rather like going to a philosophical debate and expecting a story to break out. After all, Paul's letters are full of practical advice and theological ideas not stories."[148]

This dominant view in Pauline studies has been challenged in the past three decades. An interest in narrative features of Paul's thought began to emerge, with significant figures in the Pauline guild proposing that 'story' was an integral and generative ingredient in Paul's theological

---

143. One can consult Kingsbury, *Christology of Mark's Gospel* (1983); Culpepper, *Anatomy of the Fourth Gospel* (1983); Tannehill, *Narrative Unity of Luke-Acts* (1986–1990).

144. Powell, *What Is Narrative Criticism?*

145. Resseguie, *Narrative Criticism of the New Testament*.

146. Powell, *What Is Narrative Criticism?*, 23.

147. Petersen, *Rediscovering Paul*.

148. Witherington, *Paul's Narrative Thought World*, 2.

formulations.¹⁴⁹ There is an underlying narrative that informs Paul's correspondence. Proponents of a narrative approach to Paul suggest that attention be paid to the subnarrative, the narrative contours that influence Paul's discourse and reflections.

Chief among the advocates of narrative approach to Paul is Richard B. Hays. He is considered the pioneer of contemporary study of the Pauline Letters through narrative lenses. In his 1983 monograph, *The Faith of Jesus Christ: An investigation of the Narrative Substructure of Galatians 3:1—4:11*, Hays provides methodological foundations for narratological components of Paul's theology. As the subtitle suggests, Hays argues that a narrative structure undergirds Paul's theological thought.¹⁵⁰ Taking Galatians 3:1—4:11 as a case study, Hays demonstrates that Paul's argument presupposes a story of Jesus Christ.

Reading Hays, one is reminded of Paul Ricoeur, from whom Hays undoubtedly draws his inspiration. Earlier in this chapter, we explicated Ricoeur's triple mimesis: "the world behind the text," "the world of the text," and "the world in front of the text." For Hays, as Bruce Longenecker writes, "a narrative is not 'behind' the text, detachable from it, but 'beneath' the text, undergirding it, supporting it, animating it, and giving it coherence, while also constraining its discursive options."¹⁵¹ To discern the story beneath the discourse in Paul's letters, Hays proposes that one identifies first allusions to the story and determine the story's outline. It is only then that can one inquire how the story shapes a given argument or mode of argumentation within a particular letter. Although The Faith of Jesus Christ deals only with Galatians, Hays's subsequent work offers to those who come after him a methodological basis for a narrative approach to Paul.

In 1985, as I mentioned earlier, Petersen published his famous *Rediscovering Paul: Philemon and the Sociology of Paul's Narrative World*. Proposing to identify the intersection between literary criticism and sociology, Petersen focuses on the narrative world of the Letter to Philemon and the narrative of Paul himself. He argues: "By using the literary notion of 'narrative world,' we gain a world to explore, namely the world referred to in the Letter to Philemon and the world referred to in the total corpus of Paul's letters."¹⁵²

---

149. Longenecker, "Narrative Interest in the Study of Paul," 3.
150. Hays, *Faith of Jesus Christ*, xxiii.
151. Longenecker, "Narrative Interest in the Study of Paul," 6.
152. Petersen, *Rediscovering Paul*, 1.

Put differently, Petersen, following the trajectory traced by Ricoeur and adapted by Hays, looks into the symbolic universe presupposed by Paul's theologizing. He argues that like all of the machineries for universe-maintenance, theology corresponds to the experience of problems in living within the inherited symbolic universe, whether these problems originate in failures of the universe or in competing representations of it.[153] Paul's narrative world, the symbolic universe, serves as the pre-text to his "systematic" form of reflection conveyed in the letters.

N. T. Wright and Ben Witherington III developed further this notion of the symbolic universe in Paul's letters. In his *New Testament and the People of God*, Wright argues that "worldview" (his term for "narrative world") is foundational, presuppositional to any discourse, any culture or society. For Wright, "worldviews provide the stories through which human beings view reality. Narrative is the most characteristic expression of a worldview, going deeper than the isolated observation or fragmented remark."[154] Through stories, he argues, one can discover how to answer existential questions: who are we, where are we, what is wrong, and what is the solution?[155] Hence, Wright perceives an implicit narrative, a story, imbedded in Paul's letters, and he proposes that one can understand the more limited narrative worlds of letters by placing them within the overall story world, the symbolic universe that accompanies them.[156]

Witherington takes up the same thesis in *Paul's Narrative Thought World: The Tapestry of Tragedy and Triumph* (1994). Like his predecessors, he posits that there is a story undergirding Paul's letters. He is convinced that all Paul's ideas, all his arguments, all his practical advice, all his social arrangements are ultimately grounded in a story.[157] For Witherington, Paul adapted his megastory to the particular situations, producing a symbolic universe. Consequently, good exegesis of Paul's letters need to investigate the Pauline context and his narrative thought world and to interpret the Letters as discourse, as reflection on that narrative.

The narrative approach to Paul has offered two interrelated benefits: to see history as narrative and to discover the underlying narrative of Paul's letters. But in order to fully appreciate the insights gained by applying a

---

153. Petersen, *Rediscovering Paul*, 30.
154. Wright, *New Testament and the People of God*, 122.
155. Wright, *New Testament and the People of God*, 123.
156. Wright, *New Testament and the People of God*, 405.
157. Witherington, *Paul's Narrative Thought World*, 2.

narrative approach to Paul, one needs to answer a number of questions: (1) What is the story behind Paul's letters? (2) Is there one story or are there multiple stories? (3) Is the story or are the stories linear, with plot, characterization, and a clear beginning, middle, and end, or is there a web of stories beneath Paul's letters, perhaps even rhetorical variations of a story? (4) Do all letters contain the same story or stories?

Many interpreters of the Pauline corpus who have used narrative criticism have focused primarily on Galatians and Romans. Hence, they assume that other letters have no narratives. Based on those two letters, some among Paul's interpreters have argued for a megastory, a scriptural metanarrative in Paul's letters. Longenecker summarizes this positions as follows:

> Proponents of the narrative study of Paul frequently differentiate several narrative ingredients, although their taxonomies vary. Wright for instance, prefers to speak largely of a single story operative in Paul's thinking: the 'story of God, Israel, and the world as now compressed into the story of Jesus,' or the 'story of Israel understood as the story through which the Creator God is restoring the creation, and with it the race of Adam and Eve.' Matera identified three narrative ingredients within a larger unfolding story: 'the story of Israel,' 'the story of Christ,' 'the story of his [Paul's] own life.' Like Wright, Witherington wants to maintain the integrity of an overarching macro-Story, but Witherington finds it advisable to do so by identifying four microstories within it: (1) the story of a world gone wrong; (2) the story of Israel in that world; (3) the story of Christ . . . and (4) the story of Christians, including Paul himself . . . Dunn identifies five distinct narrative ingredients: the story of God and creation, with the story of Israel superimposed upon it . . . the story of Jesus, and then Paul's own story . . . Finally, there are the complex interactions of Paul's own story with the stories of those who had believed before him and those who came to form the churches founded by them.[158]

I propose to expand the narrative approach to Paul and apply it to Phlm. I am not the first to do so. Petersen has already set the tone. And in 2013, Valan Chinnappa wrote an entire doctoral dissertation arguing that the Letter to Philemon is a narrative and demonstrating how the ἐν Χριστῷ motif is the theological matrix of the letter.[159] Following in the footsteps of my predecessors, I would demonstrate that Phlm deserves the same

---

158. Longenecker "Narrative Interest in the Study of Paul," 12.
159. Chinnappa, "The Theological Matrix of Philemon's Narrative Structure."

attention enjoyed by Galatians and Romans. There is a story (or stories) in Phlm that prompted the writing of the letter. It is the event recounted implicitly by Paul, a linear story with characters, a plot, a rhetoric, a beginning, a middle, and allusions to its end. Moreover, there is a story of Jesus, a story of Paul and his converts, namely Philemon and Onesimus, all interwoven and spatialized by Paul's discourse in the letter. But more than my predecessors, I apply insights from spatial theory to demonstrate how Paul produces a thirdspace, which I call *koinōnia*-space, an alternative worldview, where people live in transformed relationships.

Conclusion

The purpose of this chapter was twofold: on the one hand, I surveyed the interpretation history of the Letter to Philemon and discussed the different approaches and questions that guided various readers from the patristic period through the postmodern era. The survey has revealed that the typical line of inquiry among the letter's interpreters has been either the endorsement of the *fugitivus* hypothesis as set forward by John Chrysostom or its rejection by recent interpreters, particularly by African American scholars and those who identify themselves as marginal readers. Resting on the shoulders of past and recent interpreters, I have proposed combining narrative criticism and social-spatial theory in a fresh and interdisciplinary approach to the study of Phlm.

Drawing insights from narrative theorists, I have demonstrated that Phlm contains narrative features that many interpreters tend to overlook. But unlike my predecessors who have interpreted Phlm through the prism of narrative criticism, I have innovatively proposed to apply insights from social-spatial theory. As shall become clear in the subsequent chapters, social-spatial theory helps one see how the Letter to Philemon deconstructs what Edward Soja terms perceived, conceived, and lived spaces[160] in order

---

160. Both Lefebvre and Soja speak of "trialectics of spatiality" that comprises three axes: perceived space, conceived space, and lived space. Soja calls Lefebvre's *perceived space* "first space." This is the physical space, perceptible by the senses. It can be a building, a piece of land, any structure of everyday life that can be demarcated. The *conceived space* or Soja's "second space" is the mental or theoretical space. It is the signified that one sees beyond the sign, the meaning that a building represents, for example. It is a space produced by structures of power. The *lived space* or Soja's "thirdspace" is the social life with its joys and struggles. It is a space where the perceived and the conceived are experienced. (Soja, *Thirdspace*, 67, 74–75).

to produce an alternative space that I call "*koinōnia*-space," a place of radical kinship and human authenticity. Social-spatial theory will be instrumental in understanding how the different spaces Paul and his converts inhabit function both as "containers" and as "a network of relationships."[161] Insights from social-spatial theory will also help me explain how space shapes the plot in Phlm, especially as I explore how the characters negotiate strategically and emotionally the different spaces in the narrative. But we cannot really understand the spaces narrated in the text apart from the Roman Empire and its slave system. It is to this world behind the text of Phlm that we now turn.

---

161. The metaphors of space as "a container" and space as "a network of relationship" help one understand the interplay between narrative and space. See Ryan, *Narrating Space, Spatializing Narrative*, 56–57. Every storytelling involves the interplay between space as a container and space as a network. It is in negotiating the tension between containers within a network of social interactions that the narrator or storyteller helps readers or listeners come to grips with the narrative's plot.

2

Roman Slavery as a Complex Network of Relationships

Introduction

SLAVERY IN THE ANCIENT Roman Empire was not a monolithic, undifferentiated institution. Nor was it a simple system of labor. Rather, it was an institution that possessed a variety of dimensions. My purpose is to explore a number of those facets, ones that I believe help us understand Roman slavery as a complex network of relationships and hence as indispensable background to the narrative of Paul's Letter to Philemon. In brief, I examine the issues of Rome as a slave society, the relationship between slavery and Roman social hierarchies, how men and women became slaves, ancient theories of slavery and freedom, distinctions among Roman slaves, manumission, and how the slaves themselves could, and did, create some space for themselves in which they had a measure of freedom and dignity. Aware that the institution of slavery changed over time in the history of the Roman Empire, I would like to specify from the outset that I am focusing mainly on what historians call "Early Empire" (roughly between the late Republic and the end of the second century CE). I shall conclude this chapter with a brief comparative study of Roman slavery and modern forms of dehumanization as a way of preparing the ground for the interpretation of the Letter to Philemon in the context of the DRC.

Slavery in Rome

Slavery played a pivotal role in the socioeconomic structures of the Roman world. In a society where status, honor, and prestige constituted the modus vivendi of citizens, mostly among the elites, the presence of slaves was important for the exhibition of power, wealth, and influence. Whether in its Italian core or to varying degrees in its subject territories, Roman society depended on the institution of slavery.

Rome was a slave society. It was not just a society with slaves. It is common among historians to define a "slave society" quantitatively and qualitatively. In his *Slavery and Society at Rome*, Keith Bradley discusses three methods of determining a slave society. The first method applies a demographic test. This test aims to determine in a given population the degree to which slaves provide a significant source of economic power as opposed to simply being present.[1] He finds that the number of slaves and the important role they played in economic production qualified Roman Italy as a slave society similar to slave societies in the New World: Brazil, the Caribbean, and the United States.

In addition to the demographic test, Bradley applies a second method for determining a slave society. It is a qualitative method, which seeks to determine the slaves' location; that is, to determine who their owners were and what role slaves played both in the economy and other structures of the social life.[2] As I shall discuss later in this chapter, slaves dominated the production of goods and services both in Italy and in many localities in the Roman Empire, thereby providing elites with the bulk of their immediate income from property.[3] Knowing the number of slave owners and how many slaves they owned helps determine the scale of production expected from slaves and hence determines whether a society is a slave society or not. This qualitative method proves that Roman society was a genuine slaveholding society. It could be argued that the Roman Empire was the most important slave society in world history.

Bradley's third method for determining a slave society is much broader than the first two. It rests on the idea of dependent labor. Because wealthy Romans drew most of their income from exploiting unfree labor (debt bondage, serfdom, and so forth), it is possible to call their world a

---

1. Bradley, *Slavery and Society at Rome*, 12.
2. Bradley, *Slavery and Society at Rome*, 12.
3. Bradley, *Slavery and Society at Rome*, 13.

slave society or a slave economy.[4] Seen by many as a class-oriented society, ancient Rome depended heavily on slavery; the wealth, status, and leisure of elites were all built on the labor and lives of slaves.[5] Now, if Rome was a slave society, a number of questions are worth asking about the slaves themselves: What status did slaves have? Who were they? What were their origins? What ideas did they develop about this horrible institution?

According to Peter Garnsey, "a slave was property. The slave-owner's rights over his slave-property were total, covering the person as well as the labour of the slave. The slave was kinless, stripped of his or her old social identity in the process of capture, sale and deracination, and denied the capacity to forge new bonds of kinship through marriage alliance."[6] In other words, Roman slaves were chattel.

Orlando Patterson, however, is not content with a simple definition of slavery based on the idea of property. For him, ownership is far more complex than one would think. In many societies, people have all kinds of property rights upon other human beings. In fact, any person can be the object of property relations. Slaves are no different in this respect.[7] Hence, to avoid the confusion that a legalistic modern term such as property could generate, Patterson defines slavery as "the permanent, violent, domination of natally alienated and generally dishonored persons."[8]

Patterson's definition is helpful for three reasons. First, it points out the permanency and hereditary nature of slavery. Those born slaves inherit their parents' ordeal and bequeath the same heritage to their offspring unless they are freed before having descendants. The permanent and hereditary character of slavery made it different from other forms of bondage, such as debt bondage or indenture, for instance. Second, Patterson's exploration of slavery as a form of domination rather than a matter of property demonstrates the consistent workings of the institution not only in the five large-scale slave societies of history (all central to the development of Europe and European culture) that have dominated scholarly discussion to this day but across the sixty-six slaveholding societies identified in Murdock and White's Standard Cross-Cultural Sample of 186 human

---

4. Bradley, *Slavery and Society at Rome*, 13.
5. Joshel, *Slavery in the Roman World*, 9.
6. Garnsey, *Ideas of Slavery*, 1.
7. Patterson, *Slavery and Social Death*, 21.
8. Patterson, *Slavery and Social Death*, 13.

societies around the world today.⁹ Third, Patterson's emphasis on power relation in his definition of slavery is instrumental in understanding the modern forms of dehumanization after the abolition of slavery as a system. We shall come back to this last point at the end of this chapter. For now, let us understand first the nature and origins of slaves in Roman society.

Who were Roman slaves, and what were their origins? With the devastating memories of New World slavery in the United States, the Caribbean, Brazil, and elsewhere, anyone unaware of the Roman slave system might assume that Romans went to Africa to acquire slaves among black people in the sub-Saharan regions. That is the danger of approaching the ancient world with modern categories and ideologies in mind. Not everything true of the New World slavery was true of the ancient Roman slave system. Roman slavery was not based on race or on ethnicity. Roman slaves came from many places and situations. Most historians of ancient Rome agree on four major areas of Roman slave supply, namely, from war, from natural reproduction, from trade, and from piracy.

One of the characteristics of the Roman Empire was the efficiency of its military machine. The Roman military forces fought against neighbors and extended the empire by conquering most of the Mediterranean world and territory beyond. Consequently, "much is heard in the sources of enslaving a vanquished enemy en masse, a habit the Romans probably acquired as their military and political influence spiralled throughout the Italian peninsula in the fourth and early third century BC."[10] Although the first century saw a general winding down of Rome's major conquests, in subsequent centuries slavery continued to be a significant component of Roman society across the empire. In general, war slaves were conveyed without delay from the site of capture for dispersal in the marketplaces in the Roman heartland. Some slaves were sold off on the spot to itinerant dealers or distributed to the troops as a form of payment.[11]

A second source of slaves for the Roman Empire was natural reproduction among the slave population. According to Bradley, "slaves born of a slave woman took their status from their mother (that of the father was irrelevant) and were known as *vernae*."[12] These slaves were different from enslaved prisoners or those who sold themselves because they were in debt

---

9. Bodel and Scheidel, *On Human Bondage*, 6.
10. Bradley, *Slavery and Society at Rome*, 33.
11. Bradley, *Slavery and Society at Rome*, 33.
12. Bradley, *Slavery and Society at Rome*, 33.

or for other economic reasons. Living in a society obsessed with status and hierarchy, the *vernae* distinguished themselves from other slaves by being identified as home-born slaves.[13]

In addition to the home-born slaves, Roman slaves were also acquired through trade. Rome commanded a vast long-distance trade network extending well beyond the borders of the core imperial territories. Such a long-distance trade system involved both goods and human beings. A slave, like a piece of land, an animal, or an inanimate object, could be sold, lent, mortgaged, given away, or bequeathed in a will.[14] Regions surrounding the empire supplied Rome with slaves of all kinds. Bradley notes, for instance, that "in the east, the western regions of the Black Sea had been supplying the Mediterranean with slaves since the seventh century BC and from recent investigation it appears that areas to the east of the Black Sea, specifically the regions of the Caucasus, had long been involved as well."[15] In the west, it can be deduced from the distribution of Italian wine-jars discovered in Gaul that Gallic slaves were exchanged for Italian wine, as many as fifteen thousand a year.[16] Clearly, the trade system known in antiquity supplied Rome with incredible numbers of slaves to be used for different purposes.

The fourth means of obtaining slaves in the Roman Empire was through piracy. Pirates were notorious sea peoples who operated along the coastlands of the Aegean and the Mediterranean engaging in illicit activities including kidnapping and human trafficking. Bradley points out that "the island of Delos, where [Cilician pirates] dumped their victims because they knew Roman merchants were waiting there to receive them, is said to have turned over tens of thousands of slaves daily in the early second century BC."[17] Be it in distant provinces or in Italy, piracy was a widespread activity that led countless men and women into slavery in exchange for cash.

This discussion of the means by which the Roman Empire acquired its slaves (through war, natural reproduction, trade, and piracy) informs us not only about the mechanisms set in place to receive, transport, and work large supplies of slaves, but indicates the complex and variegated nature of the slave population in Rome. How did the ancients describe this varied population of slaves?

13. Bradley, *Slavery and Society at Rome*, 33.
14. Joshel, *Slavery in the Roman World*, 38.
15. Bradley, *Slavery and Society at Rome*, 36.
16. Bradley, *Slavery and Society at Rome*, 36.
17. Bradley, *Slavery and Society at Rome*, 37.

Roman Slavery as a Complex Network of Relationships

Although the Roman Empire could well be categorized as developing the largest slave institution in history, this does not mean that slavery was unique to Rome. Orlando Patterson states in the preface to *Slavery and Social Death*, "there is nothing notably peculiar about the institution of slavery. It has existed from the dawn of human history right down to the twentieth century, in the most primitive of human societies and in the most civilized."[18] Roman slavery was not a novelty. It was only one of many slave systems spread over time and space.

Inseparable from human history, slavery has generated, mutatis mutandis, different theories from philosophers, poets, lawyers, and evangelists. As a social product, slavery has been justified and sustained by intellectuals and people in power. Among these was the influential philosopher and theorist, Aristotle. His view of slavery was used by later generations in the Roman Empire to perpetuate the institution. Alongside Aristotle, we find in the first century CE Stoic philosophers and Christian writers who had opinions on the institution of slavery. It is important that we briefly explore here these different understandings of slavery and their impact on society as a whole.

Aristotle was the pioneer of what has been known as "natural slavery." In *Politics* 1254a4–18, he defines a natural slave in the following terms: "One who is a human being belonging by nature not to himself but to another is by nature a slave; and a person is a human being to another if being a man he is an article of property, and an article of property is an instrument for action separable from its owner."[19] Aristotle's definition of a natural slave emphasizes the total control of one human being by another human being. What seems natural about a natural slave is that the slave is born to be ruled by another person. The slave does not belong to himself or herself. At first, Aristotle's definition does not seem to bring anything new to the definition of the status of a slave as known throughout history. However, reading his understanding of natural slavery within the context of his moral philosophy, one can start to see his point. As a moral philosopher, Aristotle understood slavery as the opposite of freedom, the latter being the use of one's reason. Those are free who belong to themselves, and those belong to themselves who think for themselves and use their reason to pursue happiness. Those who are unable to do so are slaves by nature, and need to belong to those who can orient them and decide for them. Hence, Aristotle writes,

---

18. Patterson, *Slavery and Social Death*, vii.
19. Quoted in Garnsey, *Ideas of Slavery*, 108.

"for he is by nature a slave who is capable of belonging to another (and that is why he does so belong), and who participates in reason so far as to apprehend it but not to possess it; for the animals other than man are subservient not to reason, by apprehending it, but to feelings."[20] For Aristotle, natural slaves, unable to deliberate and decide for themselves, need to follow their masters, who can decide for them and determine the course of their lives.

Aristotle's natural slave theory was more ideological than a true description of the reality of slavery. Those recognized as slaves in the Roman Empire, as the next section shall show, did not fit into Aristotle's definition. Understood as a network of relationships, the institution of slavery was anchored on authoritative theories such as Aristotle's natural slave thesis to justify the deplorable master-slave relations. Hence, Aristotle was welcomed in a society like Rome, adamant as it was about binary understanding of social relations: the poor and the rich, the slave and the free, the male and the female, and so on. In fact, Aristotle's natural-slave theory betrays the ancient Greek philosophical tendency to organize ideas in terms of pairs of mutually exclusive polar opposites. Consequently, Roman law inherited this pattern in its legal texts, giving the impression that slavery was an essential division of society. Roman jurists felt the necessity to define and demarcate the rights and obligations of each status group. Slaves were the lowest status group of society and lived in a state of absolute subjugation.[21] Aristotle's legacy endured and deeply influenced Roman institutions. But subsequent thinkers did not all repeat Aristotle's natural-slave theory. Stoic philosophers and Christian theologians had another way of understanding slavery.

Many philosophical movements in the late fourth and third century BCE departed from mainstream philosophy as developed by Plato and Aristotle. Among these movements was Stoicism. Although there is no clear evidence of how the Stoics rejected Aristotle's natural-slave theory, one could infer from their philosophical doctrine a different perception of slaves. For Stoics, "every good man is free, and every bad man is a slave."[22] Their main concern was individual morality and the role nature plays in regulating human behavior. They did not deny humanity to a category of people and justify their subjection with theories based on natural law. Garnsey summarizes well the Stoics' take on the question slavery:

---

20. Quoted in Garnsey, *Ideas of Slavery*, 109.
21. Wiedemann, *Greek and Roman Slavery*, 1.
22. Quoted in Garnsey, *Ideas of Slavery*, 129.

> The contribution of Stoicism to slave theory was to shift the focus of attention from legal to moral slavery. In so doing they were no longer asking, as Aristotle was forced to do, how the starkest form of legal exploitation of some people by others could be justified, but how humans could free their souls from oppression by the passions and emotions, and bring their moral attitudes and behavior into line with a higher law than the law of man, the law of Nature.[23]

Although they did not oppose the institution of slavery, Stoics taught slaves to accept their slave status as it did not affect their soul but was only an exterior reality. They were given the example of Diogenes the Cynic, who, although sold into slavery, did not lose the goodness within himself. Instead, he became the master of his Corinthian master, and taught him and his household the principles of morality, which brought them out of their "slavery."

Stoic philosophy had a considerable impact on early Christian theologians like Paul. In his letters found in the New Testament, Paul's understanding of slavery echoes the Stoic moral interpretation of this dehumanizing institution. To be sure, Paul understood slavery to be a legal institution of the empire. However, as I argue in this book and as far as the Letter to Philemon is concerned, Paul proposed an alternative narrative, a messianic worldview that challenged Roman slavery on the ecclesial level and created a *koinōnia*-space, a space where both slaves and masters could live like true brothers and sisters.

Unlike Aristotle and his contemporaries, who developed theories to legitimize the institution of slavery, Stoics and Christian theologians like Paul shifted the discourse on slavery. Instead of providing masters with reasons to mistreat their slaves at will, they challenged them to reconsider their conception of slavery and freedom. In fact, their teachings were addressed to slaves as well as to masters, putting the two parties on equal footing in moral and spiritual terms. All these ideas about slavery are better understood if placed in a discussion of actual slave practices. In the next section, I shall describe the different groups of slaves known in the Roman Empire, and analyze more closely the relationships between masters and slaves both in rural and urban settings.

---

23. Garnsey, *Ideas of Slavery*, 155.

Slave Labor: Understanding the Master-Slave Relationship

In the preceding section, I examined how Rome was a slave society and the different ways human beings were acquired as chattel. In this section, I seek to discuss the new condition of those men and women acquired as slaves in the Roman Empire. I will inquire into the network of relationships that existed between slaves and their masters, and by doing so demonstrate that Roman slavery was a social network of mutual dependency between master, slave, and community—a relationship predicated on a system of dehumanization. I shall discuss the main divisions of slaves in Rome, and survey briefly their labor and its impact on the Roman economy and social status.

Discussing slave labor in the Roman Empire, Bradley writes, "For legal purposes the Romans divided slaves into two categories: those who belonged to the city household, the *familia urbana*, and those who belonged to the rural household, the *familia rustica*."[24] A general knowledge of social and political life in the Roman Empire helps in understanding this division of slaves. Rome was a remarkably hierarchical society. One's position in the social order mattered more than anything else. Social relationships were determined by one's position in the following scale of importance: nobles, senators, equestrians (social elite), municipal magistrates, freeborn Roman citizens, freed slaves (who could become citizens), and slaves.[25] As can be seen, slaves were at the bottom of the social pyramid.

Despite their low status, slaves adapted to the standards of Roman society. Needless to say, hierarchy within the slave population was predicated on the status and the possessions of slave owners. It was commonplace for slave owners to have a residence in the city and a second property in the countryside. Consequently, slaves were divided between both properties: some served in the residence as domestics; others worked in the fields. However, some slaves did both kinds of duties, depending on the wealth of their masters. Some slave owners could afford a multitude to be dispatched in different places. Thus, as Bradley suggests, "it was not the place of employment but the type of work that determined how a slave was categorized."[26] The *rustici* (the slaves who worked the fields) were considered inferior to the *urbani* (those who lived in the city).

---

24. Bradley, *Slavery and Society at Rome*, 58.
25. Joshel, *Slavery in the Roman World*, 31.
26. Bradley, *Slavery and Society at Rome*, 58.

Roman Slavery as a Complex Network of Relationships

The distinction between rural and urban slaves was important. But equally important was the fact that slaves were engaged in a variety of occupations. Bradley lists different jobs performed by Roman slaves. Slaves worked as estate managers, field hands, shepherds, hunters, domestic servants, artisans, builders, retailers, miners, clerks, teachers, doctors, midwives, wet-nurses, textile-makers, potters, and entertainers.[27] Slaves served both in the private sector and in the public administration, depending on whether they were owned by individuals, the state, communities, or temples. Their occupations ranged from the most basic tasks of footwashing and carrying water to the complex duties of stewardship and business management. To illustrate the complexity of slave labor and slaves' relationships with their masters and with society, I shall analyze the so-called *familia Caesaris* and the household of a provincial citizen described by Apuleius in his *Golden Ass*.

Familia Caesaris, that is Caesar's family, was a complex network of relationships of power and dependency. Caesar's *familia* was more than a regular nuclear family. It was the emperor's bureaucracy made up of extended family members and a large number of slaves and freedmen. Imperial slaves were assigned different responsibilities, covering both economic and political spheres.

The emperor was not just another rich man. Peter Hunt observes that from the beginning of the empire, the emperor's personal wealth was incomparably larger than that of any other individual and included property in far-flung provinces.[28] As time went by, the emperor's wealth increased. The emperor needed more hands to work in his estates, manage his property, and fulfill all the tasks of his household. Thus, he used the slaves and freedmen of his *familia* in a whole range of activities: as water-carriers, treasurers, clerks, doctors, painters, builders, pearl-setters, shoemakers, wool-weighers, and so forth. The list of slave labor in Caesar's *familia* can be found in Bradley's *Slavery and Society at Rome*.[29]

Politically, the emperor was the center of the government. Although some branches of the government were delegated to the Roman elite, namely the senate and the equestrian order, the emperor still supervised all aspects of the imperial administration. Hunt points out that central government functions, such as managing the imperial budget, needed to be taken

---

27. Bradley, *Slavery and Society at Rome*, 59–63.
28. Hunt, *Ancient Greek and Roman Slavery*, 75.
29. Bradley, *Slavery and Society at Rome*, 62.

care of at Rome. Hence, it was natural for the emperor to supervise those tasks himself.[30] To do so, he turned to his slaves and freedmen because he could not use senators as his subordinates. Hunt notes that it would have been awkward for an emperor of the traditional aristocracy to closely supervise senators and equestrians, or to have them read his mail, take his dictation, keep track of his finances, and draft responses to all the requests that came to him. The sensibilities of the aristocracy would be offended by such direct, daily, and long-term subordination to the emperor.[31] Moreover, the emperor did not always have perfect relations with the senate. A senator could at any time use his administrative power to advance his own status, and this could be to the emperor's disadvantage. To avoid such outcomes and to secure his power, wealth, and status, the emperor depended on slaves and freedmen of his *familia* to constitute his bureaucracy.

The imperial *familia* was not the only household with multiple slaves engaged in multiple tasks. As Bradley cautions, the imperial household was extraordinary only in degree not in kind.[32] Many elite households in the Roman urban families had a large retinue of slaves engaged in multiple tasks. Apuleius, in his *Golden Ass*, describes a group of slaves engaged in different tasks in the household of a leading provincial citizen. He mentions that the provincial citizen has a cook (who was married and had a son), a gatekeeper, a muleteer, a chamberlain, a physician, and several other members of the household.[33]

It can be concluded from these two examples (the *familia Caesaris* and Apuleius's provincial influential citizen) that household slaves, and slaves in general, performed various tasks to meet the needs of their masters. Even though some slaves occupied important positions (in the case of imperial slaves), their dignity was still at stake. They served the interest of a powerful man and secured his wealth, status, and power. Therefore, any attempt to assess the influence of slaves on the Roman family should consider the vast divergences in their working conditions and individual situations within the slave hierarchy. What does seem clear is that slaves were able to make the lives of the families to which they belonged very much more complicated, and in many cases, especially within an urban household, they had power to affect intrafamily relationships in a manner that far belied their lowly legal

---

30. Hunt, *Ancient Greek and Roman Slavery*, 76.
31. Hunt, *Ancient Greek and Roman Slavery*, 76–77.
32. Bradley, *Slavery and Society at Rome*, 63.
33. Apuleius, *Golden Ass*, 9:2.

Roman Slavery as a Complex Network of Relationships

status.[34] The fact that slaves could complicate things within families to which they belonged testifies to the truth that they had some agency and were able to resist slavery. It is to this point that we now turn.

Resistance and Agency

If slavery was a network of relationships based on the dehumanization of the exploited, it is not illogical to think that there must have been some forms of resistance to it. Slaves were not merely passive victims, but they also possessed agency; they played an active role in finding ways to alleviate their ordeal. In his advice to his fellow slave owners, Marcus Sidonius Falx writes:[35]

> You have as many enemies as you have slaves, as a slave owner, you must keep this traditional saying constantly at the back of your mind ... The great mass of slaves in our society is like an unexploded volcano, waiting like Vesuvius to erupt and destroy our great Roman civilization. Their conditions are not always as fair as they should be and they harbor grudges for the defeats and perceived indignities they have suffered at our hands. You should not be surprised, therefore, to find that many slaves will carry out many acts of resistance against your authority. Some of these are major and threatening, others far more minor and merely annoying.[36]

Falx's advice raises a number of questions concerning the significance of resistance on the part of slaves and the types of slave resistance: What were the objectives of such resistance and its effects on the slave system? Did resistance alleviate, worsen, or abolish slavery? It would take a whole book to tackle these big questions. Instead, I only wish to propose that Roman slaves were neither passive oppressed people nor constant virulent protesters against the institution such as arose in the Caribbean, Brazil, and the United States. But they did possess agency; there existed certain forms of resistance undertaken by slaves to reduce the burden of servitude or to exit

---

34. Edmondson, "Slavery and the Roman Family," 360.

35. The fictionalized figure of Marcus Sidonius Falx is a subject of debate among academics. However, despite the uncertainty of Falx's real existence, his notes offer us a Roman's-eye view of slavery. Describing himself as a Roman of noble birth whose family have kept slaves for generations, Falx helps one form an idea about how Roman slaveowners managed their property in the Roman Empire. Arguably, the substance of his words survives in other well-known Roman texts on slavery.

36. Falx, *How to Manage Your Slaves*, 140.

the system altogether. Hence I shall first lay out some forms of slave resistance and then focus more on the frequent practice of running away.

The best-known slave revolt recorded in Roman antiquity is the one led by the gladiator Spartacus between 73 and 71 BCE.[37] Forced to fight as gladiators, two hundred slaves disobeyed and fled. Seventy-eight of them formed a rebellion under the leadership of Spartacus to challenge the Roman army. For two years, they roamed throughout Italy with an army formed from the tens of thousands of slaves who flocked to join him, defeating a series of Roman legionary forces and posing a great threat to Rome.[38] Although Spartacus was defeated, his rebellion left an indelible mark, reminding Rome and the whole world that slaves were humans who could demonstrate their willingness to take action against excessive and dehumanizing treatment.

The Spartacus revolt was hardly the first large-scale slave revolt Rome had to deal with. Two similar slave uprisings occurred in Sicily in the later second century BCE, both of which involved huge numbers of slaves, and both of which required a substantial Roman military response. Again, as Bradley reminds us, "there is little sign that either revolt was well coordinated or planned from the outset as a general insurrection of all Sicilian slaves: each began as a localised uprising that developed almost spontaneously into a larger action according to the extant accounts."[39] Yet the harsh conditions resulting from intense exploitation were factors that contributed to the scale of slave revolts, and as far as can be discerned, the intentions of the rebellious slaves were only to extricate themselves from slavery, not to alter in any fundamental way existing social and economic structures; as in the case of Spartacus's revolt, there were no calls for ending slavery.[40]

After the suppression of the Spartacus revolt by the Roman army, there was no major slave rebellions in the Roman Empire. Any attempted rebellious act was easily annihilated. However, many forms of resistance emerged in everyday life among slaves. Those forms ranged from violent acts, such as suicide or murderous assaults on slave owners, to the far less extreme actions of lying, cheating, stealing, pretending to be sick, or working at a calculatedly slow pace, of resorting in fact to many forms of petty sabotage. As a result, slaves could cause their masters constant annoyance

37. Grenouilleau, *Qu'est-ce que l'esclavage?*, 364.
38. Bradley, *Slavery and Society at Rome*, 109.
39. Bradley, "Resisting Slavery at Rome," 365.
40. Bradley, "Resisting Slavery at Rome," 366.

and frustration.[41] Thus, everyday conflict between slaves and masters afforded agency to the maltreated.

The most significant type of resistance was running away. It is common knowledge that confronted with adversity, human beings have two options: fight or flight. When one is not strong enough to fight and secure their peace and integrity, they flee, separating themselves from the threat. Roman slaves constantly ran away from their masters. Their reasons varied. However, often the root cause of their flight was nothing else than the cruelty of slavery. When it was successful, running away offered the advantage of terminating the relationship between slave and master and thus removing the possibility of a master's retaliation.[42] Running away was not an uncomplicated endeavor for either the slave or the master. Slaves had to take their lives in their hands to run away from their masters, and, conversely, masters had to risk everything to recover their properties.

That runaway slaves were ubiquitous in the Roman Empire is attested by different sources: Documentary papyri from Roman Egypt, and classic imaginative literature, and legal sources such as the *Digest*, offer ample examples of runaway slaves and the onerous means used by their masters to recover them. Exploring the documentary papyri from Roman Egypt, Bradley discusses the content of a letter from the late third century in which a woman named Aurelius Serapias seeks the help of a district governor (*stratēgos*) in tracking down her runaway slave Serapion.[43] She is very concerned to recover a family property who was an invaluable tool for household jobs. Serapias seems to have an idea where her slave might be, but recovering him was not guaranteed.[44]

This example shows that a slave, Serapion, ran away by himself to find refuge in a concealed place. However, the papyri contain examples of other fugitives who ran away in groups of three, four, or five.[45] Given that running away was a dangerous endeavor, it is possible that some slaves feared to face this challenge as solitary pilgrims. They would have preferred to be in a small group to comfort one another, to develop better strategies of resistance when faced with adversity, and to constitute together a significant loss for their masters.

41. Bradley, *Slavery and Society at Rome*, 110.
42. Hunt, *Ancient Greek and Roman Slavery*, 147.
43. Bradley, *Slavery and Society at Rome*, 118.
44. Bradley, *Slavery and Society at Rome*, 118.
45. Bradley, *Slavery and Society at Rome*, 118.

Beloved Brother or Slave?

In their efforts to recover their slaves, masters used any means possible. One of those means was the "wanted poster." Hunt provides an example of an "Egyptian wanted poster" that reads: "If any person finds a slave named Philippos ... about fourteen years old, light in complexion, who speaks haltingly, has a flat nose, wearing a ... woolen garment and used shoulder belt, he should bring him to the army post and receive."[46]

Though incomplete and fragmentary, this Egyptian wanted poster tells us many things about Roman slavery. The slave's description shows that Roman slavery had nothing to do with race. If slavery was the peculiarity of a specific race as was the case in the New World, the master would not have had to provide many details about the slave. All would have recognized a runaway slave by the color of his or her skin. Moreover, slaves would have been more hesitant to undertake such a perilous journey, knowing that they would be easily recognizable by their skin color. Although slaves in the Roman Empire had many other distinctive signs that could help people recognize them, they could easily manage to mingle among free people without being recognized by something so obvious as skin color.

Another element revealed in the poster is the recompense promised to the slave catcher. Although in the quoted text the nature of the recompense is missing, many slave owners specified what the recompense would be. Not only did masters state the reward for helping them catch their slaves, but the law also encouraged slave catchers to help slave owners recover their slaves. In the *Digest*, Callistratus makes clear that captured runways should normally be returned to their owners but that they should be punished "more severely" if they had tried to pass as free while on the loose.[47]

From the preceding discussion, it can be concluded that Roman slaves developed different strategies to resist slavery and to find an alternative for the betterment of their lives. The slave-master relationship was imbued with an aura of unbearable humiliation and despicable dehumanization that generated resistance and revolt. Although considered animated tools, Roman slaves proved their humanity by having agency as they carried out multifaceted resistance to the horrifying system of slavery. Their actions of resistance point to the common aspiration of all human beings: freedom. In the following section, I shall discuss the practice of manumission in the Roman Empire, and see to what extent it was a happy end for Roman slaves.

---

46. Hunt, *Ancient Greek and Roman Slavery*, 149.
47. The *Digest* 11. 4.2, quoted in Bradley, *Slavery and Society at Rome*, 121.

Manumission

Despite their social death and daily torment at the hands of their masters, slaves never ceased to long for freedom. Despite the moral and legal arguments used to justify the institution of slavery in Rome, slaves continued to see their situation as an unjust fate imposed on them by a cruel society. They believed they deserved to be free like the rest of human beings. Even slave owners acknowledged this longing for freedom on the part of their slaves and used it to secure their own advantages. Consequently, manumission was a frequent practice in the Roman Empire. It was one of those practices that gives us insights into the complex network of relationships between slaves, masters, and free persons in Rome. In this section, I will discuss the frequency, the procedure, and the reasons for manumitting slaves, on the one hand; and on the other hand, I shall evaluate the impact of manumission on the relations between slaves and masters, and between masters and freedmen and freedwomen in Roman society.

Many historians agree that manumission was a well-known practice in the Roman Empire. In my discussion of social hierarchy in Rome, I pointed out that slaves occupied the lowest position, after freedmen and women. The presence of many freed slaves or ex-slaves in Rome is the first indicator that slave owners frequently manumitted some of their slaves. Because the word "many" is a vague way of quantifying the proportion of slaves that gained their freedom, I present some evidence that testifies to the frequency of manumission.

Cicero's speech in 43 BCE offers us the number of years a slave was supposed to work before he or she could earn freedom. According to Cicero, "frugal and hard-working captives" typically recovered their freedom within six years.[48] The number of years Cicero says that a slave should be kept in servitude does raise some problems. If slaves were bought and owned as tools of production, it does not seem that six years of servitude would generate enough profit for slave owners. A six-year term of enslavement may have been an exception for some slaves, but it was not a general rule for all slaves. Consequently, it has often been argued that Cicero used six years to symbolize the number of years Rome endured the tyrannical government under Julius Caesar.[49] Although Cicero's interval of six years of

---

48. Cicero, *Philippics* 3–9, 8.32.
49. Hunt, *Ancient Greek and Roman Slavery*, 119.

servitude for slaves hardly seems realistic, nevertheless his opinion testifies to the frequent practice of manumission in the Roman Empire.

In addition to Cicero's statement, one should also consider the number of epitaphs honoring slaves and ex-slaves. According to Hunt, "in several cases, historians possess sets of epitaphs numbering in the hundreds of the slaves and freed persons, the *familia*, from a particular Roman noble household."[50] The existence of epitaphs reveals two things: on the one hand, it tells us that mostly urban slaves and freed slaves were remembered through epitaphs if they served rich and noble masters capable of honoring their memories. On the other hand, it suggests that freed slaves did succeed in life and afford epitaphs that could celebrate the status they died with. It should always be kept in mind that Rome was a hierarchical society, and passing from a slave to a freed person would have been a considerable achievement worthy of recognition and honor.

A final piece of evidence for the practice of slave manumission is the existence of legal texts that determined the regulation of manumission. In the Early Roman Empire, Augustus imposed significant restrictions on manumission because it had become too frequent. Hence, new laws such as the *lex Fufia Caninia* and *lex Aelia Sentia* limited the number of slaves to be freed and the age of both slaves and masters at the moment of manumission.[51] The *Lex Aelia Sentia* stated that in principle a slave could not be manumitted before the age of thirty and that the slave-owner freeing a slave had to be twenty years old.[52] However, the law conceded a few exceptions. For instance, a slave owner under the age of twenty could manumit a slave after the council had accepted that there was a just cause for doing so. Just reasons for manumission existed where, for example, someone manumitted their father or mother, or a *paidagōgos,* or someone who had been brought up with them. Conversely, the same just reasons could be used in the case of a slave under the age of thirty.[53] Again, these legal restrictions and the other evidence demonstrate that manumission was frequent in the Roman Empire. But why and how did slave owners manumit their slaves?

Many reasons prompted masters to free their slaves, and the process could be private or public. As I stated earlier, freedom was the longing of all slaves, whether they expressed it or not. Knowing this to be true, it appears

---

50. Hunt, *Ancient Greek and Roman Slavery*, 119.
51. Dondin-Payre and Tran, *Esclaves et maîtres dans le monde romain*, 32.
52. Dondin-Payre and Tran, *Esclaves et maîtres dans le monde romain*, 32.
53. Wiedemann, *Greek and Roman Slavery*, 24–25.

Roman Slavery as a Complex Network of Relationships

that slave-owners used manumission to encourage obedience and make resistance and revolt less likely; it was a potent tool of social control.[54] When a slave knows that there is hope for freedom, he or she may patiently endure the hardships of slavery without necessarily revolting.

In a slave society like Rome, manumission was effective as an incentive. Because slavery was a network of relationships based on profit and exploitation, slaves were encouraged to save as much money as possible to purchase their freedom. In Hunt's words, manumission "allowed owners to divide up the big reward, freedom, into many small rewards and to use these to motivate slaves day after day, year after year."[55] It should be emphasized that not all slaves bought their freedom. There was a 5 percent tax imposed on manumission by Augustus.[56] Purchasing manumission was expensive, so most likely only owners would have been able to afford it, not the slaves themselves.

Owners granted manumission for other personal reasons. Falx records some of those personal reasons: many a master released a female slave because he grew affectionate towards her and wanted that relationship to become a legitimate marriage.[57] Some masters would free their slaves for helping them in carrying out crimes or in murderous actions. Others freed their slaves in large numbers because they wanted to have impressive funerals. Falx recalls, "They [slave owners] have been carried to their tombs accompanied by a great cortege of freedmen wearing their felt liberty-caps, even though some of them were slaves of the worst kind."[58] Clearly, there were both good and bad reasons for manumission in Rome.

Manumission was done both in private and in public, formally in a will, in a letter, before the praetor, or through informal verbal agreement. To be sure, manumission was a milestone for slaves. If Orlando Patterson calls slavery "social death," one could say that gaining freedom was a kind of social birth. The slave passed from a tool, from a nonperson to a person. Hence, manumission was celebrated as a major social achievement. Hunt describes the most dramatic Roman procedure before the praetor in these words: An "assertor of liberty"—often the praetor's *lictor*, his orderly—uttered a formal phrase: "I declare that, by the law of the Quirites

---

54. Hunt, *Ancient Greek and Roman Slavery*, 121.
55. Hunt, *Ancient Greek and Roman Slavery*, 121.
56. Falx, *How to Manage Your Slaves*, 167.
57. Falx, *How to Manage Your Slaves*, 169.
58. Falx, *How to Manage Your Slaves*, 171.

[an old-fashioned name for the Romans], this man is a free man." The *lictor* then touched the slave with his staff, while the master kept silent. The celebration followed as the slave was declared a free man and put on a special cap called a *pilleus*.[59] The slave was pronounced a free man or free woman. But did that mean the slave was totally free?

    I would like to end the discussion on manumission by evaluating the transition from slavery to freedom. In examples of this transition in the New World, one observes that former slaves struggle greatly to attain complete freedom in societies that had enslaved them. It is true in the United States, for instance, that slavery was abolished with the passing of the Thirteenth Amendment to the Constitution on December 18, 1865. However, the realization of true cultural, economic, and even political freedom for all in the United States today is still a matter of debate. One could also argue that many of those who came out of slavery emerged strong enough to reorient and reshape their lives in order to change history and culture and impact the world in different ways. Now, could there have been a similar reality in the Roman Empire?

    Among historians, opinions vary concerning relations between freed slaves and their former masters. For some, behind every freedman artisan or trader lurked a patron, the former master, drawing the lion's share of the profits, extracting burdensome unpaid service. Others affirm, however, that freed slaves enjoyed some independence and contributed significantly to the economic and cultural life of the ancient Rome.[60] How free, then, were freed slaves?

    In a status-driven society like Rome, nomenclature mattered. The fact that freed slaves were referred to as "freed slaves," "ex-slaves," and the like shows that those who acquired their "freedom" still bore the stigma of their past servitude. Freed slaves did not automatically become Roman citizens. Rome, unlike Greece, was more willing to expand citizenship to former slaves, but this was a very slow process, and many freed slaves suffered some political and legal disabilities before they could become full Roman citizens.[61] The stigma of servitude was also visible in the dress code for and body marks upon freed slaves. As mentioned earlier, freed slaves had special hats they wore in public to distinguish themselves from slaves, and

---

59. Hunt, *Ancient Greek and Roman Slavery*, 122.
60. Bell and Ramsby, *Free at Last!*, 1–2.
61. Hunt, *Ancient Greek and Roman Slavery*, 123.

marks imposed on their bodies by their former masters were permanent reminders of their painful past.

In addition to the imposed nomenclature and indelible body marks that tied them to their former way of life, freed slaves were not completely free vis-à-vis their former masters. The slave-master relationship was transformed into another kind of relationship: a client-patron relationship or a connection between an ex-slave and an ex-master. Roman law secured the rights of former masters by imposing some restrictions on freed slaves. In the *Digest* 37,15 one reads: "The freedman was in no sense independent of his previous owner. His obligations were both social and economic: it is to be noted that obligations of social respect (*obsequium*) assimilate the freedman's relationship to his patron to that of a son to his father."[62]

Slave masters determined the kind of relationship they wished to have with their former slaves. They demanded respect and displays of gratitude, continued labor, payments of installments to the master's progeny, and many other services encouraged by the law. Falx does not hide what a lucrative arrangement manumission was for former masters. He writes: "Freedmen are particularly useful agents to pursue your interests. I have set up numbers of my freedmen in business as bankers and moneylenders, but also in overseas trade. All these activities are highly profitable, but too vulgar for a man of high social standing to become involved with directly."[63] The same reality was lived out in the imperial *familia*, as I showed earlier. The emperor needed more hands to work in his estates, manage his property, and fulfill all the tasks of his household. Thus, he used slaves and freedmen of his *familia* in a whole range of activities, both political and economic. Thus, freedmen were not completely free because they entered a complex relationship that made most of them dependent upon their patrons.

However, the relationship of patronage that developed after manumission should not be loosely generalized to the point of understanding freed slaves only in terms of mere victims of exploitation. Just like imperial freedmen, there were many freed slaves who managed to change their situation by climbing the ladder of social hierarchy, acquiring wealth and prestige and hence impacting Roman economic and social life.

Epigraphic self-representations of freedmen on tombs and other monuments throughout the Roman landscape not only serve as evidence of the widespread practice of manumission but also indicate the social status

---

62. Quoted in Weidemann, *Greek and Roman Slavery*, 53.
63. Falx, *How to Manage Your Slaves*, 176.

of these former slaves. Koenraad Verboven points out that inscriptions that note the profession of the deceased suggest that freed slaves were proud not only of having escaped slavery but of the professions by which they achieved their freedom.[64]

In addition to their economic achievements, freedmen left their legacy even in other sectors of Roman society. According to Susan Treggiari, far from being outsiders remotely connected to the cultural life of ancient Rome, freed slaves would have been found in the family trees of countless senators, magistrates, and Roman artists, and she concludes that freedmen were at the forefront of development in the arts and industry, innovators in religious ideas, and essential participants in the change from Republicanism to *Principate*.[65]

The literature on slaves and ex-slaves was written by influential people who would convey ideas based on their biases and interests. The intrinsic truth that emerges from the Roman practice of manumission is that freedom did not always mean what it signified. While it is attested that freed slaves attained some autonomy and climbed the ladder of Roman social hierarchy, hence impacting different sectors of Roman life, it should be said that the majority of ex-slaves lived their continued servitude in a forced relationship of patronage. Free on paper, Roman freedmen and freedwomen (like descendants of slaves in America, Brazil, the Caribbean) still struggled to achieve complete freedom. Although not the end of exploitation, manumission was at least a significant step toward freedom and human dignity.

Roman Slavery and Modern Forms of Dehumanization

Throughout this chapter, we have seen that Roman slavery was a complex network of relationships similar to and yet very different from modern forms of dehumanization such as slavery in the New World. Based on Orlando Patterson's classic definition of slavery as "the permanent, violent, domination of natally alienated and generally dishonored persons," many scholars have demonstrated how slavery is a form of domination that not only plagued the Greco-Roman world but also marred other human societies around the globe.[66] I follow Patterson in the view that across cultures, slavery is best understood as a relationship of power whereby the powerful

64. Ramsby, "'Reading' the Freed Slave," 66.
65. Ramsby, "'Reading' the Freed Slave," 66.
66. Bodel and Scheidel, *On Human Bondage*, 5.

deny the dignity of the powerless through violence or other forms of inhuman exploitation. With this common element in mind, I wish to highlight some significant differences between Roman slavery and slavery in the New World on the one hand, and on the other hand, between Roman slavery and other forms of human exploitation in a society like the DRC.

Roman Slavery and Slavery in the New World: Two Significant Differences

In my discussion of the complex institution of Roman slavery, I pointed out that one of the dangers of approaching the ancient world with modern perceptions and ideologies is thinking that Roman slavery, like later forms of slavery, was based on race or ethnicity. As I interpret a first-century letter that deals with the question of slavery, I wish to make it clear that race had nothing to do with slavery in Rome, unlike in the antebellum United States, the Caribbean, or Brazil. To be sure, in the Roman Empire "Latins, Greeks, dark-skinned Syrians, black Ethiopians, and blond, blue-eyed Germans could be slaves together under one owner."[67] Both blacks and nonblacks could become slaves in Rome.

It is true, as John Nordling notes, that most blacks entered the ancient Roman world as slaves. However, there was nothing unusual about this because virtually all peoples from outside Greco-Roman society were obliged to enter the social mainstream as prisoners of war, kidnappees, foundlings from the dung heap, or debtors.[68] Such enslavement, it must be noted, happened no more frequently to blacks than to people of any other race in antiquity. William Westermann points out for example that "the number of Aethiopian or Negro slaves provable for the Roman Empire was small even in Egypt where they should be found in the largest numbers."[69]

In ancient Rome, those who suffered more from racial prejudice were Syrians and Jews. According to Cicero, Jews and Syrians were considered born for slavery.[70] Cicero's comment supports the assertion that the association of the black race or of any other people of color with slavery did not develop until early modern times. Hence, while a first-century document such as the Letter to Philemon has had much to say about New World

---

67. Osiek, "Slavery in the New Testament World," 151.
68. Nordling, *Philemon*, 72.
69. Westernmann, *Slave Systems of Greek and Roman Antiquity*, 97.
70. Cicero, *De provinciis consularibus*, 5.10.

slavery (as we saw in the interpretation history surveyed in chapter 1), modern readers should understand that race was not the criterion for slavery in Rome.

The second main difference between Roman slavery and New World slavery is the higher status slaves in the Roman Empire could enjoy in antiquity. In contrast to the primarily lower forms of slavery suffered by predominantly black slaves in the New World, many slaves in Rome enjoyed the prestige of higher education and a relatively high standing in society. As John Nordling points out, whereas white Southern plantation owners in the New World may well have feared highly educated black slaves on their plantations (or at best educated them in standard schools), Greco-Roman masters cultivated and greatly respected their highly educated slaves.[71] In fact, many slaves in Rome were far more educated than their masters. For instance, Calvinus Sabinus bought some extremely learned slaves at enormous expense so that as they fed him lines of Homer and other authors at dinner parties, he could impress his highbrow guests.[72]

Although slaves were generally dishonored people in all slave systems (according to Patterson's definition), it is important to keep in mind that Roman slaves did not suffer the stereotypes that maintained New World slaves in a permanent lower status. Even today, stereotypes such as that blacks are lazy, stupid, or ugly and hence inferior to whites, are examples of how race-based slavery denigrated and discouraged any attempt on the part of slaves to climb the social ladder. In Rome, there were some very well trained and educated slaves who would invite comparison to today's medical doctors, teachers, and university professors. Responsible slaves routinely carried out sensitive and highly technical financial transactions on behalf of their masters—the way a modern CPA or a "bonded" employee might, for example. Slaves and freemen often owned property and even other slaves.[73] Such evidence explains why the manumission rate was higher in Rome than in New World or in other slaveholding societies for that matter.

Suffice it to say that while Roman slavery and New World slavery were both dehumanizing institutions, modern readers, especially Christians who read the New Testament, should not lose sight of the significant differences between slavery in the Roman Empire and slavery in the New

---

71. Nordling, *Philemon*, 76.
72. Nordling, *Philemon*, 76.
73. Nordling, *Philemon*, 76.

World. To think that "slavery is slavery" no matter what does not do justice to history and precludes a responsible interpretation of ancient texts that deal with slavery.

Roman Slavery and Other Forms of Dehumanization

Slavery as a legal institution is a reality of the past. However, as Kevin Bales rightly puts it, "making something illegal does not make it cease to exist; making it illegal only causes it to vanish from view."[74] The problem of slavery goes far beyond the Roman Empire. It reaches back to the beginning of human civilization. And as stated earlier, I maintain that slavery is a relationship of power whereby a powerful person denies the constitutive elements of human dignity in a powerless person. Consequently, I understand slavery today as an umbrella metaphor for many forms of exploitation and dehumanization—human trafficking, sexual exploitation, rape in war zones, forced labor, debt bondage, child soldiering, unpaid and underpaid labor, and so forth.

Because this book is an interpretation of an ancient text that tackles the issue of slavery and its implications for Christians in the DRC, I wish to make it clear at the end of this chapter that I do not equate Roman slavery with all forms of dehumanizing practices in modern societies. Roman slavery was a complex network of relationships with no parallels in today's world. However, it is equally true that the noxious nucleus of slavery—whether in Rome, in the New World, or metaphorically in the New Testament and in the modern world—is the use of power in its variegated forms to deny human dignity in others. Just as they served as major sources of Roman slave supply, war, kidnapping, debt, and poverty constitute today ways through which men and women become subject to inhuman treatment.

In the DRC, slavery is a dehumanizing evil that has taken different shapes and forms. From the infamous time of the slave trade to the dark period of colonization, the DRC has experienced great humiliations. Under the Belgian colonial occupation, and especially suddenly finding themselves within the personal fiefdom of King Leopold II, the people of the Congo became victims of a particularly brutal brand of slavery enforced through torture, limb amputation, and murder. To describe this appalling disregard for human dignity, the expression "crimes against humanity" was first used. To be sure, the driving force behind this assault was

74. Bales, *Ending Slavery*, 2.

the extraction of Congo's riches, focused then on rubber and ivory.[75] Since then, the DRC, especially the eastern part, has been a space of permanent conflicts and systemic dehumanization as both neighboring countries and Western powers, in complicity with Congolese elites, loot Congo's natural resources. This looting of natural resources is also accompanied by the looting of human dignity: many children are forced to carry arms and perform hard labor, countless women are systematically raped, and many civilians are kidnapped for forced labor and sexual exploitation.

Moreover, in a country where the rule of law is quasi-nonexistent, systemic corruption has become the law of the land, and as a consequence, the most vulnerable are the perpetual prey for the mercilessly powerful Congolese elites. In universities, business, and even churches, women are constantly forced to offer their bodies in exchange for success. Many employees work without pay, or if they are paid at all, their salaries hardly take them beyond sustenance level. These are just a few examples of the many ways human dignity is trampled down in the DRC. We shall come back to this in the last chapter of this book.

Conclusion

This chapter has served a dual purpose. On the one hand, it has provided the reader with the world behind Paul's Letter to Philemon, specifically the social space as shaped and determined by the legal institution of slavery. This institution, we shall recall, was not a monolithic and undifferentiated system. Rather, it was a complex network of relationships based on the exploitation and dehumanization of 'the other.' On the other hand, this chapter has sought to contrast ancient Roman slavery with the system of slavery as it exists in the world inhabited by the modern reader (the world in front of the text). Without conducting a thorough comparative study of Roman slavery and modern slavery, the intent of this chapter has been to clarify the significant differences between these two very different sociocultural contexts, in order to enable a more responsible interpretation of the Letter to Philemon. It is to the world of this text that we now turn.

---

75. Ndaywel, *Histoire du Congo*, 123.

3

Narrative Dynamics and Spatial Negotiations in Philemon

Philemon as a Story

As stated earlier, this book proposes to read the Letter to Philemon as a narrative. Despite the obvious fact that, like other Pauline writings, the Letter to Philemon belongs to the epistolary genre, I join a large number of New Testament interpreters in considering this brief letter as a story. To be sure, the narrative structure of the letter is not as obvious as it is in conventional narrative texts such as the Gospels or the Acts of the Apostles. Beneath the epistolary discourse lies a story or even stories that undergird it and constitute the theological matrix that constructs a worldview, an alternative space for the followers of Christ.

In treating the Letter to Philemon as a narrative, I should hasten to highlight one caveat: as a letter, the text of Phlm is a moment in the story. The written text is just one moment within a long sequence of events. As Michael Gorman rightly puts it, "behind this short letter of appeal lies a fairly complicated series of events and an equally intricate network of relationships. It is like a drama with a cast of characters performing in several acts, the last act of which is still unwritten."[1] As such, the Letter to Philemon is a narrative whose scenes and plot are not easily discernible by modern readers. Understanding requires a close reading of the text itself and a consideration of the different spaces that form the sequence of events in the progression of the story's plot. But before I can attend to the narrative

---

1. Gorman, *Apostle of the Crucified Lord*, 526–27.

components of the letter, it is important that I offer here the structure that will guide my interpretation. Considering the Letter to Philemon as a drama, I adopt (with some modifications) the following sequence of four acts outlined by Gorman:[2]

Act 1: The (Relatively) Distant Past

> Scene 1: The church in Colossae is founded (perhaps by Epaphras under Paul's direction).
>
> Scene 2: Philemon believes in the gospel and becomes Paul's spiritual son.
>
> Scene 3: A church in Colossae begins to meet in Philemon's house.

Act 2: The Immediate Past

> Scene 1: Paul is in prison (somewhere in a Roman province).
>
> Scene 2: Onesimus, Philemon's slave, leaves his master's household and Colossae.
>
> Scene 3: Onesimus encounters Paul in prison, believes the gospel, and begins assisting Paul in some way.
>
> Scene 4: Paul receives news of Philemon's love and faith, as well as either direct or indirect expressions of love from him that have encouraged fellow believers.

Act 3: The Present

> Scene 1: Paul writes to Philemon, appealing to him to welcome Onesimus back as he would welcome Paul himself, as a brother rather than a slave, and to forgive any perceived debt or wrong.
>
> Scene 2: Paul sends the letter (and probably Onesimus with it) to Philemon, perhaps (though this is less certain) accompanied by someone to read and interpret the letter to the church.

Act 4: The Future (still to be written)

> Scene 1: The letter arrives in Colossae and is read to the church that meets in Philemon's house

---

2. Gorman, *Apostle of the Crucified Lord*, 529–30. The word "drama" here does not connote the technical sense of a theatrical play. Rather, it conveys the idea of a series of unfolding events following a certain sequence as is the case in the story implicitly narrated in the Letter to Philemon.

Scene 2: Philemon ponders a critical and difficult request, and finally makes a decision.

Scene 3: Both the letter and Onesimus's identity challenge the followers of Christ in Philemon's house and beyond.

Although not explicitly mentioned in the letter, the events I have just outlined are discernible through a close reading of the text itself. And since the written text is a moment in the story, the textual structure does not follow the order of events that form the four acts. Below is the classic structure of the written text:

- Verses. 1–3: Address and Greeting
- Verses 4–7: Thanksgiving and Petition
- Verses 8–22: Paul's Appeals on behalf of Onesimus
- Verses 23–25: Final Greetings

Far from being arbitrary, these four structural sections correspond to the periods of the Greek text: only one clause for the address; then, a long clause for thanksgiving followed by four short clauses for the request; and finally, three short clauses for final greetings.[3] Rhetorically, the letter's structure is important in determining what Paul communicates and how he communicates it.

The Trialectics of Spatiality in Philemon

Read through the prism of narratology, every text is an act of communication. The author employs communication strategies that consist in the management of time and space in order to construct and advance the plot. Because the negotiation of space informs the story's plot, the act of reading should be an effort to reconstruct the underlying narrative plot by attending to the narrated spaces. Since the Letter to Philemon tells a story whose plot is played out in the management of space, I propose to reconstruct in this section the three spaces that constitute the narrative world of the letter following Lefebvre's and Soja's model.

---

3. In rhetoric, a period is a complex sentence, especially one consisting of several clauses, constructed as part of a formal speech or oration.

Perceived Space

As defined earlier, perceived space is geographical space, physical space, space as perceptible by the senses. The Letter to Philemon contains several clues that allow the reader to reconstruct the geographical spaces inhabited by Paul, Philemon, Onesimus, and all the implicit recipients of this correspondence.

In the opening verse, Paul identifies himself as δέσμιος Χριστοῦ Ἰησοῦ (a prisoner of Christ Jesus). The word δέσμιος informs the reader that at the time of writing, Paul was not at the beach or in the synagogue. Rather, he was in the space-prison where space here is understood both as a container and as a network of relationships. But for the time being, I wish to understand it as a specific geographical location. As it stands, the word δέσμιος by itself does not provide the reader with sufficient information as to where Paul was imprisoned when he wrote the letter. One needs to investigate what Ricoeur calls the world behind the text to form a better idea about Paul's space of imprisonment.

Reading the Acts of the Apostles and listening to Paul's own testimony in his other letters, one discovers without much difficulty that the space-prison was almost Paul's second home. As an intrepid apostle of Jesus Christ, he suffered imprisonment for the sake of the gospel he was preaching. When cataloging his afflictions in 2 Cor 6:4–5 and 11:23–29, Paul mentioned his imprisonments, which outnumbered those of the "false apostles" who opposed him. Hence, the prison where he finds himself at the time of the composition of Phlm is just one space of incarceration among many.

As briefly discussed in the first chapter, exegetes have generally postulated three different possible locations from which Paul might have written the Letter to Philemon: Rome, Caesarea, or Ephesus. I refrain from rehearsing separate reasons for placing Paul in each of these potential spaces of imprisonment when he was writing Phlm. Suffice it to say that the majority opinion favors the Ephesian hypothesis for a couple of reasons. First, in the light of the shorter distance between Ephesus, in western Asia Minor, and the likely location of Philemon's house in the Lycus Valley, only some one hundred and twenty miles southeast, Ephesus has gained the greatest support.[4] Second, in Ephesus Paul had stayed for two years and established a school that became a mission center for Asia Minor.[5] Consequently,

---

4. Ryan, "Philemon," 179–80.
5. Barth and Blanke, *Letter to Philemon*, 124.

many of his devoted coworkers would have gone back and forth between the cities of Asia Minor proclaiming the gospel under the tutelage of the apostle Paul. Third, the Ephesian hypothesis also provides the most likely scenario to explain Paul's journey after his release from prison, which he alludes to in Phlm 20, 22: Once refreshed by his partner Philemon and given further cause for joy in Christ, Paul would then visit Philemon and his entire household.

While it is important to have an idea about the possible locations of Paul's imprisonment, the reader of the Letter to Philemon should be clear about one thing: there is no single convincing argument for one space against another. What is important and helpful for the interpretation of the letter is that the underlying narrative of Phlm, and more specifically, the word δέσμιος, helps one understand that the apostle was writing from a space of restricted freedom in one of the provinces of the geographical space called the Roman Empire. Now what about the space inhabited by Philemon, Onesimus, and the other members of Philemon's household?

In the epistolary introduction (vv. 1–3), Paul names his addressees and identifies their location: Φιλήμονι τῷ ἀγαπητῷ καὶ συνεργῷ ἡμῶν καὶ Ἀπφίᾳ τῇ ἀδελφῇ καὶ Ἀρχίππῳ τῷ συστρατιώτῃ ἡμῶν καὶ τῇ κατ' οἶκόν σου ἐκκλησίᾳ (to Philemon our beloved and coworker, to Apphia our sister, to Archippus our fellow soldier, and to the church in your house [my translation]). In reading these verses, one is faced with two interconnected questions: Was the letter primarily addressed to Philemon? If so, where was Philemon's house church located?

There is scholarly dispute about Colossae as the location of Philemon's house. The point of contention is mainly the reliability of any connections between the Letter to Philemon and the Letter to the Colossians, the latter being deemed deutero-Pauline with questionable authorship and date of composition. In this study, I side with interpreters such as Gorman, who argue that Philemon's house was most likely located in Colossae and that the letter was primarily addressed to Philemon both as Onesimus's master and as the owner of the house and, most likely, the leader of the ecclesial community that gathered in it.[6]

Of all places in the Lycus Valley, Colossae has been identified by many scholars as the most probable location for Philemon's house, to which the letter was sent.[7] When read in the light of the Letter to the Colossians, a

---

6. Gorman, *Apostle of the Crucified Lord*, 527.
7. See Lightfoot, *Colossians and Philemon*; Moo, *Letters to the Colossians and to*

number of reasons can be evoked in favor of Colossae as the location of Philemon's house. In Col 4:7 Tychicus is identified as the letter-bearer to the church in Colossae, and, as Paul indicates in 4:9 he is accompanied by Onesimus, "the faithful and beloved brother, who is one of you" (the Colossians). Moreover, Onesimus, Epaphras, and Archippus lived in that town, or at least had very close connections with the Colossian church (Col 4:12, 17; Phlm 2).

In the middle of the twentieth century, John Knox challenged this traditional consensus about Philemon as the primary addressee of the letter and Colossae as the geographical location of Philemon's house. In his book, *Philemon among the Letters of Paul* (1935), Knox argues that rather than Philemon, Archippus was Onesimus's master and the primary recipient of the letter. As we saw in the first chapter, Knox pioneered the hypothesis according to which Philemon lived in Laodicea and was the overseer of the churches in the Lycus Valley. Onesimus and Tychicus were to stay over at his house, on their way to Colossae with the letter. The goal of the letter was to persuade Philemon to use his influence on Archippus so that Onesimus would be sent back to Paul to support him in his ministry.[8]

Again, this discussion about the geographical location of Philemon's house may seem trivial at first. However, it allows a better understanding of the overall narrative, especially as we analyze the characters' negotiation of time and space to advance the plot. As in the case of Paul's space of imprisonment, it may be enough to note that Philemon's house, where the letter was destined, was located in Colossae, in the Lycus Valley, within the Roman Empire. As one reads closely the entire narrative of the Letter to Philemon, one notes that the characters and their perceived spaces (prison, Colossae, and the territory of the Roman Empire) are deeply influenced by certain worldviews. These worldviews constitute what Lefebvre and Soja call the "conceived space."

Conceived Space

Following Lefebvre's model, conceived space is the dominant space of society, a system of verbal signs ideologically elaborated by intellectuals,

---

Philemon; Fitzmyer, *Letter to Philemon*; Wright, *Paul for Everyone*; Thompson and Longenecker, *Philippians and Philemon*; Brogdon, *Companion to Philemon*; Witherington, *Letters to Philemon, the Colossians, and the Ephesians*.

8. Knox, *Philemon among the Letters of Paul*, 67–70.

professionals, and other people of power. It is the space of institutions and laws that govern human relationships. To better understand the rhetorical strategies the author employs to advance the narrative plot in Phlm, we need to reconstruct the conceived space, that is, the worldviews of all the characters involved in the story.

Both Paul and his addressees lived in the vast Roman Empire and conducted their lives according to the laws and worldview dictated by Greco-Roman institutions. One of these institutions was Roman slavery. But, unlike his addressees, who were Gentiles, Paul was a Jew whose conceived space was made up of both the Greco-Roman and the Jewish worldviews. Since I devoted an entire chapter to the discussion of Roman slavery, I would like to say a word on another world that shaped Paul's thinking, namely, the Jewish world and its understanding of slavery.

Jews were part of a world that had gone wrong, a world where the powerful could dehumanize the powerless at will. They lived in a world where slavery was taken for granted as a part of social and household life. Both Hebrew scripture and ancient Jewish literary sources demonstrate how the notion of bondage shaped the Jewish worldview, Jewish daily life, and Jewish theology. In fact, at the heart of Jewish conceived space was the exodus narrative. In national-historical and theological terms, this is the grand narrative that culminates in the great climax and point of reference for all biblical literature, namely, liberation from slavery and the revelation of God on Mount Sinai. As Robert Alter points out, the whole narrative is organized around three thematically defined spaces: Egypt (the place of bondage), the wilderness (a liminal space where freedom will be realized and new obligations incurred), and the promised destination of the exodus from Egypt.[9]

Because slavery is rooted in human wickedness and waywardness, biblical, intertestamental, Mishnaic and Talmudic traditions agree that the liberation of slaves has its solid basis in him who is called upon and proclaimed as the Lord God.[10] It is in this sense that the biblical legislation is prefaced in the following solemn and unambiguous terms: "I am the LORD your God who brought you out of the land of Egypt, out of the house of slavery" (Exod 20:1–2). Israel's conceived space would henceforth be shaped by this liberation and covenantal narrative.

---

9. Alter, *Hebrew Bible*, 208.
10. Barth and Blanke, *Letter to Philemon*, 65.

For Israel, freedom is a matter of grace and faith. They were chosen from a place of slavery to become God's people. Consequently, they transferred their loyalty from Pharaoh to YHWH. They ceased to be slaves to the created in order to be slaves to the Creator. For Israel, liberation is the transition from a bad suzerain to a good suzerain.[11] Moses makes it clear to Pharaoh, "Israel is my firstborn son. I said to you, 'Let my son go that he may worship me'" (Exod 4:22–23). God acquired Israel for a specific purpose, namely, to serve him: "For they are my servants, whom I brought out of the land of Egypt" (Lev 25:42). For the Jews, liberty is not an end in itself. "But as fear of God is proclaimed the beginning of all wisdom, so loyalty as God's covenant partners and keeping God's commandments are the purpose of liberation and the only way to remain free from the dominion of evil lords."[12]

Such a worldview served as the basis for Israel's slave legislation. Despite the sharp distinction made between Israelite and non-Israelite slaves, the biblical laws on servitude prove to have been more humane than their ancient Near Eastern counterparts. For instance, the Sabbath institution interrupted the exploitative daily relationship between all masters and all slaves. The Jubilee Year legislation is also replete with visionary elements concerning a just social order that protects foremost the weak, unfortunate, and poor among the people. "In its weekly, its heptannual, and its fifty-year cyclical forms, the Sabbath ordinance reminds of the destiny that God has set for and within his chosen people, for slave owners and slaves alike."[13] As God's covenanted people, the Israelites have assumed the condition of God's slaves and are prohibited from treating each other as slaves. According to Robert Alter, the mandatory release in the Jubilee Year is a kind of indentured servitude.[14] Freed and redeemed by God, the Israelites were to extend the same freedom to all persons as this is God's given right to be promoted and protected.

This brief discussion of the Jewish understanding of slavery should suffice to give us a picture of Paul's conceived space and the preponderant role it plays in the narrative. Remaining "a radical Jew" (as Daniel Boyarin would call him), Paul's thought and theology were replete with the Jewish worldview, including Jewish slave legislation in the light of the exodus

11. Barth and Blanke, *Letter to Philemon*, 67.
12. Barth and Blanke, *Letter to Philemon*, 80–81.
13. Barth and Blanke, *Letter to Philemon*, 71.
14. Alter, *Hebrew Bible*, 455.

narrative. We shall demonstrate how this worldview, this Jewish conceived space, comes into play for the construction of an alternative space in the Letter to Philemon.

Lived Space

Lived space, in Lefebvre's terms, is the inhabited social space, the space of human interactions as determined by laws and ideologies. In other words, it is a network of social relationships that can entertain or challenge the conceived space imposed on society by powerful people. A close reading of the story of the Letter to Philemon reveals an interesting lived space, a complex network of relationships among the different characters. Who are the characters to each other? What roles do they play both in the social structure and in the ecclesial structure? In what follows, I will focus mainly on the major characters of the story, namely, Paul, Philemon, and Onesimus, and on the basis of their different traits, reconstruct their inhabited space.

Paul

In addition to being the author of the Philemon narrative, Paul is also the narrator and one of the major dramatis personae of the narrated story. He identifies himself as Παῦλος δέσμιος Χριστοῦ Ἰησοῦ (Paul, a prisoner of Christ Jesus); an ἀδελφός (brother) to Timothy, Philemon, and Apphia (v. 1). He is a πρεσβύτης (either an old man or an ambassador or perhaps both, v. 9); a συνεργός (coworker) with Philemon, Mark, Aristarchus, Demas, and Luke (vv. 1. 25); a συστρατιώτης (fellow soldier) of Archippus (v. 2); a συναιχμάλωτος (fellow prisoner) of Epaphras (v.23); and a κοινωνός (partner) of Philemon (v. 17).

Focusing our narrative lenses on the main characters, we notice that in relation to Philemon, Paul is a brother, a partner, a friend, one who has paid a debt Philemon owed (understood here as his spiritual father), an apostle, and one who has initiated and guided Philemon in the faith and so would be in a position to tell him what to do (vv. 19–20). In relation to Onesimus, Paul is a spiritual father (v. 10). To both Philemon and Onesimus, Paul is a spiritual father and a brother, simultaneously a superior and an equal. We shall attend to these different yet interconnected roles as we discuss later the story's rhetorical dynamics.

Beloved Brother or Slave?

Philemon

From the letter's narrative, we learn that Philemon owned a slave and a house. Both properties suggest that Philemon would have been what we might call today a middle-class citizen, with a slave and with a house big enough to host an ecclesial community each week—and even a spare room for visitors (v. 22). As the paterfamilias and the principal recipient of the letter, Philemon must have been also the leader of the household church.[15] Given his roles as both a slave owner and a church leader, Philemon's lived space seems to have been a complicated experience of superiority and equality, exploitation and love, discrimination and communion, slavery and brotherhood.

For Philemon, Onesimus was just a slave, an animated tool, a means of economic production, a naturally inferior being whose human dignity was constantly denied. As Paul takes care to note, Onesimus had become useless to Philemon (v. 10). We shall come back to the rhetorical subtlties that Paul musters to prove Onesimus's usefulness to Philemon and to the cause of the gospel. For now, suffice it to note that Philemon was a master who was separated from his slave while serving the unity of all the saints, that is, the members of his household church. He was Paul's brother, son, coworker, and partner whose faith was not effective enough (v. 6) precisely because he failed to see in Onesimus "a beloved brother . . . in the flesh and in the Lord" (v. 16).

Onesimus

Onesimus is one of the dramatis personae who says no words but is only spoken for and spoken about. He is a character who does not fit into a single category as far as narrative conventions are concerned. He is both a round and a flat character. Voiceless in the narrative, Onesimus possesses several traits that make him an unpredictable character in the story. His obvious trait is that he was a slave. To borrow Patterson's language, Onesimus was a nataly alienated and generally dishonored person. He was socially dead.[16]

---

15. The expression "household church" is a disputed category in recent Pauline studies. I discuss it in more detail in chapter 4 and highlight its socioecclesial implications in the interpretation of the Letter to Philemon.

16. Patterson, *Slavery and Social Death*, 13.

Narrative Dynamics and Spatial Negotiations in Philemon

In contrast to Philemon and, arguably, to Paul, who were at the center of power, influence, and domination, Onesimus lived on the margins of society. However, Onesimus is a character that surprises and shocks the reader. Through a tactful negotiation of various spaces, he develops within the narrative, changing from a seemingly flat and static character to a more dynamic and round character.[17] He is the major character whose actions cause the writing of the letter, the construction of an alternative space for the local community and beyond, and even social change for ages to come.

Without kinship because he was considered less than human in the house of a Christian leader, Onesimus dared to raise his head in search of his undeniable dignity. He finds Paul in prison and becomes his son, his own heart (vv. 10, 12). The love and dignity he could not find in Philemon's household church, he finds in the space-prison. The encounter with a prisoner of Christ gives him a new birth, a new identity. He belongs. He matters. He feels free for a while, and hopefully the feeling of freedom remains with him the rest of his life if Philemon chooses to receive him with this new identity: as a beloved brother.

From a sociological point of view, Onesimus's audacity defies the expectations of both the intended and unintended readers of this short letter. He not only "sinned" against his master but also against the social system that oppressed him by choosing to leave the margins in order to move to the center. Consequently, to paraphrase Petersen, Onesimus's action poses a threat both to the institutionalized social system and to the sociological structures it serves, and it is in this sense that we can best appreciate the state of tension that surrounds the relationship between Onesimus and Philemon and encompasses people like Paul who have gotten involved with the guilty party.[18]

Although Petersen espouses the contested view that Onesimus was guilty of running away (a position that I oppose in this book), he has a point in highlighting the tension that Onesimus causes in the narrative. Voiceless and powerless, Onesimus's negotiation of different spaces forces the other characters—and, by the same token, all readers across time and space—out of their comfort zone. Beginning with the author and narrator Paul, all who encounter Onesimus in person or through what has become the Letter to Philemon, have to solve the tension that surrounds the

---

17. For ample discussion of characterization, see Resseguie, *Narrative Criticism of the New Testament*, 121–65.

18. Petersen, *Rediscovering Paul*, 94.

complex relationships among characters. In what follows, I will attend to the narrative dynamics and spatial negotiations that make this short letter an exceptional rhetorical gem, a delightful literary tapestry.

Rhetoric

What is rhetoric and how does it play out in the Letter to Philemon? As a component of narrative criticism, rhetoric is the art of persuasion. It breathes life into a narrative and influences how we feel and think about what the author says.[19] More than mere verbiage or imaginative turns of phrases that a speaker or writer uses to capture attention, "rhetoric delights while it persuades; it is an integral and indispensable part of every mode of discourse, whether written or spoken, for it is the means by which authors persuade us of their ideological point of view, norms, beliefs, and values."[20]

Generally, literary theorists agree that there are three kinds of rhetoric: deliberative, forensic, and epideictic. "The object of deliberative rhetoric is to exhort or dissuade; of forensic, to accuse or defend; of epideictic, to praise or blame."[21] We should specify with Frank Church that these three kinds of rhetoric were appropriate, respectively to the forum, where one's hearers had to judge the future; to the courts, where they had to judge the past; and to the marketplace or amphitheater, where they, as spectators, had to judge the art of the orator present before them.[22]

Adapted to the requirements of epistolary structure and style, the narrative of Phlm is definitely an example of deliberative rhetoric whereby Paul uses an arsenal of rhetorical devices to re-create an alternative network of social relationships among his hearers. Just like any other deliberative discourse, the Letter to Philemon divides into sections under three headings: the exordium (a prelude intended primarily to establish the appropriate mood and to secure the goodwill of the hearers); the main body or proof (where the argument is formally advanced); and the peroration, which consists of four elements: restating one's appeal, securing the hearers' favor, amplifying one's argument, and setting the hearers in an emotional frame of mind.[23] In the Letter to Philemon, the thanksgiving (vv. 4–7) serves the

---

19. Resseguie, *Narrative Criticism of the New Testament*, 41.
20. Resseguie, *Narrative Criticism of the New Testament*, 41.
21. Church, "Rhetorical Structure and Design," 18.
22. Church, "Rhetorical Structure and Design," 18.
23. Church, "Rhetorical Structure and Design," 18.

purpose of an exordium; Paul's appeal on behalf of Onesimus (vv. 8–16), constitutes the main body or proof; and the closing of the argument (vv. 17–22) serves as the peroration. Having determined the kind of rhetoric we are dealing with in the Letter to Philemon, I shall now conduct a close reading of the text and address the various rhetorical patterns and figures that create meaning and space.

Personal Names and Their Qualification

"What's in a name?" asked the character Juliet in Shakespeare's timeless classic, *Romeo and Juliet*. Unlike Juliet, who seems to imply that what matters is the person and that the name is meaningless, I contend that the name is everything. As an African, it is my belief that we live in a world where even the act of speaking is infused with power. Consequently, the act of naming creates, identifies, empowers, controls, subjugates, includes, and excludes. A name situates a person in time and space. My own name can attest to this conviction. My parents named me Okitakatshi, after my paternal grandfather, a chief of a village that bears the same name. In addition to the fact that it situates me within the geographic and social space of my family and clan, my name contains a whole program. Okitakatshi is a compound name: *Okito* (heir) and *akatshi* (leaves). Literally, Okitakatshi means "heir of leaves." This may sound weird at first, but once one discovers the philosophy behind this name-sentence, one comes to understand that my name determines my identity and destiny. In my culture, tree-leaves serve as a symbol of power. Certain leaves have the power to heal; others serve as food; and still others, as roofs for houses. A chief or a king is a person who gathers his people together the way a builder gathers leaves to roof a house; a chief or king feeds (that is, provides for) his people, and heals the wounds of the community by his wisdom and leadership. Aware of this whole range of meanings, a person named Okitakatshi (heir of leaves) feels empowered to live up to their name.

Some personal names (like Okistakatshi) contain in themselves an identity and a potential network of relationships. But other names need to be associated with certain qualifiers to serve the same purpose. Frédérique Biville is of the opinion that proper nouns and personal names take part in a system of qualification especially when associated with possessive pronouns such as *meus, tuus* and *noster*, and *veste,* as one can find in the letters of Cicero.[24] While she acknowledges that the use of possessive pronouns is generally interpreted as an indication of an affective relationship, Biville indicates that possessive pronouns can take on a variety of meanings that go well beyond the simple presumption of familiarity. Possessive pronouns are above all, in themselves, indications of interpersonal relationships, but they also take their sense from the whole system of oppositions and combinations in which they take part.[25] In the Letter to Philemon, personal names and their qualification are rhetorical devices the author employs to create meaning and transform interpersonal relationships among characters.

In the introductory verses, Paul identifies himself and other characters by name: Παῦλος δέσμιος Χριστοῦ Ἰησοῦ καὶ Τιμόθεος ὁ ἀδελφὸς Φιλήμονι τῷ ἀγαπητῷ καὶ συνεργῷ ἡμῶν καὶ Ἀπφίᾳ τῇ ἀδελφῇ καὶ Ἀρχίππῳ τῷ συστρατιώτῃ ἡμῶν (vv. 1–2). A few verses later, in the body of the letter, Paul names the slave on whose behalf the appeal is made: παρακαλῶ σε περὶ τοῦ ἐμοῦ τέκνου, ὃν ἐγέννησα ἐν τοῖς δεσμοῖς, Ὀνήσιμον (v. 10). What's in these names? Why are these names associated with other descriptive and qualifying words? Let's try to find the answer by analyzing one name at a time.

Taking a clue from the text itself, I choose to begin with the name Ὀνήσιμος in v. 10. After introducing the character Onesimus, the author explains his name in an effort to drive home an important rhetorical point: the usefulness of the slave. He refers to Onesimus as, τόν ποτέ σοι ἄχρηστον νυνὶ δὲ [καὶ] σοὶ καὶ ἐμοὶ εὔχρηστον—*the one [who was] once useless to you, but [is] now useful both to you and to me* (v. 11). In Greek, this verse functions like an explanation, an appositive note to v. 10. The author expands on the meaning of Onesimus's name. As many translators do, I inserted verbs and translated v. 11 as an independent clause to make the following point: in v. 11, the slave Onesimus is treated as a person in his own right, forming the subject of a sentence.[26] The clue for such an interpretation is taken from the etymological sense of the name Onesimus provided by the text—once useless, Onesimus can now live up to the meaning of his name: useful. We shall come back to what the text says about "the useful."

After learning from the text itself that the meaning of a name has rhetorical purpose, let's return to the first character in the story. The author and narrator is identified as Παῦλος. Appearing for the first time in Acts 13:7 in reference to the Roman proconsul in Cyprus, and then in Acts 13:9

24. Biville, "Qualification of Personal Names," 1.
25. Biville, "Qualification of Personal Names," 1.
26. Barth and Blanke, *Letter to Philemon*, 339.

in reference to the apostle known so far as Saul, Παῦλος is a transliteration of the Latin name Paulus, which means small or little. If Paul plays with the etymological sense of the name Onesimus to reveal Onesimus's true identity, we have all reason to apply the same principle to Paul's name in order to discover his rhetorical motives. In fact, I follow Alain Gignac in translating literally this name and those of other characters so as to highlight their semantic connotation.[27]

Until Acts 13:9, Luke identifies Paul as Saul. It is only after Saul encounters the proconsul Sergius Paulus that the name change from Saul to Paul occurs. Why is that, and why is it important in our understanding of Paul's self-identification in Phlm? The first missionary journey led Saul and Barnabas to Paphos where they met Sergius Paulus, whom Luke describes as "an intelligent man" desiring to hear the word of God from the missionaries. With Sergius Paulus was a Jewish false prophet named Bar-Jesus. In Acts 13:8–9, Luke takes advantage of the opposition between Bar-Jesus and Saul and identifies both characters with names so far unknown to his audience. He writes: "But the magician Elymas (for that is the translation of his name) opposed them and tried to turn the proconsul away from the faith. But Saul, also known as Paul, filled with the Holy Spirit, looked intently at him and said, 'you son of the devil, you enemy of all righteousness, full of all deceit and villainy, will you not stop making crooked the straight paths of the Lord?'" (Acts 13:8–10).

It is significant that Luke would choose this moment of spiritual warfare to change Saul's name to Paul and, for a rhetorical purpose, Bar-Jesus's name to Elymas. "In both cases," as Robert Wall explains it, "Jewish names (Saul/Bar-Jesus) are exchanged for Gentile names (Paul/Elymas) to underscore the conversion of the Roman man Sergius Paulus. In this sense, name changes cue both the Gentile mission and the nature of Jewish opposition to it."[28] By prevailing over "the enemy of all righteousness" (Acts 13:10), Saul exhibits the power of God that is in him to accomplish his mission to the pagans. Consequently, Saul adopts a Gentile name both to identify with the Gentiles to whom he is sent (represented here by Sergius Paulus) and to symbolize that he is "the little one," the instrument that God has chosen to "bring [his] name before Gentiles and kings and before the people of Israel" (Acts 9:15).

27. Gignac, "Le triangle 'Paul-Philémon-Onésime,'" 24.
28. Wall, *Acts of the Apostles*, 146.

Writing to a Gentile slave owner about a Gentile slave, Paul was fulfilling the same mission he received from God. Just as he identified with Sergius Paulus by bearing a name that means "little one," Paul identifies with the lowly, little, and marginalized Onesimus, in his correspondence to Philemon. If the etymological sense of his name is convincing enough in this regard, one should pay attention to the qualifying words that are associated with it, namely δέσμιος Χριστοῦ Ἰησοῦ. Not only is Paul "the little one," but he is also a δέσμιος (prisoner) for Christ Jesus. As many commentators have pointed out, this is the first obvious difference between the Letter to Philemon and Paul's other letters. Here, wholly unusually, "the little one" introduces himself as a δέσμιος Χριστοῦ Ἰησοῦ. He is a prisoner for Christ Jesus. Rhetorically, as will be demonstrated later when discussing the figure called an *inclusio*, Paul, "the little one," identifies himself as a prisoner since he evidently wishes to introduce a theme with which he will play several times in the letter, no doubt because of its emotive and persuasive power (vv. 9, 10, 13, 23).[29] Unlike some interpreters, such as Edward Lohse, who contend that Paul's space of imprisonment allows him to speak with greater authority to Philemon and the ecclesial community, I argue that Paul was speaking from a place of weakness to make his case.[30] To be sure, he is not Caesar's prisoner, but Christ's. In fact, as David Garland interprets it, Paul would have appreciated the double-entendre of the phrase. He is now physically locked up because of his work for Christ, but metaphorically he has been Christ's prisoner for years (see 2 Cor 2:14–17; Phil 3:12–13). The love of Christ constrains him far more than his present manacles.[31] In the context of Phlm 1, the qualifying word δέσμιος is associated with the etymological meaning of the name Παῦλος in order to highlight Paul's littleness and weakness, and prepares the reader to appreciate the relationship between Paul and Onesimus.

Alongside Paul is mentioned the name of the cosender of the letter: Timothy. Since Timothy is not one of the main characters in the story, I will not discuss the details about his name and his ministry. It is just important to note that, mentioned in most of Paul's letters, Timothy was one of the apostle's faithful and trustworthy companions. Paul calls him ὁ ἀδελφός (the brother), which implies that he is also a brother to Philemon, to Onesimus, and to all the recipients of the letter. Timothy participates in the same

---

29. Dunn, *Epistles to the Colossians and to Philemon*, 311.
30. For a full discussion of this position, see Lohse, *Colossians and Philemon*, 189.
31. Garland, *Colossians and Philemon*, 316.

brotherly social space that the letter tries to create. As an intimate of Paul and therefore fully privy to and supportive of Paul's position in the delicate affairs that form the main subject of the letter, Timothy, whose name means "honoring God," was willing to honor God by honoring Onesimus, a dishonored member of Philemon's household.

After the introduction of the author and coauthor, the recipients are named. The text mentions first the name of the main recipient who will be addressed throughout the letter: Φιλήμονι τῷ ἀγαπητῷ καὶ συνεργῷ ἡμῶν (to Philemon, our beloved and coworker). The name Philemon contains a whole program. Dividing it in two (φίλος and ἡμῶν), Gignac translates Philemon as *ami-de-nous*, that is, "our friend."[32] In the Greco-Roman world, the name Philemon generally meant "a loving or affectionate person," or, as Camille Focant translates it, *bien-aimé*, "beloved."[33] In this case, the Greek Φιλήμονι τῷ ἀγαπητῷ would be a pleonasm, unless we see in it an invitation to pass from friendship to love, that is, from an important value of the Greco-Roman world to the central value of the Christian ethos.[34] More on the virtue of love and Christian ethos in the coming chapter. For now, let us try to understand the association of the name Philemon with the qualifying word "coworker" (συνεργός).

Συνεργός is one of Paul's favorite words compounded with the prefix "συν" (meaning "with"). In reference to his fellow workers, this prefix has spatial meaning, namely, the network of partnership among those who labor with the apostle for the promotion of Christ's gospel. From other letters, we remember names such as Prisca and Aquila (Rom 16:3), Timothy (Rom 16:21), Titus (2 Cor 8:23), and Mark (Col 4:10). Even here in Phlm, Paul mentions several names of his partners for the cause of the gospel: Epaphras, Mark, Aristarchus, Demas, and Luke (vv. 23–24). It goes without saying that when Paul associates the name Philemon with the word συνεργός, he informs the reader that Philemon is his partner in the work evangelization. In his capacity as host and pastoral leader of the local congregation that gathers in his house, Philemon participates in Paul's mission to create an alternative space for Christ's followers.

Rhetorically, the name Philemon and the word συνεργός announce the various themes of the letter and prepare the ground for all the spatial negotiations that will unfold. Simply by paying attention to the conjunction καί

---

32. Gignac, "Le triangle 'Paul-Philémon-Onésime' du billet à Philémon," 24.
33. Focant, *Les lettres aux Philippiens et à Philémon*, 221.
34. Gignac, "Le triangle 'Paul-Philémon-Onésime,'" 25.

that connects τῷ ἀγαπητῷ and συνεργῷ in reference to Philemon, an attentive interpreter may wonder like Barth and Blanke: "Does καί here have the so-called 'epexegetical' sense, or does it remind of an additional element in the close relation between Paul and Philemon?"[35] When one reads closely Paul's prayer of thanksgiving (vv. 4–6), one understands that Philemon would be Paul's beloved and coworker more effectively when Philemon does what Christ expects from him: when he extends brotherhood to all, including Onesimus. To say it with Barth and Blanke, by calling Philemon our beloved coworker, Paul lays on the man a hand that is warm and heavy at the same time. Pau's hand is warm with the love that is the main theme of the epistle; Paul's hand is heavy when he appeals to Philemon to receive Onesimus: By receiving Onesimus as a brother, may Philemon continue and crown the praiseworthy work carried out so far![36]

The list of the letter's addressees continues after Philemon: καὶ Ἀπφίᾳ τῇ ἀδελφῇ καὶ Ἀρχίππῳ τῷ συστρατιώτῃ ἡμῶν καὶ τῇ κατ' οἶκόν σου ἐκκλησίᾳ (to Apphia, the sister, and Archippus our fellow soldier, and to the church in your house). The only woman to be personally mentioned in the introduction to any New Testament letter,[37] Apphia is surely blessed among women. According to Sabine Bieberstein, the mention of a woman among the letter's addressees breaks open the exclusive antithesis of two men, Philemon and Paul, which is constructed in the body of the letter. Just as with other names among the addressees, Paul associates Apphia's name with a relational word: ἀδελφή (sister). Just as Timothy, and later, Onesimus, are brothers to Paul, so Apphia, a female, is cast in the same kind of relationship to him. It is not my intent to speculate like other interpreters about Apphia's relation to Philemon and Archippus. Whether she was Philemon's wife and Archippus's mother, or the wife of Archippus, the main addressee of the letter according to Knox, Apphia stands out as a member of the Christian community summoned as a witness in what Bieberstein calls "the test of liberating praxis."[38]

What's in the name? It should be clear by now that in the Letter to Philemon, names matter. They mean everything. By linking various qualifying words with personal names, the Letter to Philemon shows itself to be a masterpiece of rhetoric; the name list at the start sets the stage for

---

35. Barth and Blanke, *Letter to Philemon*, 250–51.
36. Barth and Blanke, *Letter to Philemon*, 253.
37. Ryan, "Philemon," 218.
38. Bieberstein, "Disrupting the Normal Reality of Slavery, 106.

a delineation of relationships in a delicate network, with the expected effect of constructing an alternative space for those who are in Christ. By naming the different characters involved in this delicate network both at the beginning and at the end, the Letter to Philemon reveals that the dehumanization of one child of God should be a social concern, a public sin that makes everyone uncomfortable in their skin. Hence, all other names may be forgotten, but the name of Onesimus, "the useful one," should always be remembered as the cause and agent of spatial negotiations: he raised his head and told his story in public to effect social change.

Repetition

Another rhetorical feature discernible in the Letter to Philemon is repetition. In narrative criticism, "repetition is a stylistic device that reiterates words, phrases, themes, patterns, situations, and actions for emphasis."[39] An intentional repetition clarifies and reinforces a statement, a theme, or a motif. It calls the reader's attention to a certain structure in the narrative and the repeated words or motifs serve as the hinges of the spatial framework that the overall rhetoric is creating.

The Letter to Philemon is replete with verbal repetition. The reiteration of key words and phrases are the various techniques the author employs to negotiate space and establish a certain worldview. Without being exhaustive, I will attend to the key and most obvious repetitions in Phlm and explicate their rhetorical role in the movement of the entire narrative.

In the opening unit of the letter (vv. 1–3), the author introduces a number of key words that will later be repeated in the text to form a purposeful *inclusio*.[40] These words are the nominative δέσμιος (prisoner), the genitive phrase Χριστοῦ Ἰησοῦ (for/of Christ Jesus), the nominative ἀδελφὸς (brother), the genitive possessive pronoun ἡμων (our), and the genitive noun κυρίου (from the Lord [as part of a prepositional phrase]).

At the time of writing, Paul is a δέσμιος (prisoner). This description is repeated in various ways in vv. 10 and 23, forming both a motif and a theological theme in the letter. Outside the Philemon narrative, δέσμιος situates

---

39. Resseguie, *Narrative Criticism of the New Testament*, 42.

40. In narrative criticism, "inclusions are words, phrases, or concepts that bracket narratives or larger units such as a section of a book or even an entire book. Inclusions are framing devices that identify beginnings and endings of narratives, or underscore prominent themes and concepts of a story." Resseguie, *Narrative Criticism*, 57.

Phlm within the company of other Pauline captivity letters, namely, Philippians, Ephesians, and Colossians. We've already discussed the rhetorical meaning of the word δέσμιος. Here I wish to point out the implication of its repetition in the structural framework of the entire narrative.

The word δέσμιος forms an *inclusio* that frames the letter's first literary unit (vv. 1–3) and its last literary unit (vv. 23–25). Paul introduces himself as a "prisoner of Christ Jesus" (v. 1) and reminds his reader at the end of the letter that Epaphras is his fellow prisoner (v. 23). By the time the reader gets to v. 23, they already know that in vv. 9, 10, and 13, Paul spoke of his imprisonment as the space of Onesimus's spiritual transformation and preparation for eventual participation in the work of evangelization. To say it with John Paul Heil, Paul opens with a framework of imprisonment and partnership under grace (vv. 1–3), and closes with a framework of imprisonment and partnership under grace (vv. 23–25).[41]

The *inclusio* formed by the repeated word δέσμιος is not fully understood if severed from its qualifying modifier Χριστοῦ Ἰησοῦ. In both units that bracket the entire narrative, Paul and Epaphras are described as prisoners Χριστοῦ Ἰησοῦ. The traditional translation of this phrase has been "prisoner for Christ Jesus," rendering the Greek subjective genitive. For Joseph Fitzmyer, one of the proponents of this translation, Paul does not mean thereby that he has been imprisoned by Christ. Rather, he is imprisoned because of his relation to Christ Jesus.[42] As plausible as this translation can be, scholars such as Marion Soards have preferred the translation "prisoner of Christ" to better emphasize the subtlety of Paul's remark: "he may be in the custody of earthly governmental officials, but in fact he is captive to and under the authority of Christ Jesus."[43]

Whether one translates the phrase as an objective genitive or a subjective genitive, the repeated word and its qualifying modifier make a clear point: Since his encounter with Jesus on the road to Damascus, Paul has been taken "captive" by Christ Jesus for the sake of the gospel. Consequently, the repetition of the words δέσμιος and Χριστοῦ Ἰησοῦ forms a motif that serves an important rhetorical function in the overall narrative: Paul speaks from a space of voluntary surrender to the Lord Jesus Christ for the sake of the gospel and challenges Philemon to do the same. When the reader comes across the motif of Paul's imprisonment throughout the letter, they

---

41. Heil, "Chiastic Structure and Meaning of Paul's Letter to Philemon," 186.
42. Fitzmyer, *Letter to Philemon*, 83–84.
43. Soards, "Some Neglected Theological Dimensions," 213.

can deduce that Paul is somehow identifying with Onesimus, who was fully owned (imprisoned, so to speak) by Philemon. Thus, in the opening verse, Philemon is called to renounce his legal and yet dehumanizing power over Onesimus, because all three (Onesimus, Philemon and Paul), through common faith in one Lord, are fully owned by Jesus for the sake of his kingdom.

Another important word repeated in the text is ἀδελφός (brother). Of the 335 words in the Greek text, ἀδελφός is arguably a hermeneutical key that unlocks the earth-shaking message of the Letter to Philemon, namely, the humanization of Onesimus. The reader encounters this word for the first time in the description of Timothy. Paul calls him ὁ ἀδελφός (v.1). Then, the dative singular form of the feminine version of the same word is used in reference to Apphia in v. 2: τῇ ἀδελφῇ. In vv. 7 and 20, Paul uses it in the vocative case to directly address Philemon with more affection. When the text is performed before the assembly, the emphatic vocative would not fail to arouse an emotional reaction from both Philemon and the rest of the congregation. In both cases, Paul is calling Philemon to grant his request so as to give joy and rest to his heart. The request, as the reader would already have heard, is to receive Onesimus no longer as a slave, but as more than a slave, as a beloved brother (ἀδελφὸν ἀγαπητόν, v. 16). Repeated five times in reference to different characters in the story, the word ἀδελφός serves the rhetorical function of focusing attention on what is the nexus of Paul's appeal, that is, to concretize the filial relationship that now exists between Onesimus and Philemon.[44] More on this word will come in the discussion of kinship language.

The next repeated word I wish to discuss is ἡμῶν (our), the first person plural genitive pronoun. It may seem unnecessary to pay attention to a possessive pronoun whose use is quite normal in correspondence. However, it is my conviction that, read in the light of the words it modifies in the text, this simple pronoun plays a key rhetorical role in creating a social space, a network of relationships among those who are part of what it signifies. Repeated three times in the epistolary introdcution, ἡμῶν sets vv. 1–3 as a small, complete unit. Philemon is described as συνεργῷ ἡμῶν—our coworker (v. 1); Archippus is identified as συστρατιώτῃ ἡμῶν—our fellow soldier (v. 2); grace and peace are given to the all the recipients ἀπὸ θεοῦ πατρὸς ἡμῶν καὶ κυρίου Ἰησοῦ Χριστοῦ—from God our Father and the Lord Jesus Christ" (v. 3).

---

44. Ryan, "Philemon," 217.

Two things can be said about the repetition of ἡμῶν in these three verses. On the one hand, it establishes a network of personal relationships between the addressees and Paul, all forming the space called the church, an assembly of saints. They are partners for the same cause, namely, the gospel of Jesus Christ. On the other hand, the same pronoun establishes a connection between all the characters and God the Father as well as the Lord Jesus Christ. The latter element needs further clarification. ἡμῶν modifies the word "father." In Paul's genitive prepositional phrase, God is called "our Father (πατρὸς ἡμῶν)." The term πατήρ, (*pater* in Latin) is an interesting term in the Greco-Roman world. As Joshua Houston explains, πατήρ was a hierarchical term. The paterfamilias was the highest level of a Greco-Roman household. Hence, the term πατήρ is not necessarily one of familial warmth. Rather, it shows the authority, guidance, care, and love of God.[45] In the same vein, the term κύριος for Jesus, in the context of the Greco-Roman world, means "master" or "Lord." The two words that are connected by καὶ send a radical message to both intended and unintended readers: Not Caesar, but God is the Paterfamilias of all believers. Also, not Caesar, but Jesus Christ is κύριος, the only Master and Lord of all, including of Philemon and Onesimus.

As stated earlier, Paul was first and foremost a Jew. By calling God "our Father" and Jesus "our Lord," he is rethinking and reconstructing the Jewish notion of the people of God. As Judith Ryan explains, "The understanding of God as the Father of the people of Israel (Deut 32:6; Isa 63:16; 64:8; Jer 3:4; 19; 31:9; Mal 2:10; Sir 51:10) originates in Israel's own self-understanding as God's children (Hos 11:1; Sir 4:10; Pss Sol 17:30; Jub 1:24–25)."[46] By describing God as "our Father," Paul acknowledges not only that YHWH, the God of Hebrew Scripture, is Father to the people of Israel, but also that God is Father in a special way. God is the Father of all because he is the Creator of and the provider for all people (including Gentiles). In Rom 8:15 and Gal 4:6, Paul even goes so far as to use the more intimate Aramaic term, *abba*. Thus, by praying that the assembly in Philemon's house would receive grace and peace from God our Father and the Lord Jesus Christ, Paul announces that the new people of God, made up of both Jews and Gentiles, are in Jesus brothers and sisters of the same Father. Didn't Jesus himself teach his disciples to address God as "our Father"?

Indeed, the combination of the pronoun "our" and the word "Father" in the context of an ecclesial assembly makes one realize the frequent

---

45. Houston, *Paul's Letter to Philemon*, 71.
46. Ryan, "Philemon," 214.

scandal Onesimus witnessed in Philemon's house. As they gathered every week, the holy ones in Colossae would have inherited the apostolic tradition and prayed the Lord's Prayer, addressing God as "our Father" just as Christ taught his disciples. In this case, Matthew's version is more likely to have been characteristic of liturgical assemblies (Matt 6:9). It is not unlikely that Onesimus would have wondered: Who is truly part of the "our," and to whom is God really a father? Surely, he felt excluded. He was not a Christian while in Philemon's house. Only by departing from a space of estrangement could he eventually come to belong to the community of "our Father."

God is truly our Father inasmuch as we are in Christ. Jesus alone was fully entitled to call God "my Father," because he is truly the only-begotten Son of God, the firstborn of all creation through whom all things in heaven and earth were created (Col 1:15–16). By participation in Jesus's identity through baptism, all believers can say "our Father." As Pope Benedict XVI beautifully put it, "only within the 'we' of the disciples can we call God 'Father,' because only through communion with Jesus Christ do we truly become 'children of God.'"[47]

Against all this Judeo-Christian background, the reader of Phlm 1–3 understands that the possessive pronoun "our" is spatial in that it reconstructs the ecclesial space, the new people of God, around the God who has revealed himself as our Father in Jesus Christ. Both Philemon and all potential readers of the letter can't miss seeing how demanding this simple pronoun is: "it requires that we step out of the closed circle of our 'I.' It requires that we surrender ourselves to communion with the other children of God. It requires, then, that we strip ourselves of what is merely our own, of what divides. It requires that we accept the other, the others—that we open our ear and our heart to them."[48] The pronoun "our" requires that we, like Paul, say that we receive one another as brothers and sisters.

Kinship Language

The above discussion on the pronoun "our" in reference to God the Father and the Lord Jesus Christ invites us to address another important rhetorical element in the Letter to Philemon, namely, kinship language. Throughout the narrative, the reader discovers that family language is a space-organizing metaphor that plays an important role in the network of relationships

---

47. Pope Benedict XVI, *Jesus of Nazareth*, 140–41.
48. Pope Benedict XVI, *Jesus of Nazareth*, 141.

among characters. Timothy is called a "brother" (v. 1); God is "our Father" (v. 3); Onesimus is identified as Paul's "child" (v. 10) and as Philemon's "brother" (v. 16); Philemon is Paul's "brother," (v.20); and Paul is a "father" to both Onesimus and Philemon (v.10, 19). What is the background of this kinship language, and what could its effect be on the letter's audience?

Kinship language is by itself a vast area of research in Pauline studies. It is not my intention to offer a comprehensive analysis of it in this book. In line with the central thesis of this book and in preparation for the theological implications to be discussed in the last two chapters, I will explicate the kinship language in Phlm by focusing on the word "brother" and the notion of brotherhood. As stated earlier, Phlm 16 is the only place in the entire New Testament where a slave is directly called a "brother." Consequently, the term "brother" becomes the indispensable hermeneutical key to understanding the role of kinship language in the unifinished narrative presupposed in the Letter to Philemon. In what follows, I shall discuss, on the one hand, the meaning of brotherhood according to Paul's three different worldviews: Jewish, Greco-Roman, and Christian. On the other hand, I shall critically assess the intended and unintended readings of the word "brother" in Phlm and propose the most plausible interpretation of the word, which will guide the rest of this book.

It is common among believers to speak of God as the Father of all human beings. Consequently, all men and women are by nature brothers and sisters. Moreover, it is assumed that for Jews the fatherhood of God as demonstrated by powerful interventions in the course of history is the presupposition of a community of brothers and sisters. Events created and shaped by God encourage Israel to call God "Father" and treat one another as brothers and sisters.[49]

However, from a strictly Jewish perspective, this idea of the universal fatherhood of God and the brotherhood of man is seen as "modern and highly apologetic."[50] Louis Jacobs argues that the Bible does not speak directly anywhere of God as Father but that the idea is found by implication in Deut 14:1: "you are children of the LORD your God."[51] The inference from this verse is that because "you" are God's children, God must be your Father. For Jacobs, the "you" in this verse is language of election. "The

---

49. Barth and Blanke, *Letter to Philemon*, 427.
50. Jacobs, *Jewish Religion*, 164.
51. Jacobs, *Jewish Religion*, 164.

intimate relationship described in father-children terms is reserved for God's relationship to Israel, not for mankind as a whole."[52]

Israel's collective memory reveals that the notion of brotherhood determined the boundaries of the socioreligious space known as God's people. As God's covenanted people, Jews were brothers and sisters to each other to the exclusion of Gentiles. A brother or a sister meant a fellow Jew. Indeed, the Torah is replete with laws that define who is in and who is out. In Lev 25:35–55, Israelites are commanded to treat Israelite slaves with kindness as kinsmen, not as slaves. In Deut 17:15, Moses gives the criteria for the king who should rule over the Israelites: *One of your own community you may set as king over you; you are not permitted to put a foreigner over you, who is not of your own community*. As can be seen, Israelites' notion of kinship distinguished them from Gentiles and foreigners, and aimed to foster loving solidarity among those who shared a common blood relationship, ethnicity, and ancestry.

By stating that kinship was a boundary marker, we should also acknowledge that both insiders and outsiders could cross boundaries and be included or excluded from the covenantal family. For instance, in his book *The Beginnings of Jewishness*, Shaye J. D. Cohen explains the different ways a non-Jew could join the Jewish community and become an insider. One of those ways was through conversion. Non-Jews converted to Judaism by fulfilling the following three requirements: keeping Jewish laws, devoting oneself exclusively to the God of the Jews, and integrating socially within the Jewish community.[53] Finding in the Torah the raw material for a theology of conversion and inclusion, Cohen writes:

> According to numerous passages in the Torah and the Prophets, God, chose the Israelites to be his people and the Israelites chose God to be their Lord. Such a conception provides an ideological basis for conversion, because the link between God and his people is not "natural" but "covenantal" and would seem to allow others too to choose God to be their Lord. The Israelites became a nation by standing at the foot of Mount Sinai and binding themselves to God and the Torah through an oath. Could not gentiles too bind themselves by oath to God and the Torah and thereby make themselves into Israelites? Just as God once chose the Israelites to be his

---

52. Jacobs, *Jewish Religions*, 164.
53. Cohen, *Beginnings of Jewishness*, 156.

treasured people, could not God continue to choose individuals from among the nations to join his treasured people?[54]

Assuredly, this Jewish theology of conversion would certainly have influenced Paul's understanding of brotherhood in his mission to the Gentiles. But before getting there, we shall say a word on the Greco-Roman understanding of brotherhood.

For the Greeks, the word ἀδελφός (ἀδελφή in the feminine) literally meant co-uterine, from the same mother. More generally, it meant a near kinsman.[55] It was a widespread belief among the Greeks that Zeus, the common father of all humankind, and either Nature or a human mother's womb, or both, made all human beings brothers and sisters. The air that all of them need to breathe; the soul, as distinct from the body; the capability for being virtuous; finally death as the fate of all humankind confirmed that both free persons and slaves were equals, brothers and sisters for that matter.[56]

The notion of brotherhood played a pivotal role in Roman culture. "The Romans, who saw themselves as descendants of Romulus and Remus, considered brothers central to their public and poetic myth making, to their experience of family life, and to their ideas about intimacy among men."[57] In Roman literature, the two founding brothers represented two extremes of fraternal relationship: idealized cooperation and fratricide. Although the ideal influenced the choices Romans made, it should be noted that the experience of Roman brotherhood fell somewhere between these two extremes.

In a society shaped by honor and shame, brotherhood could be a valuable asset in a man's public career. Consequently, "appeals to fraternal *pietas* in political rhetoric found a ready audience among the elite who shared power at Rome."[58] Even outside elite social circles, brotherhood was meaningful to the Romans, who believed that kinship was a natural phenomenon that transcended social and civic status. Not only did brothers serve as models for personal relationships—namely between friends, lovers, and soldiers—but fraternal piety also came to symbolize the emotional and moral bonds that were the basis of civic society.[59] It is obvious that the

---

54. Cohen, *Beginnings of Jewishness*, 130–31.
55. Liddell and Scott, *Greek-English Lexicon*, 12.
56. Barth and Blanke, *Letter to Philemon*, 424.
57. Bannon, *Brothers of Romulus*, 3.
58. Bannon, *Brothers of Romulus*, 5.
59. Bannon, *Brothers of Romulus*, 3.

language and the notion of brotherhood in the Greco-Roman worldview is male oriented. This should not surprise modern readers as they know that Greco-Roman society vested political power in males. However, the kinship language that shaped their social space concerned both males and females. As one may find in Greco-Roman literature, the Greek ἀδελφοί and the Latin *fratres* are used for both males and females, thus translated as brothers and sisters.

From what precedes, we can see that Paul lived in a world where kinship language constructed various interpersonal relationships. Consequently, when Paul writes to his Gentile audience, he draws from both his Jewish and Greco-Roman experiences of kinship, which he reworks in the light of the Jesus-event, and proposes a fresh understanding of human relationships. As a Jew, Paul follows the Jewish theology of adoption and teaches that Gentiles have been adopted as sons and made into a people (λαός) of the God of Israel, a position previously occupied by the Israelites alone. He states this conviction very boldly when he writes to the Romans: "As indeed he says in Hosea, those who were not my people (λαός) I will call 'my people (λαός),' and her who was not beloved I will call 'beloved.' And in the very place where it was said to them, 'You are not my people (λαός),' there they shall be called children of the living God" (Rom 9:25–26). For Paul, just as Israel became God's people by standing at the foot of Mount Sinai, so Gentiles can become God's people by accepting Jesus as their Lord. Just as Abraham became righteous and a friend of God through faith, so Gentiles can also become Abraham's children through faith in Jesus. As Caroline Johnson Hodge rightly states, "Paul relies on the logic of patrilineal descent to create a new lineage for the Gentiles, a lineage that links Gentiles through Christ to the founding ancestor, Abraham. By means of this kinship-creation, Gentiles are made descendants of Abraham, adopted sons of God and coheirs with Christ."[60] The same logic undergirds the rhetorical function of kinship language in Phlm.

In the Letter to Philemon, Paul defines the social space that makes one a brother or a sister: the ἐκκλησία [church, assembly](v. 2). Those who form the ἐκκλησία in Philemon's house receive grace and peace from God the Father and the Lord Jesus Christ (v. 3). And if by ἐκκλησία Paul means God's people with whom God has entered into a saving relationship in Christ, we understand that the recipients of the Letter to Philemon form a community of brothers and sisters called by God in Christ to live in holiness and loving

---

60. Hodge, *If Sons, Then Heirs*, 5.

harmony. Just as it denoted the popular assembly of the full citizens of the *polis* or Greek city-state,[61] so ἐκκλησία was for Paul's converts an assembly of heavenly citizens, a band of brothers and sisters who participated in a reality much bigger than the Greco-Roman world, namely, the kingdom of God.

Until he met Paul, Onesimus was a brother to no one. To borrow Patterson's language, Onesimus was natally alienated and socially dead. He was denied both human dignity and Christian fellowship. By courageously leaving the margins in search of social integration, Onesimus caused the merging of the structures of the Roman Empire and the antistructures of the Church for the emergence of a *thirdspace*, an eschatological space where masters and slaves are brothers and sisters.

Away from his master, away from the household church, Onesimus found his identity in prison thanks to the ministry of a prisoner named "the small one." In v. 16, Paul urges Philemon to receive Onesimus "no longer as a slave but more than a slave, a beloved brother—especially to me but how much more to you, both in the flesh and in the Lord." If for many interpreters this verse changes everything about Onesimus and his relationships with Philemon and the rest of the community, some voices have been more skeptical and proposed alternative readings.

Commenting on this verse, Allan Callahan argues that Onesimus is not Philemon's slave, but his biological brother. For him, the Letter to Philemon is a story of the estrangement of two Christian brothers: Onesimus and Philemon.[62] Callahan bases his interpretation on the words ὡς δοῦλον (as a slave) and backs it up with some examples of bad brotherhood in the Greco-Roman world, the same world inhabited by figures that populate the incomplete narrative behind the Letter to Philemon. For Callahan, ὡς in this context means "as though," indicating that Onesimus's servile status is a thought or assertion on Philemon's part and not a point of fact. The word δοῦλος was an ambivalent term of both honor and opprobrium among early Christians. Just as Paul himself and many other Christians refer to themselves as δοῦλος τοῦ θεοῦ (a slave of God), so Onesimus could be called a δοῦλος with no indication that he was an actual slave.[63] For Callahan, Onesimus is just a brother who needs reconciliation with his brother Philemon.

Callahan evokes the estrangement of family members in late antiquity as a recurrent problem that would have affected even Paul's converts.

---

61. O'Brien, "Church," 123.
62. Callahan, *Embassy of Onesimus*, ix.
63. Callahan, *Embassy of Onesimus*, 44–45.

Paraphrasing Plutarch, Callahan espouses the view that the relation between brothers is like that of members of the body. The estrangement of brothers, then, would be like the wound of amputation. Though a serious breach, a rift between brothers nevertheless may be healed through the intercession of a mutual friend. "Similarly," Callahan concludes, "in Philemon Paul attempts to reconcile the two brothers Onesimus and Philemon. By his carefully worded appeal, the Apostle directs 'an engagement of love between brothers.'"[64]

In 2013, Alan Cadwallader saw in Onesimus, not Philemon's brother, but a slave whose identity was spoiled, and his servile status maintained through Paul's rhetoric of stigmatization and stereotyping. In his article "Name Punning and Social Stereotyping," Cadwallader argues that the Letter to Philemon exposes the labeling mechanisms and spatial manipulations used to maintain boundary distinctions that reinforce Onesimus's demeaned status.[65] According to him, Paul uses the literary device known as "name punning" to baptize the status quo among his converts. He writes: "the sweep of terms applied to Onesimos: τέκνον (v. 10), ἀγαπητός, ἀδελφός (v. 16), τὰ ἐμὰ σπλάγχνα (v. 12), ὡς ἐμέ (v. 17) and so on are not designed to deliver a change of status to Onesimos but to make his stigmatised presence less discomforting to Philemon."[66]

Speaking more specifically about brotherhood, Cadwallader contends that if the language definition of normalcy in ancient Christian communities was ἀδελφός then this is the language to which Onesimus must—impossibly—aspire.[67] Through his rhetorical moves, Paul is just playing with the meaning of Onesimus's name and bestowing upon him positive attributes so as to remove the discomfort caused by Onesimus's stigma. In Cadwallader's estimation, no one in Philemon's circle, not even Paul, considers Onesimus a brother. So the text's kinship language represents for the original readers and hearers of this letter a shocking negotiation of social space for the benefit of the powerful.

Joseph Marchal agrees with Cadwallader on name punning, manipulative kinship rhetoric in Phlm, and even goes so far as to contend that the text is a clear example of sexual exploitation against Onesimus orchestrated by the powerful apostle Paul and his partner Philemon. In his article "The

---

64. Callahan, *Embassy of Onesimus*, 52–54.
65. Cadwallader, "Name Punning and Social Stereotyping," 44.
66. Cadwallader, "Name Punning and Social Stereotyping," 59.
67. Cadwallader, "Name Punning and Social Stereotyping," 59.

Usefulness of Onesimus," Marchal submits that Phlm is a letter that discusses the utility of Onesimus and selects arguments in an effort to gain the consent of his owner. Paul's punning characterization of Onesimus based on his name (Useful) and Paul's seemingly deferential appeal to the autonomous authority of a slave owner take on different hues given the shadowy sexual use (exploitation) of slaves in the Greco-Roman world.[68]

Backing up his claims with examples from Roman culture, Marchal argues that language of love, affection, and kinship to speak about a slave are not mitigations of the imperially gendered slave system but expressions of its inner workings:

> Onesimus's name reflects his own placement within this imperially gendered slave system, since it contains a constellation of characteristics sought by owners in their slaves. The slave exists not for his or her own benefit, profit, or pleasure but for the enjoyable use of the master, and Paul's description of Onesimus in terms of his utility ἄχρηστον/εὔχρηστον reinforces the status quo of this erotically kyriarchal system [. . . E]ven when Paul enlists warmly affectionate language like "beloved" (ἀγαπητόν, v. 16) to describe Onesimus as a "brother" to both of the parties negotiating over him, it is from a context of coercion and the customary χρῆσις of slaves. Affection and the many uses of slaves can and do go together; love and obedience do in fact work together in the imperially gendered slave system.[69]

These three interpretations (Callahan's, Cadwallader's, and Marchal's) are but representative of unexpected and subversive readings of the kinship language in the Letter to Philemon. How do we appreciate them in regard to both the textual evidence and the social space inhabited by modern readers? We saw that Callahan predicated his thesis that Onesimus was Philemon's estranged blood brother on the word ὡς (as). For Callahan, ὡς δοῦλον means "as if he were a slave" or "as though he was a slave." He even evokes the text of Codex Claromontanus, *iam non quasi servum*, and translates it as "no longer a quasi-slave."[70] But this translation of both the Greek text and the Latin text is not grammatically and rhetorically correct. As Fitzmyer has plausibly demonstrated, the use of ὡς in v. 16 expresses a virtual equivalence as found in v. 17 προσλαβοῦ αὐτὸν ὡς ἐμέ—receive him

---

68. Marchal, "Usefulness of Onesimus," 751.
69. Marchal, "Usefulness of Onesimus," 760, 763.
70. Callahan, *Embassy of Onesimus*, 44.

as [you would receive] me).⁷¹ It cannot be translated "as if he were a slave," for the simple reason that such translation would convey a contrary-to-fact nuance which is absent from the text.

Moreover, Callahan's interpretation does not hold in the light of the other elements in the sentence. Rhetorically, there is a contrast between the word "slave" and the phrase "beloved brother," and the involvement of time through the use of "no longer... but." The use of the negative adverb οὐκέτι throws more light on the meaning of the sentence. It negates an extension of time beyond a certain point: *no longer, no further, no more*. As Fitzmyer points out, instead of the expected negative μηκέτι, (in a purpose clause introduced by ἵνα), οὐκέτι is used to negate the phrase ὡς δοῦλον. It thus adds emphasis to the point of view Paul wants Philemon to adopt.⁷² This point of view is Onesimus's new identity: he is kin, a brother who is loved both as a human being and as a fellow follower of the Lord Jesus Christ.

Although implausible on the grounds of textual evidence, Callahan's interpretation of the kinship language is an unexpected reading worth considering in the social context of modern readers of Phlm. Onesimus may not have been Philemon's brother in Christ by the time he sought out Paul, but he was a human being whose dignity was willfully denied by a man with power. As we have seen, the conceived space of the Greco-Roman world taught that a slave like Onesimus would nevertheless be considered a descendent of Zeus and a child of Mother Nature—and hence a brother to Philemon because they shared a common origin and breathed the same air. But because the social space Onesimus and Philemon inhabited was shaped by notions of honor and shame, of power and weakness, the denial of shared humanity between those of separate classes was socially constructed whereby the most powerful would negate another person's humanity and treat them as a slave, a mere object for their social and economic advancement.

In this context, Callahan has a point when he proposes that we see in the Onesimus-Philemon relationship two estranged brothers. A reader-response interpretation of the term "brother" should not be content with the simple fact that Paul's apostolic ministry bestows brotherhood on Onesimus (especially knowing that it is Onesimus himself who left the margins to seek out this dignity through his tactful negotiation of various spaces). Rather, readers should see the kinship language in the letter only

71. Fitzmyer, *Letter to Philemon*, 114.
72. Fitzmyer, *Letter to Philemon*, 114.

as a delayed effort to bring to the fore a reality that was long denied, a truth that was hitherto ignored. As we shall see in the last chapter of this book, Callahan's interpretation of the kinship language is instrumental in the construction of authentic human space in societies where slavery is neither a legal system as it was in Roman Empire nor a system based on race like in the New World. Powerful people around the globe continue to treat their brothers and sisters as if they were slaves.

Cadwallader's and Marchal's interpretations are more contextual, ideological, and reader oriented. Consequently, they are provocatively subversive because they do not depend on textual evidence to stand their ground. The text of Phlm does not constitute their point of departure but an appropriate terrain for the application of sociological theories that denounce the exploitation of the powerless. Both Cadwallader and Marchal as well as all the proponents of a more pragmatic reading of Phlm call modern readers to read the text of this letter from the perspective of the oppressed Onesimus. They have the merit of denouncing what seems to be a rhetoric of indirection whose purpose seems to maintain the status quo and promote the continued exploitation of the powerless. Although not personally convinced by their conclusions, I acknowledge that like Callahan, Cadwallader and Marchal challenge modern readers to approach the rhetoric in Phlm with a critical eye so as to offer a more liberating exegesis for the sake of the oppressed.

As I conclude this chapter, I do not pretend to have addressed all the narrative components of the Letter to Philemon. I purposefully focused my interpretation on certain elements that I deem important for understanding the narrative dynamics and spatial negotiations in the text. Now that we have attended to both the world behind the text and the world of the text, it is necessary that we turn to the theological significance of the letter. Having made its way into the Christian canon, the Letter to Philemon must have a theological message for those who believe in Christ. And this message, I contend, is a summons to become what we believe.

4

Live What You Believe

Koinōnia *against the Evil of Dehumanization*

Introduction

IN THE THANKSGIVING SECTION of the Letter to Philemon, Paul reveals to his audience the following prayer on behalf of Philemon: Εὐχαριστῶ τῷ θεῷ μου πάντοτε μνείαν σου ποιούμενος ἐπὶ τῶν προσευχῶν μου, ἀκούων σου τὴν ἀγάπην καὶ τὴν πίστιν, ἣν ἔχεις πρὸς τὸν κύριον Ἰησοῦν καὶ εἰς πάντας τοὺς ἁγίους, ὅπως ἡ κοινωνία τῆς πίστεώς σου ἐνεργὴς γένηται ἐν ἐπιγνώσει παντὸς ἀγαθοῦ τοῦ ἐν ἡμῖν εἰς Χριστόν—*When I remember you in my prayers, I always thank my God because I hear of your love for all the saints and your faith toward the Lord Jesus. I pray that the sharing of your faith may become effective when you perceive all the good that we may do for Christ* (vv. 4–6).

The Greek text of this verse (to which I will attend later in the chapter) is not only dense and complex, but also replete with significant theological themes that situate the Letter to Philemon within the broader structure of Pauline thought. In praying that Philemon's "*koinōnia* of faith" may become effective through the realization of the good to be done for Christ, Paul is being faithful to the general theological and ethical structure that undergirds all his writings. To be sure, Pauline scholars have identified it as an eschatological structure shaped by the indicative and the imperative of Paul's theology and ethics. Before focusing on the Letter to Philemon and its theology and ethics of *koinōnia*, I shall first prepare the ground by discussing the possibility of a coherent structure of Pauline theology and ethics.

Beloved Brother or Slave?

Is There a Coherent Structure of Theology and Ethics in Paul?

To answer this question, one has to tackle a number of interrelated questions: What is theology? Was Paul a pastor or theologian? Is there a single theology of Paul, or should we speak of theologies? And how does one go about determining a coherent structure of Paul's theology in all his Letters?

Without entering into all the intricacies of the word "theology," I wish to simply adopt its etymological definition: discourse or talk about God (from the two Greek words, *theos* and *logos*). To be more adequate, I would lean on James D. G. Dunn and add that "theology is a talk about God, and all that is involved in and follows directly from such talk, particularly the coherent articulation of the religious faith and practise thereby expressed."[1] But as simple as it is, this working definition raises questions when the word "theology" is attached to a person or a body of literature. Does Paul qualify as a theologian? If so, what is his theology?

If theology is talk about God and what such talk entails, namely, the articulation of faith and praxis, Paul is undoubtedly a Christian theologian. In fact, Pauline exegetes such as N. T. Wright and James Dunn call Paul the first and greatest Christian theologian. Describing Paul as a theologian, Dunn writes: "Paul belongs to that group of Christians who have seen it as part of their calling to articulate their faith in writing and to instruct others in their common faith, and who have devoted a considerable portion of their lives to so doing."[2] Moreover, Paul belonged to a generation "which was more creative and more definitive for Christianity's formation and theology than any other since. And within that generation it was he more than any other single person who ensured that the new movement stemming from Jesus would become a truly international and intellectually coherent religion."[3]

In reading Paul's self-description in his letters, one may object to the identification of Paul as a theologian, and surely there is textual evidence for such an objection. Nowhere in his letters does Paul identify himself as a theologian. Besides, calling Paul a theologian may sound reductionist. Paul was an apostle of Christ, a pastor, and a missionary, or, as J. Paul Sampley

---

1. Dunn, *Theology of Paul the Apostle*, 6.
2. Dunn, *Theology of Paul the Apostle*, 2.
3. Dunn, *Theology of Paul the Apostle*, 2–3.

describes him, "a preacher of his gospel and tutor of his churches,"[4] not a theologian according to the contemporary use of the word—a person who is an expert in a university discipline called theology.

However, as pertinent as the objection is, it can easily be answered as follows: Paul could not identify himself as a theologian in his letters for the obvious reason that theology as a distinct academic discipline is a later invention. Moreover, among the early followers of Christ, Paul is the first writer to go beyond a descriptive mode of communication to engage in a more discursive, argumentative form of communication. Instead of collected narratives or dispassionate treatises, Paul's letters are personal communications wherein he deals with issues of life and death for his audiences. They are substitutes for his personal defense and exposition of the truth of the gospel. They communicate his thought and convey his convictions. Consequently, to discover Paul as a theologian is to enter his thought world and engage theologically with the claims he makes and the issues he addresses, driven thereby afresh to the text itself, informed by what is to be read there, and stimulated to join in the resulting debate about what Paul has said and to join with Paul broaching issues of ongoing theological concern.[5]

To say that one has to engage with Paul's letters in order to discover his theology is another way of affirming that Paul as "real presence" is inseparable from his letters, and by the same token his letters are more than just doctrine. It is a temptation among some Christians to think of Paul's theology in terms of "what to believe." Such a view of Paul's theology is nothing but a total misconception. As a Jew, Paul could not separate faith and praxis, Torah and daily life, halakah and aggadah.[6] In Dunn's estimation, "a

---

4. Sampley, "From Text to Thought World," 3.
5. Sampley, "From Text to Thought World," 9.
6. For Rabbi Abraham Joshua Heschel, "Aggadah deals with man's ineffable relations to God, to other men, and to the world. Halakhah deals with details, with each commandment separately; aggadah with the whole of life, with the totality of religious life. Halakhah deals with the law; aggadah with the meaning of the law. Halakhah deals with subjects that can be expressed literally; aggadah introduces us to a realm that lies beyond the range of expression. Halakhah teaches us how to perform common acts; aggadah tells us how to participate in the eternal drama. Halakhah gives us knowledge; aggadah gives us aspiration . . . To maintain that the essence of Judaism consists exclusively of halakhah is as erroneous as to maintain that the essence of Judaism consists exclusively of aggadah. The interrelationship of halakhah and aggadah is the very heart of Judaism. Halakhah without aggadah is dead, aggadah without halakhah is wild." See Heschel, "Halakhah and Aggadah," par. 2 and par. 6.

theology remote from everyday living would not be a theology of Paul."[7] In fact, writing to the Corinthians, Paul mentions that Timothy has presented to this church a brief summary of his "ways in Christ."[8] Paul writes, "For this reason I sent you Timothy, my beloved and faithful child in the Lord, to remind you of my ways in Christ Jesus as I teach them everywhere in every church" (1 Cor 4:17).

This interrelationship of faith and praxis at the heart of Paul's letters is what Pauline scholars have identified as the indicative and the imperative of Paul's theology and ethics. "They agree that the structure of 'indicative and imperative' provides a good platform to understand the dialectical nature of Paul's ethical thought."[9] Despite this agreement, however, Pauline scholars offer divergent interpretations regarding the relationship between indicative and imperative. This divergence emerges from the apparent contradiction in what the two concepts mean. If "indicative" is understood as God's act of salvation in Jesus Christ, what is the significance of the imperatives (ethical commands and exhortations) in Paul's letters?

In the twentieth century, Rudolf Bultmann championed this view of Paul's theology and ethics as a coherent structure in the Pauline corpus. He placed the debate between the indicative and the imperative within the eschatological framework summarized in the phrases "no longer" and "not yet." For Bultmann, Christians no longer live according to the old *aeon* (age). They are a new creation, living under grace as God's sanctified and justified people. In other words, they live in the "indicative." But Bultmann also acknowledges that Christian believers still live and move in the present world, as the new world has not yet fully manifested. Christian existence, therefore, stands under the imperative. Although it is separated from its past and its present environment, yet this separation must be newly emphasized again and again.[10]

Unlike prior Pauline interpreters such as Martin Dibelius, W. D. Davies, and Charles H. Dodd, who saw a disconnect between the indicative and the imperative in Paul's letters, Bultmann proposed to understand the problem of the indicative and the imperative as a genuine antinomy rather than as a divided state of affairs.[11] Because of their eschatological existence,

---

7. Heschel, "Halakhah and Aggadah," paragraphs 2 and 6.
8. Sampley, "From Text to Thought World," 3.
9. Ho, *Socio-Rhetorical Interpretation of the Letter to Philemon*, 71.
10. Bultmann, *Theology of the New Testament*, 101.
11. Bultmann, "Problem of Ethics in Paul," 196.

a Christian is a justified person who lives in an old world with a new identity. Hence for Bultmann the imperative, just like the indicative, is a form of grace. A justified person can only respond by faith, and faith, as Bultmann understands it, is "man's obedience to God's act of salvation, renouncing any pretension to being capable of establishing the relationship with God on his own."[12]

For Bultmann, the fusion of indicative and imperative is made possible through love. In this respect, he speaks of the love in which the new creation becomes a reality (Gal 5:6, 6:15), and the eschatological event becoming real, so far as love is really present. For him, as Michael Parsons perceives it, indicative and imperative become one at the moment of decision.[13] By seeing the unity of indicative and imperative only in the moment of decision, Bultmann displays the influence of Heidegger's philosophy on his reading of Paul. Following in the footsteps of Heidegger, "Bultmann suggests that man truly exists *only* when he chooses his freedom in responsibility in the moment of decision, or at the decisive time (*Geschichte*). He thus locates meaning only in the present—denying that existence is a continuum at all."[14]

Building on the foundations laid by Bultmann, Victor Paul Furnish sought to develop a coherent account of the way in which the complex interrelation between theology and ethics actually plays out in Paul's letters. Like Bultmann, Furnish espouses and propels the thesis that indicative and imperative sum up Paul's ethics, and that neither aspect of Paul's thought should be kept at a distance. The indicative and imperative belong together. Furnish also concurs with Bultmann that love is the concept that ties together indicative and imperative.

But unlike Bultmann, Furnish does not understand Pauline ethics as resulting from the indicative; neither does he hold that indicative and imperative only merge at the moment of decision-making. Rather, Furnish understands the imperative as an integral part of the indicative. According to Furnish, Paul's imperative is indicative. He clearly states this view in his book *Theology and Ethics in Paul*: "The study of the Pauline ethic, therefore, is not the study of his ethical theory, for he had none, nor of his code for Christian living, for he gave none. It is the study, first of all, of the theological convictions which underlie Paul's concrete exhortations

---

12. Bultmann, "Problem of Ethics in Paul," 211.
13. Parsons, "Being Precedes Act," 103.
14. Parsons, "Being Precedes Act," 104 (italics original).

and instructions and, secondly, of the way those convictions shape his responses to practical questions of conduct."[15]

Because love is what ties together the indicative and the imperative, Furnish develops an integral framework for reading Paul's theology and ethics under three major motifs: eschatology, theology, and Christology. For Furnish, eschatology is the heuristic key to Pauline theology as a whole.[16] It helps to provide the fundamental perspective within which everything else is viewed. Through his close reading of Paul's undisputed letters, Furnish arrives at the conclusion that eschatology is an interpretive key to understanding how God operates in the present age through the grace given to humanity, and how believers can respond to God's grace and conduct their lives now with the certainty of a glorious destiny. As Alex Ho writes, "it is from this perspective that Furnish argues that Paul's exhortation is grounded in his eschatological view on the age to come, which the power of God has already manifested in this age by the gospel of Christ."[17] Consequently, there is a conflict between the values of this world and the values of God's kingdom already begun in Jesus Christ. By establishing the eschatological motif as the heuristic key to Pauline theology and ethics, Furnish can't escape the challenge of explaining how God creates this new relationship with humans and how humans participate in this new eschatological relationship. Furnish addresses this challenge by explaining the other two motifs: theology and Christology.

With regard to the theological motif that explains how God enters into a new relationship with sinful humans, Furnish writes: "The Pauline ethic is first of all radically theological because it presupposes that man's whole life and being is dependent upon the sovereign, creative and redemptive plan by his transcendent power."[18] On the basis of Rom 3–4, Furnish discusses Pauline ideas about God's power, God's faithfulness, God's righteousness, and sanctification in order to explain his own integrated view of theology and ethics in Paul. Furnish argues that God's faithfulness and truth are the basis for the creation of a new relationship between God and an unfaithful people. God's power is made manifest in his creative and redemptive plan in Jesus Christ.

---

15. Furnish, *Theology and Ethics in Paul*, 45–52.
16. Furnish, *Theology and Ethics in Paul*, 25–36.
17. Ho, *Socio-Rhetorical Interpretation of the Letter to Philemon*, 77.
18. Furnish, *Theology and Ethics in Paul*, 45–67.

According to the same logic of God taking the initiative to create a new relationship with sinful people, Furnish explains Paul's concept of sanctification in the light of 1 Thess 4:3–7. In reading this passage, he argues that sanctification is identified with God's will and God's call. Faithful to the Jewish theology of election, Paul understands that it is God who calls people and sets them apart as holy for a new relationship. Moreover, Furnish acknowledges also that for Paul, sanctification is a call from God that implies a demand for people to live a life that is worthy of the gospel. Hence, Furnish concludes, "the doctrine of sanctification in and of itself displays the unity of indicative and imperative."[19]

If God is the one who takes initiative to create a new relationship with sinful people, how do people participate in that relationship? It is through Jesus Christ, Paul would say. Furnish calls it "the Christological motif." He places Pauline Christology in the eschatological framework. For Furnish, Christ's death and resurrection constitute an eschatological event. It is an event in history but not of history. Christ's death and resurrection are God's action and the manifestation of his power. They are part of God's plan of redemption, a plan fulfilled in Jesus's self-sacrifice for us.[20] Christ's sacrifice is an act of love because it is solely motivated by God's intention to save.

Interpreting Rom 6, Furnish explicates how, through baptism, believers die and rise with Christ to new life, to new creation. The importance of newness of life is that it indicates that believers are no longer under the power of sin; they belong to Christ.[21] This belonging to Christ, as Furnish shows, is presented in a dialectical way in Paul. On the one hand, it represents that the power of God is already operative in the believer's life, and on the other hand, it is bound over to the service of God.[22] Therefore, there is a transfer of loyalty on the part of the believers: they cease being slaves to sin in order to be slaves to righteousness. Through the christological motif, Furnish demonstrates how believers, being in Christ, participate in God's redemptive plan.

Writing more than two decades later, Richard B. Hays adopted, with different amendments, Furnish's integral framework of indicative and imperative to explain the coherence of Paul's ethical thought. In his book *The Moral Vision of the New Testament*, Hays develops a theological framework

19. Furnish, *Theology and Ethics in Paul*, 34, 80–87.
20. Furnish, *Theology and Ethics in Paul*, 34, 80–87.
21. Furnish, *Theology and Ethics in Paul*, 52, 80.
22. Furnish, *Theology and Ethics in Paul*, 52, 80.

for Pauline ethics under three major themes: new creation, cross, and community. Comparing them with Furnish's three motifs, I will discuss in turn each of Hays's themes and demonstrate how Paul's ethical teachings are rooted in his theological thought.

Hays's phrase "new creation" is equivalent to Furnish's eschatology motif. Like Furnish, Hays understands that for Paul, the death and resurrection of Jesus was an apocalyptic event that signaled the end of the old age and portended the beginning of the new. It is within the cosmic drama of God's reconciliation of the world to himself that the church recognizes its role.[23] In speaking of "new creation" as an apocalyptic event, Hays specifies the origin of Paul's thought and language: "the image of 'new creation' belongs to the thought-world of Jewish apocalypticism. One of the fundamental beliefs of apocalyptic thought was its doctrine of the 'two ages': the present age of evil and suffering was to be superseded by a glorious messianic age in which God would prevail over injustice and establish righteousness in a restored Israel."[24] Paul's apocalyptic language echoes Isaiah's fervent prophetic hope for the renewal of the world and professes that such hope will find its fulfilment in the new creation, the eschatological age launched by Jesus. Consequently, instead of remaining just a future hope as in most forms of Jewish apocalyptic thought, for Paul and his churches the redemptive power of God has already broken into the present time and propels believers to act accordingly. To live in eschatological time is to walk a tightrope of moral discernment, claiming neither too much nor too little for God's transforming power within the community of faith.[25]

The second theme that unites for Hays the indicative and imperative in Paul is the cross. In Furnish's framework, this second theme corresponds to the christological motif. Unlike the Gospels, Paul's letters do not give us information about the man Jesus. Rather, as Hays notes, when Paul does refer to what Jesus did, the references point, over and over again, to the cross. "For Paul, Jesus' death on the cross is an act of loving, self-sacrificial obedience that becomes paradigmatic for the obedience of all who are in Christ."[26] For Paul as well as for all believers, Jesus's death on the cross is God's act of love for us (indicative) and at the same time a paradigm for a life of faith (imperative).

23. Hays, *Moral Vision of the New Testament*, 19.
24. Hays, *Moral Vision of the New Testament*, 19.
25. Hays, *Moral Vision of the New Testament*, 27.
26. Hays, *Moral Vision of the New Testament*, 27.

To demonstrate how Jesus's cross serves as a paradigm for believers across ages, Hays evokes Rom 15. In this unit, Paul takes Jesus's death as an example that should constrain the behavior of "the powerful," who might otherwise be inclined to despise those who are "weak in faith" (Rom 15:1). Hays's comment on this passage is illuminating: "It may seem almost ludicrous to draw an analogy between Jesus' giving up his life in crucifixion and the duty of the strong to give up eating certain foods for the sake of the weak, but the point of comparison is the voluntary surrender of prerogatives for the sake of the others."[27] As we shall demonstrate later, this is the same logic that guides Paul's ethical reasoning when he tries to persuade Philemon that treating Onesimus as a brother and a partner for the gospel should be a voluntary act, a surrender of prerogatives (Phlm 14). In the cross, then, each believer is given an example of a life lived in obedience to God's will for the good of the other. Hence, Paul's ethical thought is unashamedly cruciform.

The last theme in Hays's proposed framework neatly brings all the other components together. It is community, the body of Christ. If through Jesus's death on the cross and his resurrection God inaugurated a new creation—the eschatological age—Paul is more than certain that the community of believers is the manifestation of God's kingdom. The church, the body of Christ, is the new Israel, the new people of God living in the interval between resurrection and parousia. "According to Paul, God is at work through the Spirit to create communities that prefigure and embody the reconciliation and healing of the world. The fruit of God's love is the formation of communities that confess, worship, and pray together in a way that glorifies God."[28]

Through baptism, believers form a community of those who are "in Christ." And as Paul writes in Gal 3:28, they are no longer divided by former distinctions of ethnicity, social status, and gender. They are all children of God, brothers and sisters, members of a single family. As members of Christ's body, believers participate in God's life in Jesus (indicative), and they are called to foster the same life among themselves through acts of love (imperative). That's why, as we will argue later, Paul's indicative and imperative can be rendered in the word *koinōnia* in its double movement: *koinōnia* with God in Christ (indicative) and *koinōnia* with one another (imperative).

---

27. Hays, *Moral Vision of the New Testament*, 28.
28. Hays, *Moral Vision of the New Testament*, 32.

While the preceding analysis is by no means exhaustive, I hope to have articulated the key elements that lead many Pauline scholars to conclude that there is a coherent structure of Paul's theology and ethics. The purpose of the above discussion is twofold. On the one hand, I ventured to explain how Pauline exegetes agree that the coherent structure of Paul's theological and ethical thought emerges from a close reading of Paul's undisputed letters. And among the seven undisputed letters is the Letter to Philemon, the object of the present study. But in reading the undisputed letters for the identification of Paul's indicative and imperative, scholars have given only a cursory attention to the Letter to Philemon.[29] In response to this neglect of Phlm among Paul's authentic letters, I will demonstrate in the following pages how the Letter to Philemon is replete with the same themes found in Paul's other undisputed letters, which evidence across the whole of Paul's thought an integrated and coherent structure that encompasses both an indicative mood and an imperative mood in relation to the revelation of God in Christ.

In addition to showing that Phlm belongs among Paul's authentic letters, the preceding discussion also prepares the ground for the theological conclusion I draw in my reading of the Letter to Philemon: if Paul's theological and ethical thought is summed up in an indicative and an imperative antimony, Paul's ethic is nevertheless a narrative ethic of *koinōnia* whereby believers participate in the life of Christ through faith, and make their faith effective by living as brothers and sisters. The ethic of *koinōnia* is an antidote to the evil of dehumanization that besets the present world in various forms.

Indicative and Imperative in the Letter to Philemon

In this section, I borrow Furnish's theoretical framework of three motifs to read the Letter to Philemon. I am certainly aware that by choosing to adopt Furnish's model, I cannot escape the following objection: Why rely on a scholar whose book was written more than five decades ago? After all, Pauline scholarship has known incredible mutations in the last few decades, and Furnish's conclusions may be outdated. I would like to lean on Hays to respond to this objection.

---

29. A good illustration of this neglect of the Letter to Philemon in treating Pauline theology and ethics is volume 1 of the book *Pauline Theology*, which is called 1 Thessalonians, Philippians, Galatians, Philemon, edited by Jouette M. Bassler. Philemon appears on the title page but disappears inside the book. The authors mention it just in passing, giving more importance to the letters to churches.

In his introduction to the new edition of Furnish's *Theology and Ethics in Paul*, Hays argues that among other reasons, a scholarly work may be deemed a classic because it has shown itself to be a concise but sagacious study that entered a confused, amorphous area of inquiry and articulated balanced, synthetic judgments that have promoted the formation of a consensus. Even without making a splash, such works stand the test of time.[30] Following this logic, Furnish's work is a classic study that has stood the test of time and continues to guide conversations on Pauline theology and ethics even today. Hays himself, Furnish's former student, and James D. G. Dunn agree that Furnish offers a more coherent account of the way in which the complex interrelation between theology and ethics is actually played out in Paul's letters.[31]

However, I am aware that Furnish's work is not beyond criticism. Pauline theology has evolved, and some of Furnish's interpretive keys may need a retrospective assessment in the light of current conversations. For instance, I do not intend to embrace Furnish's emphasis on justification by faith as was the norm in his time. Rather, I adapt his framework to recent scholarship on Paul's letters in general, and on the Letter to Philemon in particular. By reading the text of Phlm in the light of Furnish's three motifs, some neglected aspects of this short letter come to light and prove to be consistent with the coherent structure of Paul's thought.

The Eschatological Motif

As stated previously, eschatology is the prism through which Paul views everything. The eschatological motif reveals how Paul reconsidered the identity of believers in the light of what God has accomplished in Jesus Christ. Believers are in the world, but they live as a new creation, the new people of God. Right in the opening verse of the Letter to Philemon, one discovers this eschatological motif in the word ἐκκλησία. As Paul identifies the recipients of his letter, he adds: καὶ τῇ κατ' οἶκόν σου ἐκκλησίᾳ—and to the church in your house (v. 2).

In order to understand how ἐκκλησία functions as an eschatological term in Phlm, one needs to attend to the different meanings that could have influenced Paul's use of it. Deriving from ἐκ-καλέω ("to call out," a verb used to summon an army to assemble), ἐκκλησία was a common word

---

30. Hays, "Introduction to Paul Furnish," 339.
31. Hays, "Introduction to Paul Furnish," 339.

in the Greek city-state. It denoted the popular assembly of the full citizens of the *polis*, or Greek city-state, hence referring to a political phenomenon functionally rooted in Greek democracy.[32] As a political term, ἐκκλησία translated the idea of participation. Every citizen, by virtue of their membership in the *polis*, had the right to speak and even propose matters for discussion.

In the Septuagint (LXX), the Greek translation of the Hebrew Bible, ἐκκλησία is the equivalent of the Hebrew *qahal* (congregation). It designates the gathering of Israel to hear the Word of God as attested in Deut 4. In his book *The Church in the Theology of St. Paul*, Lucien Cerfaux observes that Deuteronomy is the only book of the Pentateuch to use the word ἐκκλησία, and gives it a religious meaning.[33] It designates, not any kind of assembly, but the assembly summoned by God. That's why in certain instances in Deuteronomy, the term ἐκκλησία appears with the term κυριός (ἐκκλησία κυριου—Deut 23:1–8).

Cerfaux also evokes the books of Chronicles and Nehemiah, where ἐκκλησία refers to a location, a building, the consecration of the temple. Many other examples could be quoted from the LXX where ἐκκλησία is used to refer to *qahal*. Suffice it to say here that Jewish usage as attested in the LXX gives ἐκκλησία a holy meaning: God summons his people to instruct and sanctify them. Thus, there is a development in the understanding of ἐκκλησία. It moves from a purely political reality to a religious phenomenon among Jewish people living in the Greco-Roman world.

In the New Testament, the word ἐκκλησία appears 114 times, with 62 instances in Paul's letters alone.[34] Writing before other New Testament authors, Paul employed ἐκκλησία certainly as an informed inhabitant of both the Greco-Roman and Jewish worlds. Paul reworks both the idea of a popular assembly of Greek citizens and the idea of God's assembled people from the LXX around what God has accomplished in Jesus Christ. Following the logic of Deut 23, it is assumed among Pauline commentators, that whenever Paul uses the term ἐκκλησία, the genitive τοῦ θεοῦ is always implied; it is in fact found in 1 Cor 1:2, 10:32; 11:22; 15:9; in 2 Cor 1:1; Gal 1:13; found in the plural in 1 Cor 11:16; also occurring in 1 Cor 11:22; 1 Thess 2:14; and 2 Thess 1:4.[35]

---

32. O'Brien, "Church," 123.
33. Cerfaux, *Church in the Theology of Saint Paul*, 106.
34. Cerfaux, *Church in the Theology of Saint Paul*, 106.
35. O'Brien, "Church," 126; Cerfaux, *Church in the Theology of St. Paul*, 106.

In Phlm 2, the genitive τοῦ θεοῦ is absent, and I resist the temptation to suggest that it is implied. Rather, I appeal to v. 3 to argue that grace and peace ἀπὸ θεοῦ πατρὸς ἡμῶν καὶ κυρίου Ἰησοῦ Χριστοῦ—from God the Father and the Lord Jesus Christ—is the logical end of the sentence that explains the heavenly origin of ἐκκλησία in the Letter to Philemon. It is by God's grace through the Lord Jesus Christ that believers are summoned and gathered to form an eschatological community, the new people of God. The preposition ἀπό indicates that God the Father and the Lord Jesus Christ are the source, the origin of the church's life and existence. Philemon and all the recipients of the letter understand that they are more than just individuals who have gathered like Greco-Roman citizens to deliberate on important matters of the *polis*. They are God's people, summoned by him in Jesus Christ to become an alternative community to the world. They have been called out, just like Israel of old, to enter into a new covenant with God. They form a family, a household of God's children. Before I comment on the household space as an important eschatological element of the ἐκκλησία, I wish first to discuss the connection between ἐκκλησία as a community "called out" and the identity of those who form the ἐκκλησία in the light of another Pauline term, namely, "saint."

In the thanksgiving section (vv. 4–7), Paul thanks God because of Philemon's love for all the saints (πάντας τοὺς ἁγίους). The apostle also expresses his joy and encouragement, because the hearts of the saints (τὰ σπλάγχνα τῶν ἁγίων) have been refreshed through Philemon's love toward all of them. To be sure, this is not the first time that members of an ecclesial community are addressed as "saints" or "holy ones." The word ἅγιος is one of Paul's preferred terms to identify the community of believers, brothers and sisters in Christ (Rom 1:1; 1 Cor 1:2; 2 Cor 1:1; Phil 1:1; Eph 1:1; 1 Thess 3:13; 2 Thess 1:10).

More than a generic formula used for rhetorical purposes, ἅγιος specifies the kind of assembly the church has become in Christ. In other instances (Rom 1:7; 1 Cor 1:2), ἅγιος is linked to the verb "to call" in reference to the people of God as holy (1 Cor 3:17; Eph 2:21). "In Paul's eyes holiness is both a condition and a process in which the believer is involved through the work of God, of Christ or of the Holy Spirit."[36] As a Jew, Paul would certainly have understood ἅγιος in the light of the LXX passages such as Exod 19:5–6 and Lev 19:2, where the word is used to speak of the very identity of God and his people, and of the basis for right living. Maintaining the

---

36. Porter, "Holiness, Sanctification," 398.

meaning of the Hebrew word קדש, Paul conveys here the idea of being set apart, consecrated, hallowed, by contact with sacred things, and so tabooed from profane use.[37] Philemon and the congregation that meets in his house form an eschatological community whose identity is grounded in the very nature of God, who is holy.

I shall now return to the space of meeting that emphasizes the eschatological nature of ἐκκλησία. The holy ones who form the ἐκκλησία met at the household (οἶκος) of Philemon. As I have stated previously, Paul used existing institutions in the Greco-Roman world and adapted them to his evangelical ends. One such institution was the household. The household was one of the essential institutions of Greco-Roman society. It constituted the microcosm of the greater universe. For Greco-Roman ethicists, the household was perceived as the foundation of the social order as it provided the pattern for the structure and definition of larger public institutions.[38] That the cosmology of the Greco-Roman world was defined by structure and hierarchy in every realm of life is self-evident. Everything was stratified, and everyone had their own place in society.[39] The household was an arena where such hierarchy was visible: the father (the paterfamilias), wife, children, freedmen, business associates, tensants, and slaves. One will recall, for instance, that Caesar's household was the manifestation of the Roman Empire in miniature. In fact, Caesar came to be seen as a father and the state as his household. Moreover, many functions in public life were named and defined in relation to the institution of the household. One needs just notice the root οἰκ in words such as πάροικοι (resident aliens), οἰκεῖος (native), κάτοικοι (military colonists), and οἰκονόμος (administrator or steward).[40] The household was both a place and network of relationships based on loyalty and dependence. The household also provided its members with a sense of security and identity they could not easily find in the larger society.

The "household church" category has sparked much debate among New Testament exegetes and scholars of early Christian communities. Since the 2013 publication of Edward Adams's *The Earliest Christian Meeting Places: Almost Exclusively Houses?*, the notion of Pauline assemblies as "household churches" has been disputed. Adams has questioned the

37. Brown et al., BDB, 872–73.
38. Towner, "Households and Household Codes," 417.
39. Esswein, "Οἶκος of the Lord and the Church at Corinth," 87.
40. Esswein, "Οἶκος of the Lord and the Church at Corinth," 87.

traditional view that early Christians met in private houses and proposed instead various venues as possible gathering places.[41] Because this debate exceeds the scope of the present study, I will refrain from reviewing it here. Rather, I draw on the work of Annette Weissenrieder and Jan N. Bremmer and argue that the community mentioned in the Letter to Philemon met in a private house, and that the category of "household church" is theologically useful for understanding Pauline eschatology.

In his epistolary greetings, Paul connects the words ἐκκλησία and "house" when addressing a particular Christian community. This formula is found in Rom 16:3–5; 1 Cor 16:19; Col 4:15; and Phlm 2 (τῇ κατ' οἶκόν σου ἐκκλησίᾳ). How do we understand the connection between ἐκκλησία and "house"? Weissenrieder answers this question by studying the architecture of early meeting places in Corinth. I find her understanding of the conceptual models of meeting spaces in Corinth so integral and convincing that I will adopt her conclusions for understanding the meeting place in Phlm as a household in both its architectural and ecclesial senses.

Although she does not propose a specific place for the meeting of the Corinthian community, Weissenrieder understands that coming together in an assembly (*ekklesia*) is "a terminus technicus for the civic assembly."[42] Just as the political Greco-Roman ἐκκλησία was a self-generated space with behavioral rules for individuals and the community, Pauline household churches had a structural organization and procedural actions which gave a distinctive identity to their members and dictated a certain manner of behaving.[43]

Like Weissenrieder, Bremmer acknowledges that early Christians did not meet in a singular place, nor did they always gather for a singular purpose. Because early Christians met for different reasons, Bremmer distinguishes three important types of gathering place, highlighting three different functions: "places where a congregation met regularly, places where a congregation met incidentally, and places where Christians met for non-liturgical purposes."[44] Contrary to Weissenrieder, Bremmer argues that the variety of functions does not change the nature of the meeting place for early Christian communities. Surveying New Testament evidence and literary texts from 100 to 313 BCE, Bremmer plausibly concludes that

---

41. Adams, *Earliest Christian Meeting Places*, 10.
42. Weissenrieder, "Architecture," 138.
43. Weissenrieder, Architecture, 148–49.
44. Bremmer, "Urban Religion," 57–58.

houses were the normal meeting place of early Christians.⁴⁵ This is the view that guides my reading of Phlm 2. Unlike the disputed evidence from later centuries (discussed by Adams, Weissenrieder, and Bremmer), the expression τῇ κατ' οἶκόν σου ἐκκλησίᾳ in Phlm 2 reads as a reference to a household church that met regularly for liturgical purposes, and this is a critical factor in the understanding of Pauline eschatology.

Given the key role the institution of the household played in the Greco-Roman world, it is not too much to assume that it impacted Paul and his apostolic ministry. The communities founded by Paul used households as gathering places for worship and fellowship. To speak of the ἐκκλησία as a community gathered by God in Jesus, Paul uses the term "household." He describes the reality of the church and the various relationships among its members using household terms and codes. Arguably, Paul's use of household imagery seeks to depict Christians as God's family united in love, service, and care for one another. He conveys a Christian understanding of the household that gives a sense of belonging, security, and identity to those saved by Jesus. He also acknowledges differences between members of God's household and seeks to minimize these differences and instead emphasizes the shared identity of being a member within a community living in and through Jesus Christ.

By reworking the institution of the household around God and Jesus Christ, Paul establishes a clear antistructural relationship between the church and the world. In Paul's symbolic universe, the two are conceived as being spatially distinct from one another.⁴⁶ For Paul, Philemon and the holy ones who gather in his house live in the world without being of the world. They have been set apart to form an eschatological community of faith, love, and authentic fellowship within the existing world of exploitation and dehumanization.

The Theological Motif

Although Paul generally begins his letters on an eschatological basis by establishing a frame of reference for himself and for the communities that read him, the content of Paul's message is above all theological. By "theological," one should understand the centrality of God as both first cause and final end of the new life in Christ. According to Furnish, "the Pauline ethic

---

45. Bremmer, "Urban Religion," 61.
46. Petersen, *Rediscovering Paul*, 153.

is first of all radically theological because it presupposes that man's whole life and being is dependent upon a sovereign, creative, and redemptive power of God."[47] It is God who takes the initiative to create a new relationship with those who freely accept his Son as Lord and Savior.

A few themes in the Letter to Philemon introduce the reader to the theological motif in Pauline thought. Upon Philemon and the church that meets in his house, Paul pronounces the following blessing: χάρις ὑμῖν καὶ εἰρήνη ἀπὸ θεοῦ πατρὸς ἡμῶν καὶ κυρίου Ἰησοῦ Χριστοῦ—*grace and peace to you* [plural] *from God the father and the lord Jesus Christ* (v. 3). Familiar and brief as this epistolary formula may seem, this verse alone provides the audience with the basis for understanding Pauline theology. In one sentence, Paul speaks of grace (χάρις), peace (εἰρήνη), God, and Jesus. These are the pillars of Paul's theological and ethical thought that need further elaboration here.

The word χάρις (grace) is Paul's allusion to and adaptation of the customary and standard Hellenistic χαίρειν ("greetings!") as evidenced in Acts 15:23; 23:26 and James 1:1. Yet for Paul, χάρις is God's gift to those who have been called in Christ. As its use in the LXX indicates, χάρις is the privileged translation of the Hebrew חן (*ḥnn*), which means favor, grace, acceptance with men or with God (Gen 6:8; 30:27; Exod 33:12; Num 11:11; 32:5; Deut 24:1; Ruth 2:2).[48] Some scholars even argue that Paul uses χάρις to convey the idea of God's steadfast, covenant love expressed by the Hebrew word חסד (*ḥesed*).[49] Thus, instead of a mere conventional greeting, χάρις is the free, unmerited gift of God by which Philemon and the whole church have been saved.

As an assurance of divine loving presence and continued blessing, χάρις is often coupled with εἰρήνη (peace). In the LXX and the New Testament, εἰρήνη is used to translate the Hebrew word *shalom*. In Hebrew, the word *shalom* has a whole range of meaning: well-being, holistic health, safety, tranquility, absence of violence, and friendship with God and with one another.[50] When Paul uses the formula "grace and peace," he proclaims the power of God's gracious presence to effect an abundance of life in relationship with God and other people that embraces justice as its essential

---

47. Furnish, *Theology and Ethics in Paul*, 45–63.
48. Brown et al., BDB, 336.
49. Ryan, "Philemon," 213.
50. Brown et al., BDB, 1022–23.

element.⁵¹ By extending his apostolic blessing to Philemon and the entire church, Paul joins both grace and peace to echo and signify the full realization of the priestly blessing from the book of Numbers: "The Lord bless you and keep you. The Lord let his face shine upon you, and be gracious to you. The Lord look upon you and give you peace" (Num 6:24–26 my translation).

"Grace and peace" is a pronouncement that confers the fullness of divine blessing that bestows a perfection of well-being and wholeness, the fulfilment of which only God can accomplish. God's promise of peace to Israel is now vividly pictured as the establishment of God's new creation. Paul finds its most definitive and fullest expression in the salvific act of God in Christ Jesus, who effects this peace and reconciliation between God and the world in which Philemon and his household church live.⁵² As the recipients hear about God's graciousness and kindness, they are prepared to face the challenge that awaits Philemon: extend the same graciousness and kindness to Onesimus.

In the preceding chapter, I discussed the term "Father" in reference to God through Jesus Christ as we read in Phlm 3. Here, I just wish to point out that for Paul, God's fatherhood pertains not only to his fatherly role in creation but also to his kind and fatherly nature toward those who through faith in Jesus have become God's adopted children.⁵³ Moreover, the preposition ἀπό (from) is used to indicate the origin of grace and peace: God the Father and the Lord Jesus Christ. This is an important detail. In a letter where kinship language is key for understanding the eschatological space that faith in Christ creates, to refer to God as Father and the source of all blessings is an implicit call to imitating God's gratuitousness and love for all. Furthermore, that grace and peace come also from the Lord Jesus is a clear message that both masters and slaves are slaves to one master, Jesus Christ, whose lordship is not exploitation but service for the good of the other.

If Paul's greeting, "Grace and peace from God our Father and the Lord Jesus Christ," sounds the theological motif in the Letter to Philemon, so also do the themes of faith and love ground the theological motif. If out of merciful love and graciousness God takes the initiative to inaugurate a new creation and a new relationship with human beings, it goes without saying that this new relationship also entails new ways of being with God

---

51. Ryan, "Philemon," 214.
52. Ryan, "Philemon," 214.
53. Nordling, *Philemon*, 181.

and others—namely living in faith and love. These two virtues are gifts from God that make both Philemon and Onesimus, and all who believe in Christ, children of God. Because faith and love are both God's gifts and human response to God's initiative, I shall come back to their theological and ethical implications in the last section of this chapter, dedicated to the ethic of *koinōnia* in the Letter to Philemon.

The Christological Motif

There is no Pauline theology or eschatology without Christology. It is in and through Christ that God takes the initiative to inaugurate a new creation and enter into a new and everlasting covenant with his people. As may be clear by now, theology, eschatology, and Christology are not three different Pauline worldviews, but rather three aspects of the same thought. And by "the christological motif," one should not understand systematic Christology because Paul has none. Rather, the christological motif means the implicit narrative about who Jesus is and what he has done for the salvation of the world. Moreover, "the Christological motif refers to believers belonging to Christ, living in Christ, and trying to imitate Christ."[54] This last aspect will be discussed more extensively in the next section. For now, I shall explore the implications of Jesus's identity and mission under the two titles found in the Letter to Philemon: Lord and Christ.

The use of the Greek word κύριος (lord) to identify Jesus in Phlm and in other Pauline writings conforms with the general honorific sense of this term in the Greco-Roman world and its pagan religious application to certain divine figures. But beyond this popular honorific and pagan sense, there is the specific adoption of κύριος into the religious vocabulary of Greek-speaking Jews of the first century as a way of referring reverentially to God, which was paralleled to, and likely facilitated by, the use of *adonai* for God among Semitic-speaking Jews.[55] As a Jew, Paul would have used κύριος as a Greek substitute for YHWH and applies it to Jesus to make a theological point.

In Phlm 3, Paul identifies Jesus as κύριος in terms of Jesus's relationship both with God the Father and with the addressees of the letter. By stating that grace and peace for the church come from both God the Father and the Lord Jesus Christ, Paul highlights Jesus's messianic identity and

---

54. Ho, *Socio-Rhetorical Interpretation of the Letter to Philemon*, 104.
55. Hurtado, "Lord," 562.

the realization of Jewish hopes. Philemon and the entire household church understand that Jesus is not one great figure among many, one deity among many, or one master among many; rather he is Lord: that is, the manifestation of God's power and glory in the world.

Syntactically, in the expression "the Lord Jesus Christ," "Jesus" and "Christ" identify "Lord," and "Lord" defines who Jesus is for Christians and their relationship to him.[56] If Jesus is who he claims to be (that is, Lord and king), Philemon and his coreligionists are his people, his subjects, so to speak. As we saw in the preceding chapter, the rhetorical effect of this title would be that for Philemon and the other addressees, it is not the emperor but Jesus who is Lord. The force of this title is fully at play when associated with another christological term, namely, Χριστός.

Grace and peace proceed from God the Father and the Lord Jesus Christ (Χριστός). Both in Phlm and in other New Testament letters, Χριστός is used as a virtual second name for Jesus. Paul seems to take for granted the prevailing tradition of the time that Jesus is the Christ, the equivalent of the Hebrew משיח—*Mashiach* (anointed one, messiah). As James D. G. Dunn points out, Paul makes no attempt to prove that Jesus is really "the Christ" despite his suffering and death. Even by the time Paul is writing, "Christ" is no longer a title whose fitness for Jesus has to be demonstrated.[57] It is evident that Paul understands Jesus's identity in the light of his death and resurrection, so Paul transforms and transcends some early Jewish ideas about the messiah. Unlike non-Christian Jews, who did not speak of a crucified messiah or identify the messiah with God, Paul affirms that Jesus is Χριστός, the crucified messiah, the fulfilment of Israel's expectations.

Both κύριος and Χριστός are christological titles that tell the implicit story of Jesus's identity and work of redemption. Philemon and the church in his house should hear the echoes of the implicit narrative of the Jesus-event and recognize their identity and mission through their participation in Christ. Faith in Jesus as Lord and Christ should transform believers and create a community of authentic love. Jesus is both lord and messiah through his death on the cross. Consequently, his act of loving and self-sacrificial obedience becomes paradigmatic for the obedience of all who are in Christ.[58] Which is why Paul prays that Philemon's *koinōnia* of faith

---

56. Hurtado, "Lord," 566.
57. Dunn, *Unity and Diversity in the New Testament*, 43.
58. Hays, *Moral Vision of the New Testament*, 74.

in Jesus becomes effective. And it is to this ethic of *koinōnia* that we should devote the last section of this chapter.

The Letter to Philemon and the Ethic of *Koinōnia*

If all Pauline letters show evidence of a coherent and integrated narrative structure of theology and ethics, I submit that the word *koinōnia* sums up well what scholars have identified as indicative and imperative. If Paul's imperative is indicative by nature as we have explicated so far, then it is not an oversimplification to affirm that the Pauline ethic is an ethic of *koinōnia*. Simply put, I understand the ethic of *koinōnia* as an ethic of double participation: participation in the life of Jesus (identity) and participation in the work of Jesus in the world (obligation). Substantiating this claim with evidence from the Letter to Philemon, I shall demonstrate how Paul calls Philemon, and the ecclesial community by extension, to an effective participation in the cruciform love of Jesus and to an authentic brotherly relationship within the family of God gathered around the Messiah, a family where masters and slaves turn into real brothers and sisters.

The Greek term κοινωνία is a derivative of the verb κοινωνέω, whose root κοιν means "common." In classical Greek, the verb κοινωνέω conveys an array of overlapping meanings: to have or do in common with; to have a share of or to take part in a thing with another; to have dealings with or intercourse with; to share in an opinion, to agree; to form a community.[59] Following the semantic logic of the verb from which it is derived, the substantive κοινωνία means communion, association, partnership, fraternity, camaraderie. In the objective genitive, it means communion with, partnership, or fellowship. It can also mean a common gift, contribution, or alms.[60]

Paul uses the term *koinōnia* to symbolize the incorporation, the participation of Christians in the family of God's people redeemed by Jesus Christ. In this sense, it is my understanding that Paul's theology of *koinōnia* did not come ex nihilo. I submit that it is a fresh, apocalyptic development of the Jewish understanding of ברית (berit), God's covenant with the people of Israel in the light of the death and resurrection of Christ. As "a new covenant Jew,"[61] Paul sought to explain the participation of Gentiles in the new

---

59. Liddell and Scott, *Greek-English Lexicon*, 440.
60. Liddell and Scott, *Greek-English Lexicon*, 441.
61. For more details about the designation of Paul as "a new covenant Jew," see Pitre et al., *Paul, A New Covenant Jew*.

covenant ushered in by Christ. Without using the word "covenant," Daniel Boyarin is also of the view that Paul, like many Jews of the first century, was troubled by the fact that the one true God would choose one particular people, almost one family, as his people. "Why would a universal God desire and command that one people should circumcise the male members of the tribe and command food taboos that make it impossible for one people to join in table fellowship with all the rest of his children?"[62] For Boyarin, the following serves as the response to Paul's dilemma: "The birth of Christ as a human being and a Jew, his death, and his resurrection as spiritual and universal was the model and the apocalypse of the transcendence of the physical and particular Torah for Jews alone by its spiritual and universal referent for all."[63] Thus in Jesus, those who were outside the Sinaitic covenant became members of the new Israel, the universal community of God's people.

The Sinaitic covenant, we shall recall, was a solemn, reciprocal commitment: God's commitment to be Israel's God and Israel's commitment to be God's people. For Israel to be taken as God's people would come to mean "Israel becoming Yahweh's treasured possession out of all peoples."[64] Put otherwise, Israel becomes a priestly kingdom, a holy nation. In the words of John Goldingay:

> Israel is separated from other peoples in such a way as to belong distinctively to Yahweh in the way that the priesthood within a people belongs distinctively to the people's deity. As such they are a nation over which Yahweh personally reigns. They are not under the rule of some other people, as they were in Egypt. They are freed from serfdom in Egypt not so that they can be free but so that they can be given to the service of Yahweh.[65]

Being in the service of Yahweh entails keeping his commandments; this is Israel's response to God's mercy and election. In what follows, I argue that Paul reworks this covenantal theology around Jesus using the word *koinōnia*.

Koinōnia, as one of Paul's covenant words, presupposes faith. Just as obedience to the law was Israel's response to God's covenant, so faith in Jesus constitutes the response to God's covenant in Jesus Christ. No one

---

62. Boyarin, *Radical Jew*, 39.
63. Boyarin, *Radical Jew*, 39.
64. Goldingay, "Covenant," 767.
65. Goldingay, "Covenant," 770.

participates in the new creation without first believing in Jesus. "In Paul's theology and experience, this initial act of faith is the response to God's action that triggers the planned effects of that work of God in believers. More specifically, faith actualizes all the intended outcomes of Christ's death."[66] Faith in Christ represents for Paul liberation-enslavement, incorporation, and inauguration. "It liberates from the interlocking directorate of hostile powers that enslave human beings in order to make them servants of God; it incorporates people into Christ; and it inaugurates in them a new life of faithfulness made possible by the Spirit."[67]

From what precedes, we can infer that Paul understood *koinōnia* as a double movement: vertical and horizontal. Every baptized person has *koinōnia* with Jesus Christ. In virtue of their faith, they share in the divine life that Jesus's death and resurrection bring. *Koinōnia* is horizontal because *koinōnia* with Christ entails *koinōnia* with one another, *koinōnia* within the body of Christ. If the first movement is due to faith, the second, vertical movement is the manifestation of that faith, namely, love among brothers and sisters. In the words of John Jansen, "*Koinōnia* had the advantage of implying a subsisting, close relationship between those men and women who, because of the New Covenant in Christ, had reciprocal responsibilities of 'love, peace, steadfastness, kindness, goodness, faithfulness.'"[68] We could even say that Paul proposed to his churches a halakah reworked around the Jesus-event. As Christine Hayes writes, "in this age, Christ-following non-Jews are obliged to bear witness to the righteousness expressed in Torah, that is love of God and neighbor."[69]

The word *koinōnia* appears in two different forms in the Letter to Philemon. The first instance is the thanksgiving section (vv. 4–6). In this lengthy periodic sentence, Paul recounts how he remembers Philemon in his prayers and thanks God for Philemon's faith and love toward all the saints (vv. 5–6). Given that there is no other main verb after Εὐχαριστῶ in v. 4, v. 6 functions as a convoluted dependent clause containing the purpose of Paul's prayer as the conjunction ὅπως indicates. In v. 6, the end of the thanksgiving section, Paul writes: ὅπως ἡ κοινωνία τῆς πίστεώς σου ἐνεργὴς γένηται ἐν ἐπιγνώσει παντὸς ἀγαθοῦ τοῦ ἐν ἡμῖν εἰς Χριστόν—*so that the participation of your faith may become effective in the knowledge of all*

---

66. Gorman, *Cruciformity*, 125.
67. Gorman, *Cruciformity*, 125.
68. Jansen, "Appropriating New Testament Covenant Vocabulary," 31.
69. Hayes, *What's Divine about Divine Law?*, 148.

the good in us for Christ. As can be seen from my literal translation, the syntax of this verse is hard to render in English. Suffice it to note that in v. 6, Paul reveals the goal of his prayer on behalf of Philemon, namely, that Philemon's *koinōnia* of faith may become effective in knowing all the good we (believers) can do for Christ.

This first use of κοινωνία, in v. 6, reveals both the identity and the responsibility of Philemon. In fact, Paul is telling Philemon that through faith, he participates in the death and resurrection of Jesus. To be sure, it is the same syntactic structure that Paul uses when he speaks of his participation in the suffering of Christ in the Letter to the Philippians: τοῦ γνῶναι αὐτὸν καὶ τὴν δύναμιν τῆς ἀναστάσεως αὐτοῦ καὶ [τὴν] κοινωνίαν [τῶν] παθημάτων αὐτοῦ συμμορφιζόμενος τῷ θανάτῳ αὐτοῦ, εἴ πως καταντήσω εἰς τὴν ἐξανάστασιν τὴν ἐκ νεκρῶν—*to know him [Christ] and the power of his resurrection and the participation in his sufferings by becoming conformed to his death, if somehow I may attain the resurrection from the dead* (Phil 3:10–11). Hence, like Paul or like any other baptized follower of Christ, Philemon has a new identity and shares or participates in the new life inaugurated by Christ.

In addition to participation in Jesus' life and identity, κοινωνία of faith also means for Philemon communion with those who are in Christ, for the purpose of doing what is good. In other words, Paul intends to emphasize the communal character of Philemon's faith and to distinguish it from a privately invented, fabricated, or possessed virtue. For Paul faith is never a matter related to or dependent on this or that individual only. Faith implies and expresses solidarity, just as does love.[70] Faith and love are infused virtues, free gifts from God that extend beyond the individual for the glory of Christ and the benefit of the community. Given the communal nature of faith and love, it's no wonder that Paul thanks God when he hears of Philemon's love for all the saints and his faith toward the Lord Jesus (v. 5). The mention of faith and love serves as a clue for the audience to delve deeper into Paul's ethical thoughts grounded in the virtues of love, faith, and obedience.

The intriguing fact about Paul's thanksgiving prayer is both its public aspect and the petition it contains. Knowing that the letter would be performed orally before the entire congregation that met at Philemon's house, why did Paul feel the need to reveal the content of his prayer on behalf of Philemon? And what did he mean by asking that Philemon's κοινωνία of

---

70. Barth and Blanke, *Letter to Philemon*, 281–82.

faith may become effective, or a source of power (if we have to render the literal meaning of the Greek ἐνεργής)? To begin to answer these questions, we need to turn to v. 17 where κοινωνία is used in its adjectival form.

In v. 17, Paul writes: εἰ οὖν με ἔχεις κοινωνόν, προσλαβοῦ αὐτὸν ὡς ἐμέ— *If therefore you consider me a partner, welcome him as [you would welcome] me.* The adjective κοινωνός (partner) is here in the accusative singular case, translating the idea of having something in common. That Philemon's *koinōnia* of faith is not yet a source of power (ἐνεργής) to realize all the good one can do for Christ can be explained by the use of the conditional εἰ (if). For Paul, despite all that he hears about Philemon, authentic Christian faith is not effective until it translates into an inclusive *koinōnia*. Christian faith is a participation in God's power to do good, to save the lowly. Consequently, when Paul prays that Philemon's faith becomes effective or a source of energy/power, he wants Philemon's faith to create a space of authentic humanity where all are welcomed and treated with love and dignity.

The term κοινωνός, as used in v. 17, dictates a reorganization of social space. It conveys the idea of an interpersonal relationship. In the Greco-Roman commercial world, it designated those who are bound as business partners. Paul borrows this commercial and spatial language to explain the kind of relationships that exist now between those who share the same faith in Jesus. My use of "share" here does not mean "divide" but "have in common." If Philemon recognizes that by virtue of his *koinōnia* of faith he is the κοινωνός of Paul, he must receive Onesimus as if he were Paul himself. Put differently, when Philemon next sees Onesimus, he should extend his *koinōnia* to him in the same way he has extended *koinōnia* to Paul and to the saints in his household. To paraphrase Lewis Brogdon, Philemon should drink deeper from the well of faith and stop practicing exclusionary *koinōnia*.[71] A selected and exclusionary *koinōnia* hindered the conversion of Onesimus while in the house of Philemon. Now, succeeding where Philemon had failed, Paul challenges Philemon to welcome Onesimus as a partner and a brother both in the flesh and in the Lord.

It appears from the above discussion that the two uses of the term *koinōnia* in the Letter to Philemon follow the logic of Pauline theology. In the Pauline corpus, the use of the term *Koinōnia* is fundamentally religious and particularly Christocentric. Faith in Christ creates a new identity and an alternative space where all are partners for the building of God's kingdom. In this way, Paul's request to Philemon is a call to an ethic of *koinōnia*,

---

71. Brogdon, *Companion to Philemon*, 1830.

the only one capable of transforming relations of exploitation and inhumanity into authentic, humane, and Christocentric relationships.

By arguing that the goal of the Letter to Philemon is a call to an ethic of *koinōnia*, I remain faithful to the text and escape the temptation to fall on either side of Paul's interpreters. Like recent interpreters (see those mentioned in chapter 1), I go beyond the debate about whether Paul condones or condemns slavery in the Letter to Philemon. What is at the heart of the letter is rather the ethical requirement of a horizontal *koinōnia*, a cruciform love that results in reconciliation, renunciation, true freedom, and new family relationships.

In Phlm 7, Paul speaks of the joy and encouragement he has received from Philemon's love, which refreshes the hearts of the saints. And he adds in vv. 8–9: Διὸ πολλὴν ἐν Χριστῷ παρρησίαν ἔχων ἐπιτάσσειν σοι τὸ ἀνῆκον διὰ τὴν ἀγάπην μᾶλλον παρακαλῶ—*For this reason, although I have much boldness in Christ to command you to do what is required, I rather make an appeal on account of love.* By appealing to the virtue of love, Paul takes care to clarify one thing: to love is to exercise the freedom to choose. And every choice, for that matter, also involves renunciation. Essentially Christocentric, the ethic of *koinōnia* is an ethic of renunciation. For Paul, the Christian is the one who imitates the cruciform love of Jesus by renouncing certain rights and privileges for the glory of God and the good of others.

In v. 16, Paul asks Philemon to receive Onesimus, *no longer as a slave, but more than a slave, a beloved brother . . . in the flesh and in the Lord.* And he adds a very important detail in v. 21: *Having confidence in your obedience* (τῇ ὑπακοῇ σου), *I am writing to you, knowing that you will do even more than I say.* Paul is well acquainted with the conceived space of the Roman Empire in which Philemon lives. He knows that legally, Philemon has the right of life and death over his slave Onesimus. He knows that at the sight of Onesimus, Philemon might be tempted to inflict on him a punishment provided for in Roman law. Aware of Philemon's position of authority, Paul challenges him and makes a request that many would have considered impossible to make or to fulfill in the first century, namely, to consider Onesimus "a beloved brother . . . in the flesh and in the Lord" (v. 16). In other words, Paul is asking Philemon to renounce his legal rights over his slave and to radically transform the nature of their relationship.

To be sure, Paul arrives at this request after setting himself up as an example. He who had the apostolic power to command Philemon to behave in a certain way, nevertheless preferred to renounce his rights and to allow

Live What You Believe

Philemon to respond out of love and obedience to faith (vv. 8–9). And the example that Paul gives is evidently the imitation of Jesus's cruciform love as one can read in the Letter to the Philippians: *though he was in the form of God [Jesus Christ] did not regard equality with God as something to be exploited, but he emptied himself, taking the form of a slave, being born in human likeness. And being found in human form, he humbled himself and became obedient to the point of death—even death on a cross* (Phil 2:6–9).

There has been much speculation among Pauline scholars regarding the meaning of Jesus's self-emptying and the phrases that go with it: "the form of God" and "the form of a slave." Without rehearsing such speculations here, I side with Michael Gorman in acknowledging that it is generally agreed that the self-emptying is metaphorical, pointing to the complete self-lowering that becoming human involved for someone equal to God. The extent of the self-emptying is confirmed by the subsequent phrases: "taking the form of a slave, "being born in human form."[72] What we see in Phil 2:6–9 is a pattern of non-self-centered, self-giving obedience or, as Gorman puts it, "an un-Roman resume of shame, we might say, or *cursus pudorum*."[73] Being in "the form of God" and "in the form of a slave" reads as a pattern of radical self-emptying and self-giving for the good of the other. According to Gorman, Paul interprets Christ's death not only as an act of love but as an act voluntary obedience, and he expects such voluntary obedience to be the pattern of believers' existence too. "The story of the Messiah is one of radical vulnerability and downward mobility."[74]

If Jesus emptied himself of his divine glory and privileges to become a slave and suffer the infamy of the cross, if Paul could imitate Jesus by renouncing his apostolic privileges and losing his freedom for the sake of the gospel, Philemon too could renounce his socio-economic rights and privileges over Onesimus. Like Jesus, he is called to obey the will of God who wants everyone to recover their human dignity. Philemon must crucify his personal interests to favor *koinōnia* and reconciliation. He is called to change his imagination, to think within the biblical narrative, that is to say, to integrate the community of those who have allowed themselves to be transformed by the gospel.[75] He must stop considering Onesimus as useless and see him as useful, a brother both in terms of his humanity and his faith in Jesus the Messiah.

---

72. See Gorman, *Apostle of the Crucified Lord*, 507.
73. Gorman, *Apostle of the Crucified Lord*, 507.
74. Gorman, *Apostle of the Crucified Lord*, 508.
75. Wright, *Paul and the Faithfulness of God*, 15.

As I mentioned in chapter 3, Paul employs a play on words in speaking of Onesimus and his relationship to Philemon, his master. In v. 11, Paul plays on the name Onesimus, which means "useful," by choosing another word with the same meaning in both its negative and positive forms. And as Carolyn Osiek notes, there may be a further pun intended too: in Hellenistic Greek (and in modern Greek as well), the word *chrēstos* (useful) would have been pronounced exactly like *christos* (anointed one, or Christ). Thus "useless" (*achrēstos*) could also be heard as "without Christ," a description of Onesimus's situation before baptism.[76] Given that the Letter to Philemon was likely performed orally before the congregation, listeners might easily have become confused about whether "useful" or "Christ" was meant in v. 11. In fact, the aural confusion of the two Greek words is attested by historians. "There is a running disagreement among historians about whether the riots that took place in the Roman-Jewish community about 49 CE *impulsore chresto* (at the instigation of an otherwise unknown person named Chrestos) were in fact caused by animosity against Christians and their leader, Christus."[77]

If aural confusion is intended in the text, then the expected rhetorical effect is the following: the whole congregation would have understood that, previously Onesimus was without Christ. But now he is with Christ and should be considered as a brother and a partner to be loved unconditionally. Certainly, such an interpretation is more of an assumption than a conviction based on textual evidence. It may even convey a message that only those who are Christians are useful and the non-Christians are useless. Such is not my conclusion here. Rather, I point out to the play on the name Onesimus as it seeks to call attention to Onesimus' new identity and foster an ethic of *Koinōnia*. What the Roman Empire could not offer to Onesimus, Jesus has offered. As result, both Philemon and the church in his house would have to make their *Koinōnia* of faith effective by imitating Jesus in treating Onesimus as a brother.

This is where one needs to understand the goal of the Letter to Philemon. Pauline interpreters are generally divided between those who demonize Paul for not being courageous enough to denounce the evil of slavery as a system and put an end to it, and others who praise him for requesting the freedom or manumission of Onesimus. However, a responsible reading of the text reveals neither camp understands the nature of Paul's request in

---

76. Osiek, *Philippians and Philemon*, 136.
77. Osiek, *Philippians, Philemon*, 136.

this letter. Paul was an apostle, an evangelist, not an activist in the modern sense of the term. Neither Jesus, the master, nor Paul, the servant, aimed to foment popular uprising or engage in violent revolution that would destroy the small Jesus-communities. The aim of Jesus and Paul was to seek to create an eschatological space for Jesus-communities, alternative structures to the dominant social structure. It was by example, not by political activism, that Paul wanted to transform the life of his society. If in the church people treat each other as beloved brothers and sisters, those same brothers and sisters can set an example for the rest of society and radically change it from within. Slavery in the Roman Empire was a legal institution that a single individual like Paul or a minority like Christians could not overthrow overnight using free speech, as some might attempt in certain places today.

There is another dimension to the apostle's goal in his letter. Those who read Phlm only as a note requesting manumission in the Roman sense of the term completely forget the theological aspect of this letter. If his purpose were only to claim Onesimus's freedom by following the process provided by Roman law, Paul would not have written this letter. In most cases, as we saw in chapter 2, freed men and women struggled to attain economic and political freedom. Some of them could spend their entire lives working for the interest of their former masters.[78] Serving first the interests of slave owners, Roman manumission failed to offer holistic freedom. Consequently, even though buying one's freedom was seen as a great social achievement, the evil of systemic exploitation was only changing forms. This is by no means the kind of freedom Paul is asking for Onesimus. According to his letter, Paul believes that Philemon should grant Onesimus what the Roman Empire fails to offer: He should treat Onesimus like a brother, should grant him the honor of kinship, and should therefore no longer assess his dignity only in economic terms. It is by renouncing all these advantages, it is by loving Onesimus with a cruciform love that Philemon would become a good imitator of Christ and that the *koinōnia* of his faith would become effective, as Paul asks God in his prayer.

The dehumanizing evil of slavery is as old as the world. The Roman Empire was only one facet of it. The exploitative relationship that existed between Philemon and Onesimus still exists today in other forms, and it is a reality in the DRC. In the last chapter of this book, I will contextualize the conclusions of my reading of Phlm for the construction of an authentic space of human life in the DRC.

78. Weidemann, *Greek and Roman Slavery*, 53.

5

The Letter to Philemon and the Construction of a *Koinōnia*-Space in the DRC

Introduction

IN HIS FAMOUS BOOK, *Truth and Method*, Hans-Georg Gadamer writes:

> In the process of understanding, a real fusing of horizons occurs—which means that as the historical horizon is projected, it is simultaneously superseded. To bring about this fusion in a regulated way is the task of what we called historically effected consciousness. Although this task was obscured by aesthetic-historical positivism following on the heels of romantic hermeneutics, it is, in fact, the central problem of hermeneutics. It is the problem of application, which is to be found in all understanding.[1]

For Gadamer, responsible interpretation culminates in a fusion of two horizons: the horizon of the text (which is the product of a historical tradition) and the horizon of the reader, who comes to the text with all the prejudices and realities of his or her own context. Consequently, the hermeneutical task consists not in avoiding the tension between the horizon of the text and the horizon of the reader, but rather in bringing it out. The resolution of this tension is what Gadamer calls "application."

In the same line of thought, two South African biblical scholars, Jonathan A. Draper and Gerald O. West, have emphasized the need for African contextual interpretation.[2] For these two scholars, biblical interpretation in

---

1. Gadamer, *Truth and Method*, 306.
2. West, "Biblical Hermeneutics in Africa," 23–29; Draper, "African Contextual

The Letter to Philemon and the Construction of a *Koinōnia*

Africa typically consists of three poles: the pole of the biblical text, the pole of the African context, and the pole of appropriation. Draper has referred to this as a tripolar approach.[3] Both Draper and West agree that

> the biblical text and African context do not on their own participate in a conversation. For dialogue to take place between text and context a real flesh and blood African reader is required! This reader moves constantly back-and-forth between the biblical text and African context, bringing them together in an ongoing conversation which we call appropriation. How the reader moves between text and context is determined by a range of factors, including their ideo-theological orientation, their ecclesio-theological missionary heritage, their engagement with ordinary readers of the Bible in the church and community, and the important issues that require attention in the African context.[4]

Both Gadamer and the two South African biblical scholars highlight the goal of interpretation, namely, the production of meaning for the transformation of the reader and the reader's community. Such is the purpose of this chapter. Like Elisabeth Schüssler Fiorenza, I believe that there is an ethical dimension to every biblical text.[5] Therefore, I devote the last chapter of this book to the appropriation of the message of the Letter to Philemon in the context of the DRC.

To borrow Gadamer's phrase, my conclusions will denote "a fusion of horizons": the Letter to Philemon will illuminate the sociopolitical situation in the DRC, and, conversely, some aspects of Congolese society will open new ways of reading the letter. An essential implication of my contextual reading is that the evil of dehumanization that Paul's letter tries to eradicate in the domestic space inhabited by Philemon and his congregation is a pervasive phenomenon in the DRC with various facets and profound ramifications for peace and human well-being. Reading the Letter to Philemon contextually is to challenge the predominantly Christian population of the DRC to make effective their *koinōnia* of faith. In other words, Congolese Christians need to honestly assess the work of evangelization in their land, revisit their collective memory as narrativized in their national anthem, reclaim both cultural and Christian ethical values, and revolutionize their

---

Hermeneutics."
    3. West, "Biblical Hermeneutics in Africa," 21.
    4. Draper is cited in West, "Biblical Hermeneutics in Africa," 21.
    5. Schüssler Fiorenza, "Transforming the Legacy of *The Woman's Bible*," 16.

minds for the construction of a *koinōnia*-space, a country of authentic humanity.

Christianity in DRC: A Quick and Honest Assessment

In the introductory paragraph of his encyclical letter *Deus Caritas Est*, Pope Benedict XVI states the following: "Being Christian is not the result of an ethical choice or a lofty idea, but the encounter with an event, a person, which gives life a new horizon and a decisive direction."[6] A few decades before Benedict's encyclical, a Congolese Catholic priest, Jean Adalbert Nyeme, made a similar statement in his book *Munga: une éthique en un milieu africain, Gentilisme et Christianisme*:

> We know, in fact, that contact with the authentically Christian spirit constitutes for each man, each culture, each period, a real "trial by fire" and a "painful childbirth," whose outcome is beneficial! In fact, it is this trial by fire, this catharsis which is the necessary condition for the birth of the new man, that is, the man whose breath of life and wisdom blossoms admirably through the encounter with Christ . . . Only contact with Christ reveals to the Gentile all his identity, the very identity that he sensed in his generous and authentic effort without however appreciating its full scope and all its nobility.[7]

It is in the light of Benedict's and Nyeme's statements that I wish to start my assessment of the advent of Christianity in the DRC. The Congolese's contact with the authentically Christian spirit of which Nyeme speaks had taken place long before the arrival of the Belgian missionaries. According to Léon de Saint Moulin, Christian penetration in the DRC is not a recent event. He writes:

> The first evangelization, which dates back to the end of the fifteenth century, deeply marked the culture of the Kongo region, where the brass crucifixes and onomastics show that Christianity had penetrated mentalities and culture long before the colonization of the nineteenth century. Within the country, it is also possible that certain relationships between traditional accounts and biblical texts are the result of contacts with the Christian world,

---

6. Pope Benedict XVI, *Deus Caritas Est*, par. 1.

7. Nyeme, *Munga*, 98.

the latter having reached, before the appearance of Islam, Ethiopia and Sudan.⁸

If the confrontation between Congolese gentilism and Christianity dates back to the end of the fifteenth century, can we prove Nyeme right by asserting that there has been the birth of a new human person in the DRC? Has Christ revealed to the Congolese man and woman their true identity? Indeed, like Philemon and the community that gathered in his house, Congolese men and women came into contact with the genuinely Christian spirit, and this encounter has produced much good fruit. But it is also true that as was the case with Philemon and his household church, so the *koinōnia* of Congolese faith must become effective and transformative. It must become the antidote to dehumanization and the cornerstone for building a united, beautiful, and humane DRC.

It is a truism to say that the DRC is a deeply religious and particularly Christian country. As Theodore Trefon observes, "anyone interested in contemporary Congolese politics and society cannot fail to be fascinated by religion and its epiphenomena—the dynamics of churches, religious identities, ever-renewed forms of solidarity, faith and belief systems—and particularly the way in which they manifest themselves in an urban context."⁹ Since the arrival of the Portuguese on Congolese soil in the fifteenth century, the sons and daughters of this part of central Africa have adhered to Christianity overwhelmingly. By distributing the population of cities in the DRC by religion, Saint Moulin arrived at the following results: "In all the cities of the Congo, nearly 95% of the population declare themselves Christian: 66% claim to be Catholic, 23% Protestant, and 4.1% Kimbanguists."¹⁰ It should be noted that these statistics go back to 1975, a time when the phenomenon of "revivalist churches" was still almost nonexistent. For more than two decades now, Christianity has enriched itself with a new space of discourse known as *églises de réveil* (revivalist churches). Found on almost every street corner in large Congolese agglomerations, revivalist churches have made the Congolese space the home of an effervescent Christianity.

These few statistics on evangelization suffice to show that the Word has really become flesh and blood in the DRC. By professing the Christian faith, the DRC as a whole has chosen to adopt Christian values as reference points for daily life. Just as Paul gives thanks for Philemon's love and faith,

---

8. De Saint Moulin, *La place de la religion*, 78.
9. De Saint Moulin, *La place de la religion*, 78.
10. De Saint Moulin, *La place de la religion*, 46.

we too can only give thanks for the faith that the Congolese show towards God the Father and the Lord Jesus. Our thanksgiving is all the more justified in view of the impact that the Christian faith has had on the interior, social, cultural, and political life of the Congolese people.

One must admit that Christianity found fertile ground in Africa, and more precisely in the DRC. Congolese men and women are deeply religious people in the sense that they have always believed in a Superior Being. For them, as Nyeme points out, God is everything. He is heaven. He is earth. It is to him, the source and origin of all reality and life, that ultimately everything belongs. Theirs is a God of life, and their very lives flow from God.[11] It is in the Christian faith that the Congolese find their identity, their raison d'être, their mission in the world, and, above all, the hope to live a more meaningful and fulfilled life.

In the very DNA of the Congolese people is the conviction that to live is always to live with. Such conviction, in line with the gospel message, has engendered a remarkable solidarity among Congolese Christians across denominations. Commenting of this value of Congolese Christianity, Saint Moulin writes:

> Another, more internal feature of Congolese Christianity brought to light by surveys in urban areas is a spontaneous ecumenism. We consider it as a value insofar as believers consider themselves brothers and support each other, contrary to the traditional teaching in the West that contact between members of various Churches usually leads to indifference and abandonment of religious practice.[12]

Catholics, Protestants, Kimbanguists, and members of revivalist churches form a space of solidarity and mutual aid that is particularly appreciable in a country where the economic crisis continues to rob the people of God of their dignity. This willingness to live together as brothers and sisters, it should be emphasized, is nothing other than the Christianization of the black African vision of the world, which promotes solidarity, hospitality, and friendship as indispensable values for the construction of an authentically human space.

This spontaneous ecumenism, this desire for solidarity and communion are the fruit of an interior transformation which is intended to spread and impact all layers of Congolese society. The Christians of the DRC, especially those of the Catholic Church, concur with the idea that all authentic

11. Nyeme, *Munga*, 37–39.
12. De Saint Moulin, *La place de la religion*, 75.

evangelization pursues the holistic salvation of the human person: spiritual and material. In the words of Cardinal Laurent Mosengwo, "through evangelization, the Church leads man to God. This is the theological or vertical dimension. But she also reveals to man his dignity as a man and makes every effort to free him from everything that prevents him from fully living his life as a son of God: this is the horizontal dimension. Cooperation for human development is thus an integral part of the mission of the Church."[13]

Thus in the DRC, churches play an important sociopolitical role insofar as they are spaces for reflection on and awareness of social problems. By speaking of God, they make a contextual interpretation of the sacred scripture and propagate a vision of the human person and society that is in conformity with God's plan. It is in this context that we must recognize the work of the assembly of Congolese Catholic bishops known as CENCO—Conférence Episcopale Nationale du Congo—that is, the National Episcopal Conference of Congo. These bishops, representing the unified voice of the population, both Catholics and non-Catholics, have tirelessly and boldly defended inalienable rights and promoted authentic values such as the reconstruction of the country, national unity, the territorial integrity of the DRC, its defense and national sovereignty, nonviolence, peace, the protection of people and their goods, national reconciliation, and dialogue in freedom, justice and truth.[14]

Throughout the history of the DRC, the Catholic Church in particular has continued to oscillate between two roles in the reconstruction of the country and the democratic process: that of facilitator and that of critic. Figures such as Cardinal Joseph Malula, Cardinal Laurent Monsengwo, Bishop Nicolas Djomo, and the priest Apollinaire Malu Malu have been pivotal in the many dialogues for peace, reconciliation, and fair democratic elections in the DRC.[15] For example, during the thirty-two years of President Mobutu's dictatorship, Malula opposed resistance to Mobutu's determination to do away with some Christian traditions and values in the name of the "authenticity campaign."[16] After Malula, Monsengwo also opposed Mobutu and aligned himself with some Western powers calling for negotiations for a unified Congo.[17] Monsengwo continued his prophetic

13. Mapwar, *Église et société*, 12.
14. Mapwar, *Église et société*, 13.
15. For a deeper discussion of the role of Catholic bishops in the DRC, see Okitafumba Lakola, "Self-Understanding of the Congolese Church," 195–201.
16. Turner, *Congo*, 116.
17. Turner, *Congo*, 117.

mission even during Joseph Kabila's administration, denouncing all the evils that tried to make the Congolese slaves on their own soil. Although some analysts have accused Catholic prelates of trying to be involved with politics and advance their political career, bishops and the Catholic Church as a whole, with the cooperation of some Protestants, have been strongly involved in the struggle for justice, peace, and human dignity in the DRC.

After this brief assessment of the work of evangelization, we are in a better position to answer our initial question: Is the *koinōnia* of faith effective among Congolese Christians? The short answer is not yet. In fact, the fact that the Catholic Church and other religious denominations continue to defend the inalienable rights of people and advocate authentic Christian values is sufficient proof that the Christian faith is not yet effective in the DRC. Like Philemon who, though a Christian and probably the leader of the household church in Colossae, continued to exploit Onesimus, so denying him all humanity, the Christians of the DRC, especially the powerful who control the sociopolitical and economic space, profess their *koinōnia* in the life of Christ without letting themselves be transformed by the message of freedom and human dignity that this Christian faith dictates. Like Philemon, the Congolese oppressors must make their *koinōnia* of faith effective by creating an authentic living space where love, human dignity, freedom, justice, unity, and solidarity reign.

If at the heart of slavery as a system lies the deliberate denial by the powerful of the slave's humanity and God-given dignity for personal interests, one has to admit that the enslavement of the Congolese people is a perennial evil. The Congolese "Philemons" along with their foreign allies have remained comfortable in their exploitation of the poor "Onesimuses," who ask nothing more than their right to live as human beings. The evil of dehumanization with its many facets makes the DRC a domestic space where the population, like Onesimus, struggles to be treated like a brother or a sister. In the next section, I discuss the history of the struggle for human dignity in the DRC and highlight the pillars on which an authentic *koinōnia*-space must be built.

The National Anthem or the Narrativization of Congolese Collective Memory

We have seen that in order to successfully construct a *koinōnia*-space, an authentic living space where Philemon and Onesimus could henceforth call each other brothers and live in harmony, Paul began by implicitly narrativizing the perceived space, the conceived space, and the lived space he shared with his new converts. By doing so, he was able to identify the evil of dehumanization that plagued the Roman Empire in general, and the Christian community in particular. He therefore proposed an alternative vision of the world based on the indicative of the salvation accomplished by Jesus and the ethical imperative that is a logical response to it. In this section, I will follow Paul's logic. To construct a *koinōnia*-space in the DRC, we must begin by paying attention to the way in which the Congolese narrativize their own space, their history, and their aspirations. And more than anything else, the Congolese national anthem, "Debout Congolais" (Arise Congolese), is an inspired account that conveys the consciousness and the *état d'âme* of the Congolese people. Composed by the Reverend Simon-Pierre Boka and lyricized by Joseph Lutumba, the captivating Congolese national anthem reads as follows:

> CHOIR:
> Debout Congolais,
> Unis par le sort,
> Unis dans l'effort pour l'indépendance,
> Dressons nos fronts longtemps courbés
> Et pour de bon prenons le plus bel élan, dans la paix,
> O peuple ardent, par le labeur, nous bâtirons un pays plus beau qu'avant, dans la paix.
>
> VERSE:
> Citoyens, entonnez l'hymne sacré de votre solidarité,
> Fièrement, saluez l'emblème d'or de votre souveraineté, Congo.
>
> REFRAIN:
> Don béni, *Congo* des aïeux *Congo*,
> O pays *Congo* bien aimé *Congo*,
> Nous peuplerons ton sol et nous assurerons ta grandeur.
> *Trente juin* O doux soleil *trente juin* du trente juin,
> *Jour sacré* Sois le témoin *jour sacré* de l'immortel serment de liberté
> Que nous léguons à notre postérité pour toujours.[18]

---

18. Lutumba, "Debout Congolais." The words in italics in the refrain are meant to be sung by a choir, while the other words in the refrain are meant to be sung by soloists.

In English, the following translation has been adopted:

CHOIR:
Arise, Congolese, united by fate,
United in the struggle for independence,
Let us hold up our heads, so long bowed,
And now, for good, let us keep moving boldly ahead, in peace.
Oh, ardent people, by hard work we shall build,
In peace, a country more beautiful than before.

VERSE:
Countrymen, sing the sacred hymn of your solidarity,
Proudly salute the golden emblem of your sovereignty, Congo.

REFRAIN:
Blessed gift *Congo* of our forefathers *Congo*,
Oh country *Congo* that we love *Congo*,
We shall people your soil and ensure your greatness.
30th *June* Oh gentle sun 30th *June* of 30th June,
Sacred day Be witness *sacred day* of the immortal oath of freedom
That we hand on to our children forever.[19]

    According to Etiti Yomo Djewiro, words and expressions jostle in the minds of the "Debout Congolais" authors; their true magic sometimes escapes the grasp. Carefully choosing sentences that arouse confidence and consent among the Congolese people, the authors of this anthem mix together the indicative and the conditional, the past, the present, and the future to reveal not only the euphony of their words but also the essential soul of a people.[20] This essential soul, this *état d'âme* of the Congolese people is their love for life, a better life, a life worthy of the human person. In what follows, I venture, not to conduct a detailed analysis of the "Debout Congolais," but to draw from it the intergenerational collective consciousness of a people who have spared no effort in the struggle for their life and dignity.

    Through a close reading, we notice that the structure of the "Debout Congolais reveals a double movement: retrospective and prospective. Retrospectively, this beautiful text of the national anthem takes the reader on a journey into a dark past of exploitation and dehumanization of the Congolese in their own domestic space. It then brings back the reader to the present to prove the resilience of a people determined to stand up, to raise its

19. Lutumba, "Debout Congolais."
20. Djewiro, *Comprendre le "debout congolais"*, 8–9.

long bowed brow in order to build a dignified and habitable domestic space for all. It is from their collective memory, from the story of their struggles and victories, that the Congolese people must draw strength and gain the most momentum to build a more beautiful home than before.

Collective Memory

The "Debout Congolais" recounts without recounting. The words conceal behind the musical eurhythmy the uninterrupted waves of the intergenerational consciousness, the deconstruction of nothingness, of emptiness, of an imposed narrative. Each word refers to another word; the words are entangled like the rainforest liana vines: words swinging in a forest of words—the most flamboyant of which announce the beginning of a revolution.[21] The narrative behind the text invites the reader to discover the story of a people who, despite the oppression imposed on them by hostile external and internal forces, have never given up the fight for their human dignity.

This history of struggle began with the arrival of Europeans in the Cuvette Centrale basin. When Diego Cao, the Portuguese explorer, arrived in the Kongo basin in 1482, the Kongo kingdom was one of the largest and best organized Bantu kingdoms.[22] But very quickly, this organization and this desire among the Bantu people to live together in peace was confronted with evil powers. The arrival of several European explorers into this part of the African continent triggered a merciless domination by foreigners over indigenous peoples and led to the slave trade and to the slavery that spread across the so-called New World beginning in the sixteenth century. According to David Van Reybrouck,

> The Atlantic slave trade lasted roughly from 1500 to 1850. The entire west coast of Africa was involved in it, but the area around the mouth of the Congo most intensively. From a strip of coastline some four hundred kilometers (250 miles) long, an estimated four million people were put on transport, equaling almost a third of the entire Atlantic slave trade. No less than one in every four slaves on the cotton and tobacco plantations of the American South came from equatorial Africa.[23]

21. Djewiro, *Comprendre le «debout congolais»*, 8–9.
22. Omba, *Debout Congolais pour ta Patrie*, 700.
23. Van Reybrouck, *Congo*, 23.

It would be an understatement to say that the international slave trade had an enormous impact on Central Africa in general, and in Congo in particular. Regions were torn apart, lives destroyed, and horizons shifted. The traditional authority of tribal chieftains was shaken to the foundations. Centuries-old social forms were eroded. Anarchy reared its head. Political ties based on village and family were elbowed out by new economic alliances between traders.[24]

Faced with this dehumanizing injustice, the Bantus of Congo did not surrender like cowards to the powers of darkness. Despite the complicity of some locals who sold their brothers and sisters to slave traders, the Congolese people in general greatly resisted foreign powers.[25] Students of the history of Congo may recall resistance struggles such as the Battle of Ambuila, the intransigence of the young Kimpa Vita (nicknamed the African Joan of Arc), and the bravery and exploits of Ngongo Lutete against Arab domination in the lands of the Great Lakes region.[26]

The invasion by European explorers and the ensuing slave trade cleared the ground for another great crime of humanity: colonization. It was from November 15, 1884, to February 26, 1885, that the biggest mafia in the history of the world was taking shape and form in the German capital: the infamous Berlin Conference. Capturing well the ill intent of Western powers, some historians have called this whole process "the scramble for Africa."[27] John Akare Aden and John H. Hanson explain: "Seven European powers, led by Britain, France, and Germany and including Italy, Portugal, Spain, and the Belgian monarch Leopold II, carved up the continent. These powers engaged in diplomacy among themselves to set terms for dividing the continent into 'spheres of influence' before they moved to extend effective occupation through force into those spheres."[28]

24. Van Reybrouck, *Congo*, 25.

25. This fact is well attested by historians such as John Akare Aden and John Hanson. They write: "During the trans-Atlantic slave trade Europeans negotiated with African elites for the right to build and reside in forts and other coastal enclaves. For years Europeans remained content to stay on the coast and engage in commerce with Africans who traveled to them. Commerce remained an activity that brought benefits to all parties, and Europeans made contacts with a plethora of local authorities further and further in the interior, offering treaties of trade and protection. These were but the first steps in a process that culminated in European colonial rule in Africa." Akare Aden and Hanson, "Legacies of the Past," 47.

26. Omba, *Debout Congolais pour ta Patrie*, 700.

27. Aden and Hanson, "Legacies of the Past," 47.

28. Aden and Hanson, "Legacies of the Past," 47.

Sharing Africa among themselves like a birthday cake at the end of the Berlin Conference, the seven European powers decided the fate of Africa without the African people. To the Belgian monarch, King Leopold II, was given the geographical space known today as the Democratic Republic of the Congo. As Reybrouck describes it, "on June 1, 1885, King Leopold II awoke in his palace at Laeken a different man: in addition to being king of Belgium, from that day on he was also sovereign of a new state, the Congo Free State."[29]

"The Congo Free State"? The irony of such a joke could only be entertained by a greedy person like Leopold II. It is true that for Leopold II and the Belgian government after him, this beautiful name sounded like the advent of the "liberating," "saving," and "civilizing" mission of colonization. But in truth, the Congo Free State symbolized the slavery of the Congolese and the freedom of the Belgians to transform this rich space into an economic free-trade zone for the benefit of the Western powers of the time.

From the day he was proclaimed the head of the state of Congo in 1885 until his death in 1909, Leopold II never set foot in his private property, Congo. Both Leopold II and the Belgian government to which he transferred his colony in 1908 acted in Congo not as philanthropists but as unashamed greedy people who would treat humans like living tools to acquire wealth. In the light of the crimes committed by Leopold II and the Belgians, Joseph Conrad went as far as to describe Congo as the "heart of darkness."[30] Unsurprisingly, many people, especially Western media, have misunderstood Conrad and interpreted the "heart of darkness" as Congo's innate savagery. But as Thomas Turner points out, most journalists who advance this interpretation "seem not to realize that Joseph Conrad had concluded that the ultimate darkness lay in the hearts of white men in their white buildings in Europe, sending their agents to rape and kill in Central Africa."[31]

Blatantly oblivious to the real motivation behind colonization, King Baudouin of Belgium said the following on June 30, 1960, Congo's Independence Day:

> The independence of Congo is the end result of the work started with the exceptional personality of King Leopold II, which he tackled with determined courage and which has been continued with persistence by Belgium.

29. Van Reybrouck, *Congo*, 57.
30. Conrad, *Heart of Darkness and Other Tales*, 2002.
31. Turner, *Congo*, 5.

> It represents a defining moment in the destination, not only of Congo itself, but I have no hesitation in saying it, of all of Africa. For 80 years, Belgium has sent the best of its sons to your country, first to liberate the Congo Basin from the horrible slave trade that thinned out your populations, later to bring the different peoples—who used to be enemies—closer together and prepared to form together the largest of the independent African states; finally to bring a happier life to the different regions of Congo that you represent here in the same parliament.
>
> At this historic moment, our thoughts must turn to the pioneers of the emancipation of Africa, and those who, after them, made Congo what it is today. They deserve our admiration and your appreciation, for it was they who, by sacrificing their best strengths and even their lives to a great ideal, brought you peace and enriched your moral and material possessions. They must never be forgotten, neither by Belgium nor by the Congo.
>
> When Leopold II embarked on the great work that is being crowned today, he did not come here as a conqueror but as a bringer of civilization. From the start, Congo has opened its borders to international trade, without Belgium ever exercising an exclusive right focused solely on its own interests. Congo has been given railways, all kinds of sea and air lines, which, by connecting your populations with each other, have promoted their unity and expanded the countries to the world. A medical service, which was set up several decades earlier, has been patiently organized and has delivered you from many devastating illnesses. Numerous and remarkably well-equipped hospitals have been built. Agriculture has been improved and modernized.[32]

Coming from a descendant of the monarch who managed Congo as his private property, these remarks were far from surprising. The revolting thing is that they deliberately ignore the barbarism and dehumanization of which the Congolese were victims. It was in the open that the Belgians inflicted inhuman treatment on Congolese subjects, thus committing enormous human right abuses for many years. What a beautiful civilization! What a fine antidote to the slave trade! Fortunately, Congo has minds like Patrice Emery Lumumba to tell the true story of this unique space in the heart of Africa. Also speaking on June 30, 1960, after King Baudouin, Lumumba aptly summed up the collective memory of a valiant people in the following terms:

---

32. Quoted in Lumumba, "Discours de l'indépendance."

Men and women of the Congo,

> Victorious independence fighters,
> I salute you in the name of the Congolese Government.
>
> I ask all of you, my friends, who tirelessly fought in our ranks, to mark this June 30, 1960, as an illustrious date that will be ever engraved in your hearts, a date whose meaning you will proudly explain to your children, so that they in turn might relate to their grandchildren and great-grandchildren the glorious history of our struggle for freedom.
>
> Although this independence of the Congo is being proclaimed today by agreement with Belgium, an amicable country, with which we are on equal terms, no Congolese will ever forget that independence was won in struggle, a persevering and inspired struggle carried on from day to day, a struggle, in which we were undaunted by privation or suffering and stinted neither strength nor blood.
>
> It was filled with tears, fire and blood. We are deeply proud of our struggle, because it was just and noble and indispensable in putting an end to the humiliating bondage forced upon us.
>
> That was our lot for the eighty years of colonial rule and our wounds are too fresh and much too painful to be forgotten.
>
> We have experienced forced labor in exchange for pay that did not allow us to satisfy our hunger, to clothe ourselves, to have decent lodgings or to bring up our children as dearly loved ones. Morning, noon and night we were subjected to jeers, insults and blows because we were "Negroes." Who will ever forget that the black was addressed as "tu," not because he was a friend, but because the polite "vous" was reserved for the white man?
>
> We have seen our lands seized in the name of ostensibly just laws, which gave recognition only to the right of might.
>
> We have not forgotten that the law was never the same for the white and the black, that it was lenient to the ones, and cruel and inhuman to the others.
>
> We have experienced the atrocious sufferings, being persecuted for political convictions and religious beliefs, and exiled from our native land: our lot was worse than death itself.
>
> We have not forgotten that in the cities the mansions were for the whites and the tumbledown huts for the blacks; that a black was not admitted to the cinemas, restaurants and shops set aside for "Europeans"; that a black travelled in the holds, under the feet of the whites in their luxury cabins.
>
> Who will ever forget the shootings which killed so many of our brothers, or the cells into which were mercilessly thrown those

who no longer wished to submit to the regime of injustice, oppression and exploitation used by the colonialists as a tool of their domination?

All that, my brothers, brought us untold suffering.

But we, who were elected by the votes of your representatives, representatives of the people, to guide our native land, we, who have suffered in body and soul from the colonial oppression, we tell you that henceforth all that is finished with.[33]

By rejecting the Belgian thesis according to which colonization was a philanthropic work for the benefit of the Congolese, Lumumba certainly did not mean to deny certain benefits arising from the presence of Belgians in Congo—these included the end of the slave trade, centered as it was on Arab traffickers; the education of Congolese men; the building of infrastructure; and even the expansion of the Christian faith. But at the heart of Lumumba's speech is the denunciation of the evil of colonization. No one can pretend to civilize a people by denying them all freedom and all dignity. Therefore, the "benefits" of colonization can only be called so as long as they served the interests of the oppressors. Instead of the Arabs, it was the Belgians who oppressed and enslaved the Congolese on their own soil. The infrastructure was a set of facilities used for the economic activities of Belgium. Education of the Congolese was kept at a minimum and aimed to form assimilable and manipulatable indigenous elites who would serve the interests of the colonizers. Evangelization took place under the prism of Belgian nationalism and imposed a purely European Christ.

After June 30, 1960, it was time for a new beginning. The history of Congo had to be written henceforth in Congo and by the Congolese, as Lumumba famously announced: "The Republic of the Congo has been proclaimed and our beloved country's future is now in the hands of its own people. Brothers, let us commence together a new struggle, a sublime struggle that will lead our country to peace, prosperity and greatness."[34]

Sixty years after independence, can we say that Lumumba's dream has come true? The honest answer is a painful no. The results of sixty years of independence have made the DRC an oppressive domestic space for millions of Congolese. What happened after the Belgians left? Why did the native population not avoid the evils of the colonial era? President Felix Tshisekedi responds in his speech for Independence Day, June 30, 2020:

33. Quoted in Buchakuzi, *Pleure, Ô Noir, frère bien-aimé*, 84–86.
34. Quoted in Buchakuzi, *Pleure, Ô Noir, frère bien aimé*, 86.

> The total lack of trust among national political actors the day after the proclamation of our independence is the combined result of inexperience, the youth of the political class and the unhealthy game of external covetousness. This failed start led our country, a country with yet exceptional promises, unto a downward road which may have seemed endless and which has spared no sector of national life.[35]

There is no one to blame for this postcolonial crisis except for the Congolese elite itself. Congolese political leaders are sons and daughters of the land, but in reality they behave like slave-masters. Like the Belgians before them, they are driven by nothing else but personal interests. President Tshisekedi, one of them, found the courage and the appropriate words to reveal this mentality: "In sixty years, we have gradually let our political class turn into a kind of mafia, and we have made it the main model of success for our youth. From independence to the present day, our practice of politics has had the main effect of diluting efficiency, diluting responsibilities and, in the end, of doing harm instead of serving."[36]

Since independence, entering the political sector has garnered more interest than any other arena in society, because politicians can earn good money fast. As the Congolese historian Isidore Ndaywel rightly points out, the creed of all political officials, with rare exceptions, has been *j'y suis, j'y reste*, that is, I am here and I will stay as long as possible. The only relevant practice has been limited to the elaboration of strategies to gain and to retain power, following the corollary principle of *Ôte-toi de là que je m'y mette!* (Get out of here so that I may take over).[37]

For Congolese rulers, politics is not a ministry or a service, but a business. Like their European counterparts and allies, Congolese politicians treat their own brothers and sisters like slaves who have only one right, that of being pitied by their leaders. They appear as magnanimous men and women capable of distributing bags of flour, cartons of chicken and milk, sacks of salt, and T-shirts to the unfortunate. The improvement of social life and the concern for the common good are never among their priorities. Like Philemon, Congolese politicians have only one concern, namely, to maintain their social status at the expense of the poor, powerless, and marginalized Congolese Onesimus. Instead of serving, their power enslaves

---

35. Tshisekedi, "60ème Indépendance du 20 Juin 2020."
36. Tshisekedi, "60ème Indépendance du 20 Juin 2020."
37. Ndaywel, *L'audace de dresser le front pour un autre Congo*, 95.

and dehumanizes. And as one may well guess, such a way of leading can only engender frustration, grievance, and revolt within the population.

The geographical space known as the DRC has been a perennial hot spot, and a playing field for hostile powers. From the earliest days of the fledgling nation, overt intervention by Western governments has resulted in far-reaching and often tragic consequences for the government and for the people of the DRC. Much of this intervention has been extensively documented through contemporary sources and historical accounts.[38] Almost immediately after independence was declared, certain Western powers stepped in to reshape the government of the DRC according to their own objectives; a series of calamitous events swiftly ensued: The Western powers manipulated the first president, Joseph Kasavubu, and incited him to get rid of the courageous and threatening prime minister, Patrice Emery Lumumba.[39] After his speech on Independence Day, Lumumba was seen as the enemy of Western interests, and the plot to eliminate him was under way. In 1961, with the help of Colonel General Joseph Mubutu, Kasavubu sidelined Lumumba. On January 17, 1961, Lumumba was executed and dissolved in sulfuric acid in Katanga (the southern province of the DRC), under Belgian supervision, and in the presence of Katangan and Belgian officials and officers.

The same Mobutu who helped Kasavubu and the enemies of Congo eliminate the undesirable Lumumba ousted Kasavubu by a coup d'état and proclaimed himself the president of Congo on November 25, 1965. Initially, Mobutu gave some hope to the Congolese by pretending to adopt Lumumba's nationalist approach. He opposed Belgian cultural imperialism and called for a return to authenticity, a kind of cultural nationalism. Among other things, he changed the country's name from Congo to Zaire, which was a Portuguese deformation of the Kongo word "Nzandi," meaning river.[40] Christian names and European attire, including the suit and tie, were strictly forbidden. In the economic sphere, Mobutu's measures seemed to give locals a greater share in the country's resources. However, it became clear to most locals that Mobutu was transferring ownership of Congolese businesses to mostly European political cronies. They hired

---

38. Prunier, *Africa's World War*; Stearns, *Dancing in the Glory of Monsters*; Ndaywel, *L'audace de dresser le front pour un autre Congo*.

39. Van Reybrouck, *Congo*, 303–5.

40. Turner, *Congo*, 10.

incompetent Congolese to run these businesses and focused only on accruing short-term profit and disorganizing the economy.[41]

Supporters of Lumumba and those who could no longer endure Mobutu's dictatorship formed rebellions that caused bloodshed and turmoil in Congo. The Mayi-Mayi, the Mulelists, the Simba, and the Lumumbist's Armée Populaire de Libération (the People's Liberation Army) are among the rebel groups who fought Mobutu's regime of terror. After thirty-two years of ruthless dictatorship and state-organized pillage, in 1997 Mobutu, weakened by cancer, was finally ousted by another Congolese warrior, Laurent-Désiré Kabila.

A longtime opponent of Mobutu, Kabila was the head of a coalition referred to as the AFDL, the Alliance des forces démocratiques pour la libération du Congo (the Alliance of Democratic Forces for the Liberation of Congo). Although Kabila spearheaded this rebellion, the truth is that he only performed the job of providing a Congolese face for the Rwando-Ugandan invasion into Congo, frustrating at the same time the efforts of the United Nations to investigate the massacres of Rwandan Hutu refugees in the Congolese forests.[42] As AFDL gained strength and popularity, international firms and corporations who continuously covet Congo's mineral resources signed deals with the rebel leader Kabila to secure their place in the war of partition and pillage that would soon start.[43] On May 17, 1997, Kabila's troops, a majority of whom were Rwandese and Ugandan soldiers, conquered the capital city, Kinshasa. This victory brought Mobutu's dictatorship (and also what's called the First Congo War) to an end, and inaugurated a new era known as the AFDL administration, with Kabila as the president of the DRC.

Laurent-Désiré Kabila's regime represented for the Congolese a new departure. Initial actions heralded the advent of liberation from Mobutu's oppressive regime. Discipline, public order, and the rule of law began to be a lived reality. Soldiers and police officers received their pay; they did not get much, but at least they got it regularly. For the first time in decades, teachers and civil servants could start saving up for a bicycle. The towering inflation receded significantly, and the country's currency *nouveau zaïre*, now the *franc congolais*, regained its value.[44]

---

41. Turner, *Congo*, 10.
42. Turner, *Congo*, 16.
43. Turner, *Congo*, 16.
44. Van Reybrouck, *Congo*, 434–35.

Very soon, however, these initial signs of hope turned out to be elusive. The enthusiasm and hysteria for Kabila quickly dwindled. Frustration grew on every side because of Kabila's authoritarian and Marxist-like ideology. The Congolese who had hoped that Kabila would succeed where Mobutu had failed witnessed the rise of another dictator. The legitimacy of the constitution, the parliament, the government, and the electoral committee of the transitional years before his inauguration, landed in the trash can. As Van Reybrouck sums it up, "rather than an instate full-blown democracy, the new government reverted to an extremely authoritarian regime in which everything revolved around the person of Kabila himself."[45]

Things got only worse when Kabila revealed his true colors to his Rwandan, Ugandan, and other international allies. Having no choice in the face of a growing protest by the population against the vexing foreign interference, Kabila turned his back to his allies, broke his promises to Rwanda and Uganda, and decided to expatriate all Rwandan and other foreign soldiers. This decision turned Kabila's friends into the merciless enemies of his regime. This was a great opportunity for Western powers such as the United States of America to do away with Kabila, who became unsatisfactory to them. To be sure, "Kabila refused to abandon his Marxist ideology, revoked several Western mining company contracts, and turned to China, Cuba, and Venezuela for advice on economic development."[46] Here lies the primary cause of Kabila's assassination by one of his bodyguards on January 16, 2001. Again, it was a Congolese soldier who provided a Congolese face to this horror planned outside of Congo's borders.

Before his assassination, Kabila witnessed the beginning of what would become the First Congo War or the First African World War.[47] As usual, the invasion of Congo by Rwanda and Uganda required the participation of some naïve, greedy, and frustrated Congolese citizens. The Second Congo War, which began in 1998, came under the guise of the movement known as RCD (Rassemblement Congolais pour la Démocratie—Congolese Rally for Democracy). Lasting until 2003, this conflict has become a source of episodic terror that destabilizes the Congo in its eastern part to this day.

The Second Congo War, which sought to oust Kabila, was an extremely complex conflict. "No fewer than nine African countries and some thirty local militias took part. It was the showdown on an African scale, with

---

45. Van Reybrouck, *Congo*, 434.
46. Turner, *Congo*, 40.
47. Van Reybrouck, *Congo*, 440.

Congo as the central theater of war."[48] Laurent-Désiré Kabila's son, Joseph Kabila, inherited his father's conflicts and even bequeathed them to the current president, Felix Tshisekedi. As may have become clear now, the unending war in eastern Congo is a war of aggression motivated by greed and grievance: Rwanda covets the DRC's eastern province of Kivu and seeks to annex it to the Rwandan national territory. Alongside Rwanda, many other African countries and Western powers, with the help of greedy Congolese leaders, use armed conflicts to plunder the DRC's natural resources.

To be sure, the DRC is one of the richest countries in the world in terms of natural resources. It has the second-largest rainforest in the world, after the Amazon. Gold, diamonds, copper, cobalt, tin, uranium, and coltan, are among the many minerals that make the DRC one of the most coveted countries in the world. No one can appropriately talk about modern technology without Congo. For instance, 60 percent of the world's coltan is found in the DRC. This is the precious mineral needed for electronics such as smartphones, tablets, computers, gaming consoles, jet engines, printers, and so forth.[49]

Becoming a playground for greedy, powerful individuals, companies, and nations, the DRC is a space where human rights are constantly trampled down. The people of eastern Congo in particular have been abused and treated like slaves in their own country. Since 1996, local as well as foreign soldiers fighting in that region have committed atrocities that amount to crimes against humanity. As many volunteers and aid workers in that region have attested, "the Democratic Republic of Congo may be the worst place in the world to be a woman or a child."[50] Rape has been used as a weapon of war. Various armed groups have systematically raped women and girls in large numbers. Many of those rapes have resulted in pregnancies. Even worse, some victims have been infected with HIV and then been victimized again when their husbands and families have repudiated them.[51]

In terms of casualties, the wars in the DRC have developed into the deadliest conflict since World War II.[52] Van Reybrouk substantiates this statement with the following horrifying statistics: "Since 1998 at least three million and perhaps as many as five million people have been killed in

---

48. Van Reybrouck, *Congo*, 440.
49. Crisis in Congo, accessed January 20, 2022 (https://congojustice.org).
50. Turner, *Congo*, 120.
51. Turner, *Congo*, 120.
52. Van Reybrouck, *Congo*, 440.

hostilities in Congo alone, more than in the media-saturated conflicts in Bosnia, Iraq, and Afghanistan put together. And their number continue to rise."[53] In addition to living as victims of war, touched by rape and killing, many Congolese who live around mining areas have been displaced from their homes to clear the way for the plundering of Congo's natural resources. Further, children have been forced to carry arms and perform manual labor.

The conflict in the DRC is complex, and I resist the temptation to endlessly discuss its consequences. Suffice it to say that what is happening in the DRC is the deliberate denial of human dignity of countless men and women by powerful and greedy people. And as I stated earlier, there are many to blame for this evil, but the Congolese elite is primarily responsible. Since the advent of Europeans until today, greedy Congolese leaders have been manipulated and used to enslave their brothers and sisters. Rebellions, pillaging, lawlessness, and many other practices that plague the DRC take place because the Congolese participate in them.

It is true that the DRC is one of the most tormented inhabited spaces in the world. But it is equally true that the Congolese are one of the most valiant and indomitable peoples of the earth. Despite its long history of suffering from the beginning of the slave trade through colonization, in the struggle for independence, through Mobutu's thirty-two years of brutal dictatorship, and in the civil wars and wars of aggression that have raged from 1996 to the present day, the Congolese people have never lost hope. Their dream to build a better Congo where all live as brothers and sisters is not buried. Anytime they sing the "Debout Congolais," they are more than motivated to raise their bowed heads and resolve to boldly move forward.

Arise, Congolese: Raise Your Bowed Heads and Keep Moving Boldly Ahead

Freedom is not free. True freedom is achieved through suffering and sacrifice. As we saw in the first chapter, the history of the interpretation of the Letter to Philemon has revealed a neglect of Onesimus's agency among early Pauline exegetes. Paul's voice, as important as it is, and the actions Philemon would have to take to determine Onesimus's fate, dominate the narrative. Consequently, a casual and inattentive reading of the letter may give the reader the impression that the whole narrative is about Onesimus,

---

53. Van Reybrouck, *Congo*, 440.

with the latter playing no major role. But read closely through the lenses of narrative criticism, the letter shows how Onesimus is a subversive and revolutionary character who managed different spaces to gain his dignity and freedom. In the words of the "Debout Congolais," Onesimus raised his bowed head, took his life into his hands and went away in search of his freedom. He went to Paul, seeking an alternative domestic space where his human dignity would be recognized, protected, and promoted. Onesimus was ready to sacrifice his life to claim his right to dignity and his place in the domestic space called humanity.

Following Onesimus's example, the Congolese people need to understand that it is time to truly rise, raise their bowed heads, and boldly move ahead to obtain their dignity and build for themselves a space of authentic human life on the soil of their ancestors. Their destiny cannot be reduced to a posture of wandering and despair. But rather, as Godefroid Ka Mana puts it, "We are destined to create, impose and spread the Congolese miracle all over the world. The miracle of a country that will have overcome the fatality of despair to invent a destiny of greatness, prosperity, vital splendor and development in the true and global sense of the term."[54] To successfully make Congo a more beautiful country than before, as we sing in the national anthem, we must revolutionize our imagination and create cracks in the system of dehumanization put in place by the powerful. This revolution will be possible only if the Congolese (1) recognize their identity and become aware of their dignity, (2) reclaim and live out traditional-cultural values in the light of their Christian faith, and (3) revolutionize minds and renew hearts.

Congolese Quid?

In his encyclical letter *Fides et Ratio*, Pope John Paul II writes: "The admonition *Know yourself* was carved on the temple portal at Delphi, as testimony to a basic truth to be adopted as a minimal norm by those who seek to set themselves apart from the rest of creation as 'human beings', that is as those who 'know themselves.'"[55] This truth about human identity led the Roman pontiff to the following conclusion: "a cursory glance at ancient history shows clearly how in different parts of the world, with their different cultures, there arise at the same time the fundamental questions which

---

54. Quoted in Ndaywel, *L'audace de dresser le front pour un autre Congo*, 144.
55. Pope John Paul II, *Fides et Ratio*, par. 1.

pervade human life: Who am I? Where have I come from and where am I going? Why is there evil? What is there after this life?"[56]

One cannot really know how to behave unless they know who they are. Put otherwise, action is rooted in identity. To know what you ought to do or what's expected of you in various situations, you must have a sense of who you are. In one of his articles back in 1950, Lumumba called on his compatriots to understand this guiding principle: "Self-knowledge is the foundation of all evolution and the cornerstone of all moral improvement. It allows us to take stock of our intellectual and moral store: our good or bad habits, our intellectual, moral and physical abilities."[57] Now the fundamental question is, do the Congolese people truly know themselves or has their identity been imposed upon them by others?

In a pithy formula that has become a cliché by which many refer to the Congolese people today, Youweri Museveni, the current president of Uganda, defined the Congolese elite as BMW, which stands for beer, music, and women. This initialism gives a measure of contempt and opprobrium that, more than in the simple thought of the Ugandan leader, serves as the most condescending description of the Congolese people by others around the world. What is worse is that many Congolese, exasperated by the crises that the country has been going through, end up assimilating this serious insult. Without embarrassment, some Congolese harm their own reputations by calling their compatriots BMWs. Some even go as far as to call their countrymen lazy, concerned only about their stomach and their genitals.[58] BMW is but one of the many examples of a "received identity" that should be deconstructed. Beer, music, and licentiousness should not constitute the soul of the Congolese people. What defines the Congolese is their genius, their ethic of hard work, and their love for a life of dignity and greatness. To define "Congolese" is to evoke the cultural values as well as the Christian values that form the core of Congolese identity.

Reclaiming and Living Cultural and Christian Values

In order to successfully construct a *koinōnia*-space for Philemon, Onesimus, and other members of the ecclesial community, Paul begins by recalling the values that distinguish Christians from the rest of the world. With

---

56. Pope John Paul II, *Fides et Ratio*, par 1.
57. Quoted in Buchakuzi, *Pleure, O Noir, frère bien-aimé*, 50–51.
58. Nzinga, *Stratégies de domestication d'un peuple*, 314.

The Letter to Philemon and the Construction of a *Koinōnia*

a great command of *captatio benevolentiae*, the apostle Paul highlights the essential Christian values that characterized Philemon's relationship with the members of his household church: faith and love translated into hospitality, service, and communion—all summed up in the phrase "*koinōnia* of faith." Transformed by faith in Christ, Philemon is challenged to extend his koinōnia to all, including to the slave Onesimus. The same challenge lies before Congolese Christians. We need to reclaim and live out essential values such as faith, love, solidarity, and unity.

In a deeply religious and predominantly Christian nation like the DRC, faith should be the ultimate foundation for the construction of a *koinōnia*-space. Before being children of the same land inherited from our ancestors, we are first and foremost children of God, hence, brothers and sisters both in the flesh and in the Lord. Pope Francis understood this well when he wrote the following in his encyclical letter on fraternity and social friendship: "As believers, we are convinced that, without an openness to the Father of all, there will be no solid and stable reasons for an appeal to fraternity. We are certain that 'only with this awareness that we are not orphans, but children, can we live in peace with one another.' For 'reason, by itself, is capable of grasping the equality between men and of giving stability to their civic coexistence, but it cannot establish fraternity.'"[59] Faith in a transcendent Other, whom Paul calls God our father (Phlm 3), opens one to the transcendent truth that all people are created equal and endowed by their creator with an undeniable dignity. It is to restore this dignity that Jesus became man and died for all humans. Consequently, like Philemon, the powerful leaders of the DRC are called to recognize the transcendent truth and accord their life and actions with this truth. This is the same appeal Pope John Paul II was making to the powerful of this world in general when he wrote:

> If one does not acknowledge transcendent truth, then the force of power takes over, and each person tends to make full use of the means at his disposal in order to impose his own interests or his own opinion, with no regard for the rights of others. People are then respected only to the extent that they can be exploited for selfish ends. Thus, the root of modern totalitarianism is to be found in the denial of the transcendent dignity of the human person who, as the visible image of the invisible God, is therefore by his very nature the subject of rights which no one may violate—no individual, group, class, nation or State. Not even the majority of a social body may violate these rights, by going against the minority,

---

59. Pope Francis, *Fratelli Tutti*, par. 272.

by isolating, oppressing, or exploiting it, or by attempting to annihilate it.[60]

In a country where mediocrity and corruption have infiltrated even spaces of worship, it is more than urgent for religious leaders to awaken the transcendent truth of human dignity in their hearts and in the hearts of their faithful. It is regrettable to notice that religious leaders in the DRC are among the most corrupt leaders in Congolese society. Knowing that money can change a pastor's sermon and public discourse, Congolese political leaders approach leaders of various religious groups with cash to advance their agenda. Unashamedly, those religious leaders then do all they can to convince their congregations, who live in misery, to maintain the corrupt political elite in power.

Even when they have a chance to launch the electoral process by choosing a suitable candidate to serve as the chairman for the CENI—the Commission Electorale Nationale Indépendente (the Independent National Electoral Commission), religious leaders cannot let their faith unite them for a noble cause. Over the three previous electoral cycles, at this phase of the process, the eight recognized religious denominations have always been divided, the Catholic Church finding itself alone against all the others and denouncing a stranglehold by the regime on the designation of a favored candidate, who in turn would manipulate the election result in favor of the incumbent administration.[61] Religious leaders should imitate Paul, who rather than imprisoning the truth for selfish and evanescent profits, became a prisoner of Christ for the truth of the gospel and called his congregations to follow his example. As the Conference of the Congolese Bishops have demonstrated throughout the history of the DRC, religious leaders, especially the Christian church, cannot and must not remain on the sidelines in the building of a *koinōnia*-space, or fail to "reawaken the spiritual energy" that can contribute to the betterment of society. It is true, as Pope Francis reminds us, "that religious ministers must not engage in the party politics that are the proper domain of the laity, but neither can they renounce the political dimension of life itself."[62]

---

60. Pope John Paul II, *Centissimus Annus*, par. 44.

61. Teller Report, accessed January 24, 2022 (https://www.tellerreport.com/news/2021-27-25-drc=religious-denominations-on-the-same-line-before-the-appointment-of-the-president-of-fthe-ceni.S1lPlya9Cd.html).

62. Pope Francis, *Fratelli Tutti*, par. 276.

The Letter to Philemon and the Construction of a *Koinōnia*

If faith is the ultimate foundation on which authentic human relations should be built, then we have to acknowledge that the visible expression of faith is love. Effective *koinōnia* of faith is possible only when one's love for God extends to the other, especially the marginalized and the powerless. Every Congolese Christian who reads the Letter to Philemon should be challenged by this appeal to authentic love. For many people today, especially in the DRC, "politics" is a distasteful word, mainly because of the mistakes, corruption and inefficiency of the Congolese political elite. In reading the Letter to Philemon in their sociopolitical context, Congolese readers are confronted with a call to social and political charity.

Social and political charity. What is that? Is it possible? From the Letter to Philemon, we learn that Paul gives thanks to God for Philemon's love toward *all* the saints, and he prays that Philemon's *koinōnia* of faith becomes effective by perceiving the good that believers like him can do for Christ (Phlm 6–7). Two things emerge from Paul's prayer for Philemon. On the one hand, he rejoices that Philemon's love is social in that it seeks the common good, the good of others. On the other hand, he prays that this social charity would be all the more grounded in faith in Jesus so as to extend to the slave Onesimus, who has endured the pain of an exclusive *koinōnia* practiced by Philemon.

In the same vein, evoking the social doctrine of the Catholic Church, Pope Francis describes social and political charity as follows: political charity is born of a social awareness that transcends every individualistic mindset. Social charity makes us love the common good; it makes us effectively seek the good of all people, considered not only as individuals or private persons, but also in the social dimension that unites them.[63] For Francis, effective social and political love "makes it possible to advance towards a civilization of love, to which all of us can feel called. Charity, with its impulse to universality, is capable of building a new world."[64]

Social and political charity is fundamentally sacrificial, cruciform. It is an act of the will whereby a person decides to set aside their personal interest in order to will and seek the good of the other. The Congolese reader cannot fail to see in the Letter to Philemon a summons to this kind of charity and to an ethic of renunciation for the good of the other. Paul says to Philemon, "I preferred to do nothing without your consent, in order that your good deed might be voluntary and not something forced" (v. 14). Like

---

63. Pope Francis, *Fratelli Tutti*, par. 182.
64. Pope Francis, *Fratelli Tutti*, par. 183.

Philemon, the Congolese elite should find in the ethic of renunciation an authentic form of social and political charity. They should understand that elected officials ought to serve first the interest of others, especially those on society's margins. This kind of charity, according to Pope Francis, is the heart of politics. It is always a preferential love shown to those in greatest need; it undergirds everything we do on their behalf.[65] Politicians are called to tend to the needs of individuals and peoples.[66] And to tend to the needs of others takes strength and tenderness, effort and generosity, abnegation and sacrifice.

A *koinōnia*-space is also a space where love fosters unity and solidarity. And these two values are among the ancestral values that form the core identity of the Congolese people. The exercise of solidarity makes the Congolese aware of building an environment favorable to a harmonious and lasting development of life in their homes and in their human community. Also, the Congolese hold in esteem generosity and prodigality as the building blocks of a human city that has some chance of survival and happiness.[67]

Because greed and selfishness have threatened to erode such fundamental values, a contextual reading of the Letter to Philemon becomes necessary to help the Congolese people reclaim what makes them authentically human. There is nothing good that can be built in disunity. Democracy is another form of *koinōnia* in that it calls for the participation of all citizens for the common good. Consequently, government leaders should promote respect for other people's opinions and especially heed the cry of those who suffer in zones of conflicts, war, and exploitation.

It is regrettable to note that these core values tend to disappear today, and this is due, in part, to the manipulation by the colonizers who introduced mistrust and division between brothers and sisters of the same land. With their "divide and reign" policy, they created factions among the population to annihilate a possible united opposition to their imperialism. Sadly, after the colonizers, their Congolese counterparts, that is, the political elite, espoused the same policy. Even today, elected members of the parliament, senators, and even governors impose candidates of their own making and liking to run local administrations in their provinces of origin for the obvious selfish reason of securing their reelection. Such imposed leadership increases tensions, grievances, and ethnic conflicts in local communities. An

---

65. Pope Francis, *Fratelli Tutti*, par. 187.
66. Pope Francis, *Fratelli Tutti*, par. 188.
67. Nyeme, *Munga*, 105.

example of a conflict ignited by the political elite is the recent emergence of the rebel group known as Kamuina Nsapu in the Kasai-Central province.[68] Communal clashes broke out after Kamwina Nsapu, a traditional chief, called for a popular uprising in June 2016 with the aim of removing all state institutions and security forces from the region. His followers had wanted his chiefdom to be officially recognized by the authorities. Kamwina Nsapu was killed two months later when the police raided his house, and his followers vowed to avenge his death. Beheadings, rape, enslavement, and mutilation were among the many atrocities caused by this conflict.[69]

Unless we recover the shared passion to create a community of belonging and solidarity worthy of our time and culture, our energy and our resources, the illusion of individual happiness that misleads the Congolese elite will collapse and leave many in the grip of anguish and emptiness. To put it differently, for Pope Francis, "the notion of 'every man for himself' will rapidly degenerate into a free-for-all that would prove worse than any pandemic."[70]

In addition to the values discussed above, we must also mention the republican values that constitute the Congolese national motto and mission statement, namely, justice, peace, and work. Justice is the bedrock of any democracy. With the adjective "democratic" in its name, the DRC aspires to bring about justice in order to guarantee the proper functioning of institutions. To construct a space of authentic human life for all, the Congolese must advocate for the independence of justice and the rule of law. Without justice, there will never be peace in a country where rebels and warlords become government leaders without being held accountable for their acts of violence and terror. Without justice and peace, dignifying work and decent wages will only be an illusion for the majority of Congolese. Job opportunities for all should be a priority in a country that seeks true development. But how can the DRC become a space of justice, peace, and work without the revolution of minds and the renewal of the political elite?

---

68. Ndaywel, *L'audace de dresser le front pour un autre Congo*, 138.

69. BBC News, "DR Congo's Kasai Crisis," accessed January 28, 2022 (https://www.bbc.com/news/world-africa-44613147).

70. Pope Francis, *Fratelli Tutelli*, par. 36.

The Revolution of Minds: Congolese, Become the Best Version of Yourself

Although the general situation in the DRC leaves a great deal to be desired, it is far from being hopeless. The potential to construct a better Congo, a space of authentic *koinōnia* and human flourishing lies latent in each Congolese man and woman. What is needed is a revolution of minds and a resolute determination to be *debout*, as we sing the national anthem, that is, to rise like Onesimus and take charge of a glorious and dignified destiny. And to this end, Godefroid Ka Mana's *cri de coeur* remains a permanent challenge. The following is both a translation and a paraphrase of Ka Mana's words:

> We Congolese men and women, we are not condemned to be a people of irrationality, immorality, existential absurdity, despairing contradictions and endemic disorganization. We are not condemned to the law of misery, poverty, and debt. We are not condemned to ever live under the yoke of a ruthless world order, horrors of wars of predation and furors of delirious tropical despotisms. We are not condemned to endlessly err in debilitating spiritualities which engulf us in the stupidity and naïveté of a nation that only prays, sings, and complains without ceasing about their unfortunate situation while the country, like a sinking boat, is taking on water from every side. We are not condemned to believe that the reconstruction of our country depends on the genius of foreign people to whom we offer our minerals so that, in exchange, they may build for us roads, sport spaces, as if we did not have minds capable of creativity and organization for the construction of our nation. We are not condemned to live in the fear of neighboring countries whom we accuse of trying to balkanize our country, but rather establish a defense system that respects and honors our central place in Africa and in the world. Our destiny should never be reduced to a posture of inertia and despair. Rather, we are destined to create, to impose and spread wide and far the "Congolese miracle." This miracle is, undoubtedly, the grandeur of a country that would have conquered the fatality of despair in order to invent a destiny of greatness, prosperity, splendor, and holistic development.[71]

Ka Mana's words resound like a reader's response to the Letter to Philemon and a blueprint for the construction of a *koinōnia*-space in the DRC. His appeal for a revolution of minds and renewal of hearts is reminiscent of Paul's appeal to the Romans: "Do not be conformed to this world, but be

---

71. Quoted in Ndaywel, *L'audace de dresser le front pour un autre Congo*, 143.

transformed by the renewing of your minds, so that you may discern what is the will of God, what is good and acceptable and perfect" (12:2). For this revolution to take place, three areas of Congolese society should play an important role. Those areas are the family, the school, and the church.

First, the family. In interpreting the Letter to Philemon, we saw that the family or the household was one of the essential institutions of Greco-Roman society. It constituted a microcosm of the bigger universe. For Greco-Roman ethicists, the household was perceived as the foundation of the social order, as it provided the pattern for the structure and definition of larger public institutions. And because of the household's central role in the transformation of society, Paul challenges his converts, who at the time gather in households, to become builders of a renewed world called the kingdom of God.

The same holds true in the context of the DRC. In the words of Pope John Paul II, "the family, which is founded and given life by love, is a community of persons: of husband and wife, of parents and children, of relatives. Its first task is to live with fidelity the reality of communion in a constant effort to develop an authentic community of persons."[72] Consonant with the African understanding of the institution called the family, John Paul's definition highlights what is at the heart of this book, namely, *koinōnia*.

The family is the primary space where individuals learn to live in love and community. They participate in something that both creates and transcends them. As Phambu Ngoma-Binda describes it, the family is an ethicocultural institution of vital importance for democracy and development.[73] Unlike the restricted Western understanding of family as nuclear (father, mother, and children), the African family is fundamentally extended, interdependent and solidary. It is a space that nurtures ethical and cultural values such as love, tolerance, humility, honesty, sincerity, discipline, realism, and abnegation. In the family, the child learns interdependence, the rule of law, and obedience in freedom, which later become republican values that leaders of a nation need to demonstrate.[74]

Congolese families must become what they truly are: spaces of life, love, and human dignity. A wounded and broken family is more prone to producing broken individuals who can cripple the life a community. It is true that there is no family that does not know how selfishness, discord,

---

72. Pope John Paul II, *Familiaris Consortio*, par 18.
73. Ngoma-Binda, *Rôle de la femme et de la famille*, 78.
74. Ngoma-Binda, *Rôle de la femme et de la famille*, 83.

tension, and conflict violently attack and at times mortally wound its own communion. Hence there arise the many and varied forms of division and grief in family life. But these wounds and divisions can be healed through reconciliation between brothers and sisters, as Paul encouraged between Philemon and Onesimus. All members of the family, each according to his or her own gift, have the grace and responsibility of building, day by day, the communion of persons, making the family "a school of deeper humanity." This happens where there is care and love for the little ones, the sick, and the aged; where there is mutual service every day; where there is a sharing of goods, of joys and of sorrows.[75]

The second area that can foster a revolution of minds in the DRC is the school. Explaining the role of education in the development of a society, Ilhan Ozturk writes:

> Education in every sense is one of the fundamental factors of development. No country can achieve sustainable economic development without substantial investment in human capital. Education enriches people's understanding of themselves and the world. It improves the quality of their lives and leads to broad social benefits to individuals and society. Education raises people's productivity and creativity and promotes entrepreneurship and technological advances. In addition it plays a very crucial role in securing economic and social progress and improving income distribution.[76]

Now more Congolese children than ever before have access to school all over the country. Back in 2018, the United Nations Children's Fund (UNICEF) released the following statistics about education in the DRC: "The Democratic Republic of Congo has made significant progress towards universal access to primary education in recent decades. The net attendance rate increased from 52% in 2001 to 78% in 2018."[77] Moreover, there are thousands of universities and colleges across the country producing millions of graduates each year. It is true that in a poor country with more than 90 million people, there is still work to be done in making school available to more children, especially those in remote provinces or conflict zones.

---

75. Pope John Paul II, *Familiaris Consortio*, par. 21.

76. Ozturk, "Role of Education in Economic Development," 1.

77. UNICEF, Education, accessed January 26, 2022 (https://www.unicef.org/drcongo/ce-que-nous-faisons/education).

However my emphasis here is not so much on the availability of school. Rather, I am concerned with the quality of the available schools.

The alarming situation regarding education in the DRC since the colonial period is that more people are being schooled than are being educated. As Ndaywel, a renowned Congolese university professor, testifies, the Congolese education system has been producing plenty of schooled people with impressive diplomas, but it has not been offering to society formed, competent, and creative leaders who move the country in the right direction.[78] To demonstrate how this reality has been an ongoing scandal since the time of Mobutu, Ndaywel evokes Mobutu's frustration with the Congolese elite:

> Observe well my entourage from 1965 to this day. It is not just the military that constitutes my main collaborators. I am surrounded essentially by university and college graduates and all that our national elite at its best can offer in disciplines such as science, economy, law, etc. They all hold either a licentiate or a doctorate in all those disciplines. It is assumed that they are all well-formed and equipped with knowledge and ethical principles required of their personality. But who asks them to steal the common good? Who commands that they work two hours instead of eight? And to give just one example. During the last colloquium we had on higher education, I must say that I was impressed by the eloquence and all the pertinent suggestions offered by a certain university professor. Right after that colloquium, I appointed him as a member of the government and put him in charge of the sector of higher education. But guess what? In just a few months, he granted more than two hundred fifty state scholarships only to the people of his tribe to go study in Europe. Worse still, he excelled in financial mismanagement and a complete lack of knowledge about his sector. He is notoriously incompetent. And sure enough, I fired him.[79]

Just like many other institutions in the DRC, education has been chaotic and ineffective. Schools and universities have become simply a lucrative business. Qualified teachers and professors, decent libraries, and a more research-oriented learning system are lacking in the DRC's education system. Even in schools where some rigor and quality may still exist (for example, in certain Catholic and Protestant institutions), corruption has in many cases had a crippling effect on the good efforts of these institutions.

---

78. Ndaywel, *L'audace de dresser le front pour un autre Congo*, 144.
79. Ndaywel, *L'audace de dresser le front pour un autre Congo*, 145.

In a country where education is not among the priorities of the central government, teachers and professors are subject to the politics of marginalization and pauperization.[80] As a consequence, their motivation decreases, whereas their propensity toward corruption increases. In most cases, what guarantees a student's success in school is not hard work, but money and (for female students) good looks. Without buying the professor's class notes, paying for additional hours of review or for different quizzes, there is no guarantee of passing any given class in many universities. For girls, it's even worse. There is a widespread phenomenon known among Congolese students as PST—Points Sexuellement Transmissibles (Sexually Transmitted Grades). Female students may offer or be forced to offer their bodies instead of money to pass a class.

As can be seen, the education system in the DRC is more enslaving than it is liberating. It is incumbent upon Congolese leaders to treat their fellow citizens as brothers and sisters by investing in the education sector. If it is true that education is about inspiring the mind, not filling the head, the general situation in the DRC is that both inspiration and knowledge are sorely lacking. Without a revolution in the Congolese education system, the existence of *koinōnia*-spaces will remain a merely utopian ideal.

In addition to the family and the school, the church ranks as the third area that can promote a revolution in minds and a renewal of hearts in the DRC. In the previous section, I briefly discussed the role of the Christian church as well as other religious organizations in fostering changes of mind and heart among their congregants. The prophetic role of the church in the DRC should not be the responsibility of the one denomination called the Catholic Church. Other Christian denominations for whom the Letter to Philemon is the Word of God should make the concern for the dignity of the human person their own.

Church leaders should remember that the church exists to evangelize. And as Pope Paul VI reminded us, "Evangelizing means bringing the Good News into all the strata of humanity, and through its influence transforming humanity from within and making it new."[81] Like the apostle Paul, church leaders have the duty to preach the Word of God in a way that seeks the transformation of the mind and the heart, not in self-seeking way that leads to brainwashing the faithful. The church should challenge people to make effective their *koinōnia* of faith. As Paul VI puts it, "the church evangelizes

---

80. Ndaywel, *L'audace de dresser le front pour un autre Congo*, 144.
81. Pope Paul VI, *Evangelii Nuntiandi*, par. 18.

when she seeks to convert, solely through the divine power of the message she proclaims, both the personal and collective consciences of people, the activities in which they engage, and the lives and concrete milieu which are theirs."[82]

As the Congolese Catholic bishops have rightly pointed out, echoing Isa 62:6, the prophetic role of the religious leaders in the DRC is that of *veilleurs* et *éveilleurs des consciences* (watchmen and awakeners of consciences).[83] In this context, the prophetic role is a question of affecting and as it were upsetting, through the power of the gospel, human criteria of judgment, determining values, points of interest, lines of thought, sources of inspiration, and models of life that contrast with the Word of God and the plan of salvation.[84] This affecting and upsetting ministry is what Walter Brueggemann calls the dialectic of criticism and the energizing of prophetic task.[85]

Unlike Paul, who could not denounce explicitly the evil of slavery in his appeal to Philemon, church leaders in the DRC have more freedom to be fully, unabashedly prophetic in calling evil by its name. The only reason they might shrink from such roles is because they themselves are participating in the evil of dehumanizing their brothers and sisters. Like Philemon, a church leader in his household, many religious leaders in the DRC today need to experience authentic, personal conversion in order for their message to affect political leaders.

Signs of Hope

The construction of a *koinōnia*-space in the DRC is an ambitious project, but not a utopia. There exist men and women who embody the *koinōnia* ethic contained in the Letter to Philemon. I would like to end this chapter by evoking only two examples of individuals who have been responsible for positive change in their local communities: Nicolas Djomo Lola and Denis Mukwege.

Nicolas Djomo has been the bishop of the Diocese of Tshumbe in rural central DRC since November 1997. His appointment as a bishop coincided with the beginnings of the First Congo War.[86] To say the least, Djomo

---

82. Pope Paul VI, *Evangelii Nuntiandi*, par. 18.
83. Mapwar, *Église et Société*, 21.
84. Pope Paul VI, *Evangelii Nuntiandi*, paragraph 19.
85. Brueggemann, *Prophetic Imagination*, 33.
86. Okitafumba, "Self-Understanding of the Congolese Catholic Church," 199.

knows firsthand what it means to be a bishop in a time of crisis. During the heat of the Congo Wars, between 1996 and 2003, militias destroyed schools, roads, and parishes across the Tshumbe diocese, and thousands fled the region. Even after war subsided, most people continued to eke out a living through bare-bones subsistence farming. But in the face of the crisis that ravaged his diocese, Djomo raised his head and decided to rebuild his community. James J. Carney summarizes well Djomo's actions:

> Djomo's humanitarian vision stems in part from his vision of himself as a local pastor who remains with his sheep. Unlike many other religious leaders and nearly all political leaders in the Tshumbe region, Djomo stayed with his people throughout the 1998 to 2003 war. Given Tshumbe's juxtaposition between the eastern heartland of the conflict and Congo's capital of Kinshasa, many militias operated in the region. Hundreds of parishes and schools were destroyed, and over one million local residents lacked basic necessities such as soap, salt, and medicine. In response, Djomo collaborated with the Dutch government to import 12 tons of medicine into Tshumbe. In 1998, Djomo arranged for the importation of 700 tons of food, clothing, books, and kitchen supplies. Djomo also worked to bring back Tshumbe's internally displaced people, focusing in particular on the hundreds of local women who had become embroiled in Kinshasa's thriving wartime prostitution industry. Through Djomo's mediation, over 1,000 women made the 1,500 kilometer river journey from Kinshasa back to Tshumbe.[87]

Moreover, Djomo has also invested in the education of the youth. One of Djomo's proudest initiatives is Tshumbe's new l'Université Notre Dame de Tshumbe (UNITSHU), founded in 2006, the first Catholic university in the region. Led by Franciscan Sister Rebecca Walo, the first Congolese woman to receive a doctorate in mathematics, the university includes programs in nursing, education, business, agriculture, and law. For Djomo, the university is a key part of Congo's overall search for peace and social stability.[88]

Djomo's actions for his marginalized community left no one indifferent. As Okitafumba notes, "Djomo's legacy reached the headquarters of the DRC's church and that of central Africa. He successively served as the president of the Association of Bishops' Conferences of Central Africa for two terms (2002–7) and as CENCO's president for two terms from 2008

---

87. Carney, "Bishop Is Governor Here," 107–8.
88. Carney and O'Keefe, "Bishop Builds Bridges of All Kinds after Congo's Long War."

to 2016. During these years, Djomo was a tireless advocate of the dignity and inalienable rights of the victims of war."[89] In a documentary realized in 2013, Djomo reports,

> This richness of [minerals] does not right now help the Congolese people. They call them in French "les minéraux de malheur" (the minerals of misery). Last year [2012], I went to the US Congress for testimony in a public hearing. Congressmen told me that indeed at least two thousand companies are dealing with armed groups. These minerals are the occasion to attract wars from outside and inside [of the DRC] because provoking instability the fighters can loot the minerals, purchase weapons, and commit atrocities against the population including rape. That is why the minerals are not the richness for the population, but it is the misfortune, the misery for them right now.[90]

As a beacon of hope in the seemingly limitless scale of human suffering, the Catholic diocese led by Djomo could stand for any community in the DRC. Djomo's *koinōnia* of faith is not just vertical. It also extends horizontally in concrete actions of love toward others. But in case one may think that such an effective *koinōnia* of faith is only possible for bishops or Catholics, I wish to discuss briefly the work of another Congolese citizen: Denis Mukwege.

As one can read on the website for the Mukwege Foundation, "Dr Denis Mukwege is a world-renowned gynecologist, human rights activist and Nobel Peace laureate from east Congo. He has become the world's leading specialist in the treatment of wartime sexual violence and a global campaigner against the use of rape as a weapon of war."[91] In 2018, Mukwege won the Nobel Peace Prize for his work in war-torn eastern Congo. As a surgeon, Mukwege has helped thousands of victims of sexual violence in armed conflicts in the DRC. Both on a national and an international level he has repeatedly condemned the impunity of mass rape and has criticized the Congolese government and other countries for not doing enough to stop the use of sexual violence against women as a strategy and weapon of war.[92]

89. Okitafumba, "Self-Understanding of the Congolese Catholic Church," 200.

90. O'Keefe, dir., *Tokimane*, accessed February 9, 2022 (https://vimeo.com/78791938).

91. Mukwege Foundation, "October 23, 2018," accessed February 9, 2022 (https://www.mukwegefoundation.org/story/dr-denis-mukwege).

92. Nobel Prize, "Denis Mukwege Facts," accessed February 9, 2022 (https://www.nobelprize.org/prizes/peace/2018/mukwege/facts).

Like the majority of the Congolese population, Mukwege is a Christian (a Pentecostal). Like Djomo's, Mukwege's *koinōnia* of faith proves effective in his concern for the marginalized. In his recent book, *The Power of Women*, he writes: "It's unusual for a man to campaign for women's rights. I know this . . . I defend women because they are my equals—because women's rights are human rights, and I am outraged by the violence inflicted on my fellow humans. We must fight for women collectively."[93]

To fight for women collectively, Mukwege founded Panzi Hospital in Bukavu in 1999. As a space of life and social reintegration, this hospital as well as the Mukwege Foundation have helped women injured during childbirth and thousands of victims of rape in eastern Congo. Unlike foreign human right activists who tend to be paternalistic toward the Congolese victims of atrocities, Mukwege treats them as equals—as better than equals: as brothers and sisters. He notes: "My role has always been to amplify the voices of others whose marginalization denies them opportunities to tell their stories. I stand at their side, never in front."[94]

For Mukwege, the women he treats and whose dignity he restores are not just passive victims with no agency. Like Onesimus, they raise their heads and tell their stories in order to call everyone to a new consciousness. They become survivors and builders of a space of humanity for others. Mukwege makes it clear to his readers: "The backdrop might appear bleak, for the lives of many women in this book have, like my own, been overshadowed by violence. But these women are each a light and an inspiration, demonstrating how the best instincts of humanity—to love, to share, to protect others—can triumph in the worst-possible circumstances."[95]

Djomo and Mukwege are just two examples of Congolese Christians who have demonstrated that an ethic of *koinōnia* is possible. If Jesus is really Lord for more than 93 percent of the Congolese population, then I pray, like Paul, that their *koinōnia* of faith may become effective in realizing all the good that they can do for Christ and for their country. For after all, the powerful and the powerless, the rich and the poor in the DRC, should be no longer masters and slaves, but brothers and sisters in the flesh and in the Lord.

---

93. Mukwege, *Power of Women*, 7, 10.
94. Mukwege, *Power of Women*, 10.
95. Mukwege, *Power of Women*, 12.

General Conclusion

CENTRAL TO THIS STUDY is the claim that the Letter to Philemon constructs a *koinōnia*-space, a space of radical kinship that challenges both the noxious nucleus of Roman slavery and modern systems of dehumanization in the DRC. Considering the content of Paul's prayer in vv. 4–6 and his challenging request in v. 16 as the hermeneutical keys to the whole letter, I have argued that the message of Phlm is a summons to an ethic of *koinōnia* among the followers of Christ. Consequently, the statement, "not a as slave, but a beloved brother in the flesh and in the Lord" (v. 16) is kinship language that dictates a reorganization of social space not only in Philemon's household but also in the domestic space of the DRC.

The distinctive contribution of this examination lies in both the methodology employed to study the Letter to Philemon and the application of its conclusions in the sociopolitical context of the DRC. In regard to the methodology, I have offered a new framework for the study of Phlm. Employing an interdisciplinary approach, my work innovatively combines both narrative criticism and social-spatial theory to put forward a plausible interpretation of Phlm.

Joining a growing number of biblical scholars who advocate a narrative approach to Paul's letters (including Richard Hays, N. T. Wright, Norman Petersen, Ben Witherington III, and David Rhoads), I draw upon insights from narrative theorists such as Gérard Genette, Paul Ricoeur, and Seymour Chatman to demonstrate that Phlm contains narrative features that many interpreters tend to overlook. But more than my predecessors who have interpreted Phlm through the prism of narrative criticism, I have applied insights from social-spatial theory. Relying on spatial theorists such as Henri Lefebvre and Edward Soja, I have reconstructed the three spaces that constitute the narrative world of Paul's Letter to Philemon: perceived space, conceived space, and lived space. As discussed in chapter 3, this reconstruction of the different spaces Paul and his audience inhabit has allowed me to attend to Phlm's narrative dynamics and rhetorical features such as plot, characterization, identification and naming, repetition, and kinship language. Arguably, taking narrative criticism and social-spatial theory together as lenses through which one can interpret the Letter to Philemon departs from the typical dialectical line of inquiry that has dominated Western scholarship on Phlm, namely, the endorsement or rejection of the *fugitivus* hypothesis based on the interpretation of v. 16. My methodological framework confronts the subversive message of this short letter with various forms of human exploitation beyond the Western world.

As chapter 4 demonstrates, my narrative and spatial interpretation of Phlm brings to light the neglected theological aspects of the Letter to Philemon and proves that the themes of this short letter are consistent with the coherent structure of Paul's thought found in other undisputed Pauline letters. To be sure, the interplay between the indicative and the imperative in Phlm calls for an effective faith. Thus, *koinōnia* of faith means new creation, new personal and corporate identity, and transformation of exploitative and dehumanizing relationships into authentic, humane, and Christocentric relationships.

Reading Phlm as a native of the DRC has challenged me to answer the question that is inevitably present on the minds of people in my country: What does a letter about a slave and his master in the first century of our era have to do with us today in the DRC? It is my conviction that this study has been significant in showing how the noxious nucleus of slavery (the denial of the essentially constitutive qualities of a human being) in the Roman Empire is similar to the yoke of exploitation and dehumanization unleashed by the greedy Congolese elite and their foreign patrons upon and against many Congolese people within the space of the DRC.

Just as the Letter to Philemon tackles the embarrassing paradox of a Christian who treated another human being as a non-human, my contextualization and appropriation of Phlm seeks to challenge the 93 percent of the Congolese population that identify themselves as Christians and yet fail to treat one another as brothers and sisters in the flesh and in the Lord. In the light of my careful interpretation of the construction of a *koinōnia*-space in the Letter to Philemon, I propose an ethic of *koinōnia* as the foundation upon which Congolese people can construct a domestic space of human dignity and social prosperity. More concretely, I propose that Congolese

Christians (1) honestly reassess the work of evangelization on their soil; (2) revisit their collective memory as narrativized in the national anthem ("Debout Congolais"); (3) reclaim and live out both cultural and Christian ethical values; and (4) revolutionize their minds and renew their hearts so that they can truly build "un pays plus beau qu'avant."[1]

As I conclude this work, I acknowledge that my interpretation of the Letter to Philemon is by no means an exhaustive effort. Rather, this project has defined a trajectory for my future research on Paul in general, and on the Letter to Philemon in particular. If the Letter to Philemon were the only Pauline text that we have, how could its narrative inform and transform leadership in the church today? How could Onesimus's agency inspire contemporary movements against sexual harassment, domestic violence, and the dehumanization of immigrants and refugees? How can a summons to an ethic of *koinōnia* encourage reconciliation and the reintegration of survivors of sexual assaults and human trafficking into the community? These questions are avenues of further investigation. I hope that readers have found and will continue to find in my study of Phlm a template for transformative interpretation of texts across the whole of Scripture.

---

1. Lutumba, "Debout Congolais."

Bibliography

Adams, Edward. *The Earliest Christiafn Meeting Places: Almost Exclusively Houses?* LNTS. Early Christianity in Context. London: Bloomsbury T. & T. Clark, 2013.

Aden, John Akare, and John H. Hanson. "Legacies of the Past: Themes in African History." In *Africa*, edited by Maria Grosz-Ngaté et al., 32–55. 4th ed. Bloomington: Indiana University Press, 2014.

Alter Robert. *The Hebrew Bible: A Translation and Commentary*. Vol. 1, *The Five Books of Moses, Torah*. New York: Norton, 2019.

———. *The Art of Biblical Narrative*. Rev. ed. New York: Basic Books, 2011. Kindle.

Apuleius. *The Golden Ass*. Translated by P. G. Walsh. Oxford World's Classics. Oxford: Oxford University Press, 1994.

Aquilina, Mike. *The Fathers of the Church: An Introduction to the First Christian Teachers*. Exp. ed. Huntington, IN: Our Sunday Visitor, 2006.

Auerbach, Erich. *Mimesis: The Representation of Reality in Western Literature*. Translated by Willard R. Trask. Princeton: Princeton University Press, 1953.

Augustine. *On Christian Doctrine*. Translated by J. F. Shaw. Boston: Neeland Media, 2010. Kindle.

Bales, Kevin. *Ending Slavery: How We Free Today's Slaves*. Berkeley: University of California Press, 2007.

Bannon, Cynthia J. *The Brothers of Romulus: Fraternal Pietas in Roman Law, Literature, and Society*. Princeton: Princeton University Press, 1997.

Barnett, Clive. Review of *Thirdspace: Journeys to Los Angeles and Other Real-and-Imagined Places*, by Edward W. Soja. *Transactions of the Institute of British Geographers* 22 (1997) 529–30.

Barth, Markus, and Helmut Blanke. *The Letter to Philemon*. ECC. Grand Rapids: Eerdmans, 2000.

Barton, Stephen C. "Paul's Sense of Place: An Anthropological Approach to Community Formation in Corinth." *New Testament Studies* 32 (1986) 225–46.

Baslez, Marie-Françoise. "Esclaves fugitifs et droit d'asile dans l'Orient hellénisé à l'aube du Christianisme." In *Épire, Illyrie, Macédoine . . . Mélanges offerts au Professeur Pierre Cabanes*. Textes réunis par Daniel Berranger-Auserve, 315–48. Collection ERGA, Recherches sur l'Antiquité 10. Clermont-Ferrand: Presses Universitaires Blaise Pascal, 2007.

BBC News. "DR Congo's Kasai Crisis: War Crimes Committed by Both Sides, UN Says." June 26, 2018. https://www.bbc.com/news/world-africa-44613147.

Bibliography

Beker, J Christiaan. *Paul the Apostle: The Triumph of God in Life and Thought.* Philadelphia: Fortress, 1980.

Bell, Sinclair, and Teresa Ramsby, eds. *Free at Last! The Impact of Freed Slaves on the Roman Empire.* London: Bristol Classical, 2012.

Benedict XVI, Pope. *Deus Caritas Est: Encyclical Letter to the Bishops, Priests, and Deacons, Men and Women Religious and All the Lay Faithful on Christian Love.* Vatican City: Libreria Editrice Vaticana, 2005.

———. *Jesus of Nazareth.* Vol. 1, *From the Baptism in the Jordan to the Transfiguration.* Translated by Adrian J. Walker. New York: Doubleday, 2007.

Bieberstein, Sabine. "Disrupting the Normal Reality of Slavery: A Feminist Reading of the Letter to Philemon." *JSNT* 23.79 (2000) 105–16.

———. "Philemon: A Reading under Apphia's Critical Eyes." In *Feminist Biblical Interpretation: A Compendium of Critical Commentary on the Books of the Bible and Related Literature*, edited by Luise Schottroff and Marie-Theres Wacker, 848–56. Grand Rapids: Eerdmans, 2012.

Biville, Frederique. "The Qualification of Personal Names by the Possessive Adjective in the Letters of Cicero." In *What's in a Name? The Significance of Proper Names in Classical Latin Literature*, edited by Joan Booth and Robert Maltby, 1–11. Swansea: Classical Press of Wales, 2006.

Bodel, John, and Walter Scheidel, eds. *On Human Bondage: After Slavery and Social Death.* The Ancient World: Comparative Histories. Chichester, UK: Wiley-Blackwell, 2017.

Booth, Wayne C. *The Rhetoric of Fiction.* 2nd ed. Chicago: University of Chicago Press, 1983.

Boyarin, Daniel. *A Radical Jew: Paul and the Politics of Identity.* Contraversions. Berkeley: University of California Press, 1994.

Bradley, Keith R. "Resisting Slavery at Rome." In *The Cambridge World History of Slavery.* Vol. 1, *The Ancient Mediterranean World*, edited by Keith Bradley and Paul Cartledge, 362–84. Cambridge: Cambridge University Press, 2011.

———. *Slavery and Society at Rome.* Key Themes in Ancient History. Cambridge: Cambridge University Press, 1994.

Bremmer, Jan N., et al. "Urban Religion, Neighbourhoods and the Early Christian Meeting Places." *Religion in the Roman Empire* 6.1 (2020) 48–74.

Brogdon, Lewis. *A Companion to Philemon.* Cascade Companions. Eugene, OR: Cascade Books, 2018.

Brookins, Timothy A. "'I Rather Appeal to *Auctoritas*': Roman Conceptualizations of Power and Paul's Appeal to Philemon." *CBQ* 77 (2015) 302–21.

Bruce, F. F. *The Epistles to the Colossians, to Philemon, and to the Ephesians.* NICNT. Grand Rapids: Eerdmans, 1984.

Brueggemann, Walter. *The Prophetic Imagination.* 2nd ed. Minneapolis: Fortress, 2001.

Buchakuzi Kanefu, Rodrigue, ed. *Pleure, Ô Noir, frère bien-aimé: Anthologie des textes de Patrice Emery Lumumba, Premier Ministre de la RD Congo 1960–61.* Ethics Praxis 4. Geneva: Globethics.net, 2015.

Bultmann, Rudolf. "The Problem of Ethics in Paul." In *Understanding Paul's Ethics: Twentieth Century Approaches*, edited by Brian S. Rosner, 195–216. Grand Rapids: Eerdmans, 1995.

———. *Theology of the New Testament.* Vol. 1. Translated by Kendrick Grobel. New York: Scribner, 1951.

Bibliography

Burnet, Régis. "Épitre de saint Paul à Philémon." In *La Bible en ses traditions: Définitions suivies de douze études*, edited by Ecole biblique et archéologique française de Jérusalem, 181–96. Jerusalem: Ecole biblique et archéologique française de Jérusalem, 2010.

Cadwallader, Alan. "Name Pruning and Social Stereotyping: Re-inscribing Slavery in the Letter to Philemon." *Australian Biblical Review* 61 (2013) 44–60.

Callahan, Allen Dwight. *Embassy of Onesimus: The Letter of Paul to Philemon*. New Testament in Context. Valley Forge, PA: Trinity, 1997.

———. "Onesimus Fugitivus: A Defense of the Runaway Slave Hypothesis in Philemon." *JSNT* 41 (1991) 97–119.

———. "Paul's Epistle to Philemon: Toward an Alternative *Argumentum*." *HTR* 86 (1993) 357–76.

Carney, James Jay. "'The Bishop Is Governor Here': Bishop Nicholas Djomo and Catholic Leadership in the Democratic Republic of the Congo." In *Leadership in Postcolonial Africa: Trends Transformed by Independence*, edited by Baba G. Jallow, 97–122. Palgrave Studies in African Leadership. New York: Palgrave Macmillan, 2014.

Carney, James J., and John J. O'Keefe. "Bishop Builds Bridges of All Kinds after Congo's Long War." *National Catholic Reporter*, April 5, 2014. https://www.ncronline.org/news/world/bishop-builds-bridges-all-kinds-after-congos-long-war.

Cerfaux, Lucien. *The Church in the Theology of Saint Paul*. Translated by Geoffrey Webb and Adrian Walker. Freiburg: Herder & Herder, 1959.

Chatman, Seymour. *Coming to Terms: The Rhetoric of Narrative in Fiction and Film*. Ithaca: Cornell University Press, 1990.

———. *Story and Discourse: Narrative Structure in Fiction and Film*. Ithaca: Cornell University Press, 1978.

Chinnappa, Valan. "The Theological Matrix of Philemon's Narrative Structure." STD diss. Jesuit School of Theology of Santa Clara University, 2013.

Church, F. Forrester. "Rhetorical Structure and Design in Paul's Letter to Philemon." *HTR* 71 (1978) 17–33.

Cohen, Shaye J. D. *The Beginnings of Jewishness: Boundaries, Varieties, Uncertainties*. Hellenistic Culture and Society 31. The S. Mark Taper Foundation Imprint in Jewish Studies. Berkeley: University of California Press, 1999.

Conférence Episcopale Nationale du Congo (CENCO). "Notre rêve d'un Congo plus beau qu'avant: Message de la Conférence Épiscopale Nationale du Congo au peuple Congolais à l'occasion du Cinquantième Anniversaire de l'Indépendance de la RD Congo." Kinshasa, June 24, 2010. *Actes de la CENCO & Documents* 1 (2010) 11–25.

Conrad, Joseph. *Heart of Darkness and Other Tales*. Edited with an introduction and notes by Cedric Watts. Oxford World's Classics. London: Oxford University Press, 2002.

Crisis in the Congo. http://www.congojustice.org.

Culpepper, R. Alan. *Anatomy of the Fourth Gospel: As Study in Literary Design*. FF. New Testament. Philadelphia: Fortress, 1983.

Dahl, Alstrup Nils. "The Particularity of the Pauline Epistles as a Problem in the Ancient Church." In *Neotestamentica et Patristica: Eine Freundesgabe, Herrn. Professor Dr. Oscar Cullmann zu seinem 60, Geburtstag überreicht*, 261–71. NovTSup 6. Leiden: Brill, 1962.

Decock, Paul Bernard. "The Reception of the Letter to Philemon in the Early Church: Origen, Jerome, Chrysostom and Augustine." In *Philemon in Perspective: Interpreting a Pauline Letter*, edited by D. Francois Tolmie; assisted Alfred Friedl, 273–88. BZNW 169. Berlin: de Gruyter, 2010.

Bibliography

"Denis Mukwege Facts." The Nobel Prize, 2018. https://www.nobelprize.org/prizes/peace/2018/mukwege/facts.

De Saint Moulin, Léon. *La place de la religion dans la société à Kinshasa et en RD Congo*. Cahiers Africains 94. Paris: L'Harmattan, 2019.

Devereaux, Constance, and Martin Griffin. *Narrative, Identity, and the Map of Cultural Policy: Once upon a Time in a Globalized World*. Farnham, UK: Ashgate, 2013.

DeVos Craig S. "Once a Slave, Always a Slave? Slavery, Manumission and Relational Patterns in Paul's Letter to Philemon." *JSNT* 82 (2001) 89–105.

Dondin-Payre, Monique, and Nicolas Tran, eds. *Esclaves et maîtres dans le monde romain: Expressions épigraphiques de leurs relations*. Rome: Ecole française de Rome, 2017.

Draper, Jonathan A. "African Contextual Hermeneutics: Readers, Reading Communities, and Their Options between Text and Context." *Religion and Theology* 22.1–2 (2015) 3–22.

Dunn, James D. G. *The Epistles to the Colossians and to Philemon: A Commentary on the Greek Text*. NIGTC. Grand Rapids: Eerdmans, 1996.

———. *The Theology of Paul the Apostle*. Grand Rapids: Eerdmans, 1998.

———. *Unity and Diversity in the New Testament: An Inquiry into the Character of Earliest Christianity*. Philadelphia, Westminster, 1977.

Djewirio, Etiti Yomo. *Comprendre le "debout congolais": Commentaire hymnologique et perspectives de construction du Congo démocratique*. Essai. Paris: Persée, 2015.

Edmondson, Jonathan. "Slavery and the Roman Family." In *The Cambridge World History of Slavery*. Vol 1, *The Ancient Mediterranean World*, edited by Keith Bradley and Paul Cartledge, 337–61. Cambridge: Cambridge University Press, 2011.

Elliott, Scott S. "'Thanks, but No Thanks': Tact, Persuasion, and the Negotiation of Power in Paul's Letter to Philemon." *NTS* 57 (2011) 51–64.

Esswein, Mitchell Alexander. "The Οἶκος of the Lord and the Church at Corinth: Understanding οἰκονόος and οἰκονομία in Paul's First Epistle to the Corinthians." *BN*, N.F. 172 (2017) 87–110F.

Falx, Marcus Sidonius. *How to Manage Your Slaves*. Commentary by Jerry Toner. Foreword by Mary Beard. London: Profile, 2014.

Fitzgerald, John T. "Theodore of Mopsuestia on Paul's Letter to Philemon." In *Philemon in Perspective: Interpreting a Pauline Letter*, edited by D. Francois Tolmie; assisted by Alfred Friedl, 332–63. BZNW 169. Berlin: de Gruyter, 2010.

Fitzmyer, Joseph A. *The Letter to Philemon: A New Translation with Introduction and Commentary*. AB 34C. New York: Doubleday, 2000.

Fludernik, Monika. "Histories of Narrative Theory (II): From Structuralism to the Present." In *A Companion to Narrative Theory*, edited by James Phelan and Peter J. Rabinowitz, 36–59. Blackwell Companions to Literature and Culture 33. Malden, MA: Blackwell, 2005.

Focant, Camille. *Les lettres aux Philippiens et à Philémon*. Commentaire biblique: Nouveau Testament 11. Paris: Cerf, 2015.

Foucault, Michel. *The Archaeology of Knowledge*. Translated by A.M. Sheridan Smith. World of Man. London: Tavistock, 1972.

———. *L'archéologie du savoir*. Bibliothèque des sciences humaines. Paris: Gallimard, 1969.

———. "Of Other Spaces." Translated by Jay Miskowiec. *Diacritics* 16.1 (1986) 22–27.

Francis I, Pope. *Fratelli Tutti: Encyclical Letter on Fraternity and Social Friendship*. Vatican, Rome: Libreria Editrice Vaticana, 2020.

BIBLIOGRAPHY

Friedl, Alfred. "St. Jerome's Dissertation on the Letter to Philemon." In *Philemon in Perspective: Interpreting a Pauline Letter*, edited by D. Francois Tolmie; assisted by Alfred Friedl, 289–316. BZNW 169. Berlin: de Gruyter, 2010.

Friedman, Susan Stanford. "Spatial Poetics and Arundhati Roy's *The God of Small Things*." In *A Companion to Narrative Theory*, edited by James Phelan and Peter J. Rabinowitz, 192–205. Blackwell Companions to Literature and Culture 33. Malden, MA: Blackwell, 2005.

Furnish, Victor Paul. *Theology and Ethics in Paul*. New introduction by Richard B. Hays. NTL. Louisville: Westminster John Knox, 2009. Kindle.

Gadamer, Hans-Georg. *Truth and Method*. 2nd ed. Translated by Joel Weinsheimer and Donald G. Marshall. London: Continuum, 1975.

Garland, David E. *Colossians and Philemon*. The NIV Application Commentary Series. Grand Rapids: Zondervan, 1998.

Garnsey, Peter. *Ideas of Slavery from Aristotle to Augustine*. The W. B. Stanford Memorial Lectures. Cambridge: Cambridge University Press, 1996.

Genette, Gérard. *Discours du récit: essai de méthode*. In *Figures III*. Collection Poétique. Paris: Seuil, 1980. Kindle.

———. *Narrative Discourse: An Essay in Method*. Translated by Jane E. Lewin. With a foreword by Jonathan Culler. Ithaca: Cornell University Press, 1980.

Gignac, Alain. "Le triangle 'Paul-Philémon-Onésime' du billet à Philémon: Lorsque la petitesse, l'amitié et l'utilité construisent une identité discursive." In "Constructions des identités religieuses: hommages à Jean Duhaime." Special issue *Théologiques* 24.2 (2016) 17–40.

Goldingay, John. "Covenant." In *NIDB* 1:767–78.

Gorman, Michael J. *Apostle of the Crucified Lord: A Theological Introduction to Paul and His Letters*. 2nd ed. Grand Rapids: Eerdmans, 2017.

———. *Cruciformity: Paul's Narrative Spirituality of the Cross*. Grand Rapids: Eerdmans, 2001.

Grant, Richard. *Africa: Geographies of Change*. Oxford: Oxford University Press, 2014.

Grenouilleau, Olivier. *Qu'est-ce que l'esclavage? Une histoire globale*. Bibliothèque des histoires. Paris: Gallimard, 2014.

Hawthorne, Gerald F. et al., eds. *Dictionary of Paul and His Letters: A Companion of `Contemporary Biblical Scholarship*. Downers Grove, IL: InterVarsity Press, 1993.

Hayes, Christine. *What's Divine about Divine Law? Early Perspectives*. Princeton: Princeton University Press, 2015.

Hays, Richard B. *The Faith of Jesus Christ: An Investigation of the Narrative Substructure of Galatians 3:1—4:11*. SBLDS 56. Chico, CA: Scholars, 1983.

———. "Introduction." In *Theology and Ethics in Paul*, by Victor Paul Furnish, 27–44. NTL. Louisville: Westminster John Knox, 2009.

———. *The Moral Vision of the New Testament: Community, Cross, and New Creation; A Contemporary Introduction to the New Testament Ethic*. San Francisco: HarperSanFrancisco, 1996. Kindle.

Heil, John Paul. "The Chiastic Structure and Meaning of Paul's Letter to Philemon" *Bib* 82 (2001) 178–206.

Herman, David. "Histories of Narrative Theory (I): A Genealogy of Early Developments." In *A Companion to Narrative Theory*, edited by James Phelan and Peter J. Rabinowitz, 19–35. Blackwell Companions to Literature and Culture 33. Malden, MA: Blackwell, 2005.

Bibliography

Heschel, Abraham Joshua. "Halakhah and Aggadah: Balancing between the Importance of Jewish Behavior and the Meaning That Jews Find in Those Behaviors Creates a Productive Tension That Defines Jewish Life." My Jewish Learning, n.d, reprinted with permission from *Between God and Man*. https://www.myjewishlearning.com/article/halakhah-and-aggadah.

Ho, Alex Hon. *A Socio-Rhetorical Interpretation of the Letter to Philemon in Light of the New Institutional Economics: An Exhortation to Transform a Master-Salver Economic Relationship into a Brotherly Loving Relationship*. WUNT 2/444. Tübingen: Mohr Siebeck, 2017.

Hodge, Caroline Johnson. *If Sons, Then Heirs: A Study of Kinship and Ethnicity in the Letters of Paul*. Oxford: Oxford University Press, 2007.

Houston, Joshua Seth. *Paul's Letter to Philemon: A Historical and Exegetical Commentary*. Murfreesboro, TN: Heart & Soul, 2020. Kindle.

Hubbard, Phil, et al., eds. *Key Thinkers on Space and Place*. London: Sage, 2004.

Hunt, Peter. *Ancient Greek and Roman Slavery*. Hoboken, NJ: Wiley, 2018.

Hurtado, Larry W. "Lord." In *Dictionary of Paul and His Letters: A Companion of Contemporary Biblical Scholarship*, edited by Gerald F. Hawthorne et al., 560–69. Downers Grove, IL: InterVarsity, 1993.

Jacobs, Louis. *The Jewish Religion: A Companion*. Oxford: Oxford University Press, 1995.

James, Henry. "The Art of Fiction." *Longman's Magazine*, September 4, 1884, 502–21. In *A Victorian Art of Fiction: Essays on the Novel in British Periodicals, 1830–1900*, edited by John Charles Olmsted, 285–306. London: Routledge, 2016.

———. *The Art of the Novel: Critical Prefaces*. 1934. Reprint, with an introduction by R. P. Blackmur and a new foreword by Colm Tóibín. Chicago: University of Chicago Press, 2011.

Jansen, John F. "Appropriating New Testament Covenant Vocabulary in Ecumenical Commitment." *Austin Seminary Bulletin*. Faculty ed., 96 (March 1981) 27–37.

Jeal, Roy R. *Exploring Philemon: Freedom, Brotherhood, and Partnership in the New Society*. SemeiaSt 2. Rhetoric of Religious Antiquity 2. Atlanta: SBL Press, 2015.

John Paul II, Pope. *Centissimus Annus: Encyclical Letter to His Venerable Brother Bishops in the Episcopate, the Priests and Deacons, Families of Men and Women Religious, All the Christian Faithful, and to All Men and Women of Good will on the Hundredth Anniversary of "Rerum Novarum."* Vatican City: Libreria Editrice Vaticana, 1991.

———. *Familiaris Consortio: Encyclical Letter to the Episcopate, to the Clergy, and to the Faithful of the Whole Catholic Church on the Role of the Christian Family in the Modern World*. Vatican City: Libreria Editrice Vaticana, 1981.

———. *Fides et Ratio: Encyclical Letter to the Bishops of the Catholic Church on the Relationship between Faith and Reason*. Vatican City, Rome: Libreria Editrice Vaticana, 1998.

Johnson, Matthew V. et al., eds. *Onesimus, Our Brother: Reading Religion, Race, and Culture in Philemon*. Paul in Critical Contexts. Minneapolis: Fortress, 2012.

Joshel, Sandra R. *Slavery in the Roman World*. Cambridge Introduction to Roman Civilization. Cambridge: Cambridge University Press, 2010.

Kingsbury, Jack Dean. *The Christology of Mark's Gospel*. Philadelphia: Fortress, 1983.

Knox, John. *Philemon among the Letters of Paul: A New View of Its Place and Importance*. Rev. ed. New York: Abingdon, 1959.

Kreitzer, Larry J. *Philemon*. Readings—A New Biblical Commentary. Sheffield: Sheffield Phoenix, 2008.

Bibliography

Lakoff, George, and Mark Johnson. *Metaphors We Live By*. Chicago: University of Chicago Press, 1980.

Lampe, Peter. "Affects and Emotions in the Rhetoric of Paul's Letter to Philemon: A Rhetorical-Psychological Interpretation." In *Philemon in Perspective: Interpreting a Pauline Letter*, edited by D. Francois Tolmie, assisted Alfred Friedl, 61–77. BZNW 169. Berlin: de Gruyter, 2010.

———. "Keine Sklavenflucht des Onesimus." *ZNW* 76 (1985) 135–37.

Latham, Alan. "Edward Soja." In *Key Thinkers on Space and Place*, edited by Phil Hubbard et al., 269–74. London: Sage, 2004.

Lefebvre, Henri. *Critique de la vie quotidienne*. Vol. 1, *Introduction*. Les Témoins. Paris, Grasset, 1947.

———. *Critique of Everyday Life*. Vol. 1, *Introduction*. Translated by John Moore and Gregory Elliott; introduced by Michel Trebitsch. London: Verso, 2008.

———. *La production de l'espace*. 4th ed. Société et urbanisme. Paris: Anthropos, 2000.

———. *The Production of Space*. Translated by Donald Nicholson-Smith. Oxford: Blackwell, 1991.

Liddell, G. Henry, and Robert Scott, eds. *Greek-English Lexicon*. Founded upon the Seventh Edition of Liddell and Scott's Greek-English Lexicon. London: Oxford University Press, 1997.

Lightfoot, J. B. *St. Paul's Epistles to the Colossians and to Philemon*. The Epistles of St. Paul 3. London: Macmillan, 1892.

Lohse, Eduard. *Colossians and Philemon*. Translated by William R. Poehlmann and Robert J. Karris. Hermeneia. Philadelphia: Fortress, 1971.

Longenecker, Bruce W. "Narrative Interest in the Study of Paul: Retrospective and Prospective." In *Narrative Dynamics in Paul: A Critical Assessment*, edited by Bruce W. Longenecker, 3–16. Louisville: Westminster John Knox, 2002.

Lumumba, Patrice-Emery. "Discours de l'indépendance." Delivered as part of the Independence Day ceremonies on June 30, 1960. In *Les discours prononcés par le Roi Baudouin Ier, le Président Joseph Kasa-Vubu et le Premier Ministre Patrice-Emery Lumumba lors de la cérémonie de l'indépendance du Congo* (pamphlet) 8–10. https://archiv.kongo-kinshasa.de/dokumente/lekture/disc_indep.pdf.

Lutumba, Joseph. "Debout Congolaise" [Arise Congolese]. 1960. National Anthems. https://nationalanthems.info/cd.htm.

Mapwar, Bashuth Faustin-Jovite, ed. *Église et Société: Le discours socio-politique des évêques de la Conférence Épiscopale Nationale du Congo et la Transition politiquede l'Eglise Catholique du Congo (CENCO)*. Messages, Déclarations et Points de presse des Évêques de la Conférence Épiscopale Nationale du Congo et la Transition Politique (1996–2006) 2. Documents du Christianisme Africain 9. Kinshasa: Facultés Catholiques de Kinshasa, 2008.

Marchal, Joseph A. "The Usefulness of Onesimus: The Sexual Use of Slaves and Paul's Letter to Philemon." *JBL* (2011) 749–70.

Marguerat, Daniel, ed. *La lettre à Philémon et l'ecclésiologie paulinienne*. Colloquium Oecumenicum Paulinum 22. Leuven: Peeters, 2016.

Marguerat, Daniel, and Yvan Bourquin. *La Bible se raconte: Initiation à l'analyse narrative*. Pour lire les récits bibliques. Paris: Cerf, 1998.

Martin Ralph P. *Colossians and Philemon*. NCB. Grand Rapids: Eerdmans, 1981.

Mayer, Wendy. "Who Came to Hear John Chrysostom Preach? Recovering a Late Fourth-Century Preacher's Audience." *ETL* 76 (2000) 73–87.

Bibliography

McKittrick, Katherine. "bell hooks." In *Key Thinkers on Space and Place*, edited by Phil Hubbard et al., 189–94. London: Sage, 2004.

McKnight, Scot. *The Letter to Philemon*. NICNT. Grand Rapids: Eerdmans, 2017.

Moo, Douglas J. *The Letters to the Colossians and to Philemon*. Pillar New Testament Commentary. Grand Rapids: Eerdmans, 2008.

Mukwege, Denis. *The Power of Women: A Doctor's Journey of Hope and Healing*. New York: Flatiron, 2021. Kindle.

Mukwege Foundation. "October 23, 2018: Dr Denis Mukwege." n.d. https://www.mukwegefoundation.org/story/dr-denis-mukwege.

Ndaywel è Nziem, Isidore. *Histoire du Congo: Des origines à nos jours*. Histoire. Brussels: Cri Afrique, 2011.

———. *L'audace de dresser le front pour un autre Congo: La saison sèche e st pluvieuse*. Préface de Léon de Saint Moulin. Paris: L'Harmattan, 2018.

Ngoma-Binda, Phambi. *Rôle de la femme et de la famille dans le développement: Argument pour la justice et l'égalité entre les sexes*. 2nd ed. Droits de devoir. Kinshasa: Mediaspaul, 2015.

Nordling, John G. "Onesimus Fugitivus: A Defense of the Runaway Slave Hypothesis in Philemon." *JSNT* 41 (1991) 97–119.

———. *Philemon: A Theological Exposition of Sacred Scripture*. ConcC. St. Louis: Concordia, 2004.

Nyeme Tese, Jean-Adalbert. *Munga: une éthique en un milieu africain, Gentilisme et Christianisme*. Dissertation en vue de l'obtention du grade de Docteur en Théologie (Pontificia Universitas Urbaniana). Ingenbohl: Imprimerie du Père Théodose, 1975.

Nzinga Makitu, Germain. *Stratégies de domestication d'un peuple: BMW comme armes de distraction massive*. Paris: Edilivre, 2014. Kindle.

O'Brien, Peter T. "Church" In *Dictionary of Paul and His Letters: A Companion of Contemporary Biblical Scholarship*, edited by Gerald F. Hawthorne et al., 123–31. Downers Grove, IL: InterVarsity Press, 1993.

Okitafumba Lokola, Raphaël. "The Self-Understanding of the Congolese Church during War: CENCO in the Grip of the Greatest Modern Humanitarian Crisis." *Journal of Religious History* 44 (2020) 187–211.

Økland, Jorunn J., et al., eds. *Constructions of Space III: Biblical Spatiality and the Sacred*. LHBOTS 540. London: Bloomsbury T. & T. Clark, 2016.

O'Keefe, John, dir. *Tokimane*. Produced by Oakswing Productions LLC. Vimeo, uploaded November 6, 2013. https://vimeo.com/78791938.

Omba Ben, Olive. *Debout Congolais pour ta Patrie, l'héritage du Patrimoine légué à la génération de ses successeurs*. Cape Town: Nicole Mampuya-MN Redaction, 2016. Kindle.

Osiek, Carolyn. *Philippians, Philemon*. ANTC. Nashville: Abingdon, 2000.

———. "Slavery in the New Testament World." *TBT* 22.3 (1984) 151–55.

Ozturk, Ilhan. "The Role of Education in Economic Development: A Theoretical Perspective." *Journal of Rural Development and Administration* 33 (2001) 39–47.

Pao, David W. *Colossians and Philemon*. Zondervan Exegetical Commentary on the New Testament 12. Grand Rapids: Zondervan, 2012.

Parsons, Michael. "Being Precedes Act: Indicative and Imperative in Paul's Writing." *EvQ* 60 (April 1988) 99–127.

Patterson, Orlando. *Slavery and Social Death: A Comparative Study*. Cambridge: Harvard University Press, 1982.

Bibliography

Paul VI, Pope. *Evangelii Nuntiandi: Apostolic Exhortation to the Episcopate, to the Clergy, and to All the Faithful of the Entire World* Vatican City: Libreria Editrice Vaticana, 1975.

Petersen, Norman R. *Rediscovering Paul: Philemon and the Sociology of Paul's Narrative World*. 1985. Reprint, Eugene, OR: Wipf & Stock, 2008.

Phelan, James, and Peter J. Rabinowitz, eds. *A Companion to Narrative Theory*. Blackwell Companions to Literature and Culture 33. Malden, MA: Blackwell, 2005.

Pitre, Brant, et al. *Paul, A New Covenant Jew: Rethinking Pauline Theology*. Grand Rapids: Eerdmans, 2019.

Philo, Chris. "Michel Foucault." In *Key Thinkers on Space and Place*, edited by Phil Hubbard et al., 121–28. London: Sage, 2004.

Porter, Stanley E. "Holiness, Sanctification." In *Dictionary of Paul and His Letters: A Companion of Contemporary Biblical Scholarship*, edited by Gerald F. Hawthorne et al., 397–402. Downers Grove, IL: InterVarsity Press, 1993.

Powell, Allan M. *What Is Narrative Criticism?* GBS. New Testament Series. Minneapolis: Fortress, 1990.

Ramsby, Teresa. "'Reading' the Freed Slave in the Cena Trimalchionis." In *Free at Last! The Impact of Freed Slaves on the Roman Empire*, edited by Sinclair Bell and Teresa Rmsby, 66–87 London: Bristol Classical, 2012.

Resseguie, James L. *Narrative Criticism of the New Testament: An Introduction*. Grand Rapids: Baker Academic, 2005.

Rhoads, David M. "Performing the Letter to Philemon." *Journal of Biblical Storytelling* 17 (2008) 1–12.

Rhoads, David M., and Donald Michie. *Mark as Story: An Introduction to the Narrative of a Gospel*. 1st ed. Philadelphia: Fortress, 1982.

Ricœur, Paul. *Temps et récit*. Vol. 3, *Le temps raconté*. L'Ordre philosophique. Paris: Seuil, 1985.

Ryan, Judith M. "Philemon." In *Philippians and Philemon*, 167–261. SP 1. Collegeville, MN: Liturgical, 2005.

Ryan, Marie-Laure, et al. *Narrating Space, Spatializing Narrative: Where Narrative Theory and Geography Meet*. Theory and Interpretation of Narrative. Columbus: The Ohio State University Press, 2016.

Sampley, J. Paul. "From Text to Thought World: The Route to Paul's Ways." In *Pauline Theology*. Vol. 1, *1 Thessalonians, Philippians, Galatians, Philemon*, edited by Jouette M. Bassler, 3–14. SymS 4. Minneapolis: Fortress, 1991.

Schaff Philip, ed. *Chrysostom: Homilies on Galatians, Ephesians, Philippians, Colossians, Thessalonians, Timothy, Titus, and Philemon*. NPNF[1]. Peabody, MA: Hendrickson, 1994.

Schüssler Fiorenza, Elisabeth. "Introduction: Transforming the Legacy of *The Woman's Bible*." In *Searching the Scriptures*. Vol. 1, *A Feminist Introduction*, 1–26. New York: Crossroad, 1993.

Shields, Rob. "Henri Lefebvre." In *Key Thinkers on Space and Place*, edited by Phil Hubbard et al., 208–13. 2nd ed. London: Sage. 2010.

Simmel, Georg. *On Individuality and Social Forms: Selected Writings*. Edited and with an introd. by Donald N. Levine. Heritage of Sociology.

Sleeman, Matthew. "Lukan Narrative Spatiality in Transition: A Reading of Acts 11:19—12:24 for Its Spaces." In *Constructions of Space III: Biblical Spatiality and the Sacred*, edited by Jorunn J. Økland et al., 151–68. LHBOTS 540. London: Bloomsbury T. & T. Clark, 2016.

Bibliography

Soards, Marion L. "Some Neglected Theological Dimensions of the Letter to Philemon." *PRSt* 17 (1990) 209–19.

Soja, Edward W. *Postmodern Geographies: The Reassertion of Space in Critical Social Theory*. Radical Thinkers. London: Verso, 1989.

———. *Thirdspace: Journeys to Los Angeles and Other Real-and-Imagined Places*. Cambridge: Harvard University Presss, 1996.

Tannehill, Robert C. *The Narrative Unity of Luke-Acts: A Literary Interpretation*. 2 vols. FF. New Testament. Philadelphia: Fortress, 1986–1990.

Thompson James W., and Bruce W. Longenecker. *Philippians and Philemon*. Paideia. Grand Rapids: Baker Academic, 2016.

Tolmie, D. Francois, ed. *Philemon in Perspective: Interpreting a Pauline Letter*. Assisted by Alfred Friedl. BZNW 169. Berlin: de Gruyter, 2010.

———. "Tendencies in the Research on the Letter to Philemon since 1980." In *Philemon in Perspective: Interpreting a Pauline Letter*, edited by D. Francois Tolmie; assisted by Alfred Friedl, 1–27. BZNW 169. Berlin: de Gruyter, 2010.

Towner, Philip H. "Households and Household Codes." In *Dictionary of Paul and His Letters: A Companion of Contemporary Biblical Scholarship*, edited by Gerald F. Hawthorne et al., 417–19. Downers Grove, IL: InterVarsity, 1993.

Trefon, Theodore. *Congo's Environmental Paradox: Potential and Predation in a Land of Plenty*. African Arguments. London: Zed, 2016.

Tshisekedi, Felix. "60ème Indépendance du 20 juin 2020." https://www.presidence.cd/uploads/files/60e%CC%80me%20Anniversaire%20de%20L%E2%80%99Inde%CC%81pendance%20de%20la%20RDC.pdf.

Tull, Patricia K. "Narrative Criticism and Narrative Hermeneutics." In *The Oxford Encyclopedia of Biblical Interpretation*. Vol 2, *Metaphor Theory and Biblical Texts–Womanist Interpretation*, edited by Steven L. McKenzie, 37–46. The Oxford Encyclopedia of the Bible. New York: Oxford University Press, 2013.

Turner, Thomas. *Congo*. Malden, MA: Polity, 2013.

UNICEF. Education. n.d. https://www.unicef.org/drcongo/ce-que-nous-faisons/education.

Van Dyke, Robert. "Paul's Letter to Philemon: An Appeal Above and Beyond the Law." *STRev* 41 (1998) 384–98.

Van Reybrouck, David. *Congo: The Epic History of a People*. Translated by Sam Garrett. New York: Ecco, 2013.

Wall, Robert W. *The Acts of the Apostles*. In *The New Interpreter's Bible Commentary*. Vol. 9, *Acts, Introduction to Epistolary Literature, Romans, 1&2 Corinthians, Galatians*, 1–292. Nashville: Abingdon, 2015.

———. *Colossians & Philemon*. IVP New Testament Commentary Series. Downers Grove, IL: InterVarsity, 1993.

Wiedemann, Thomas, ed. *Greek and Roman Slavery*. London: Routledge, 1981.

Weissenrieder, Annette. "Architecture: Where Did Pauline Communities Meet?" In *Paul and Economics: A Handbook*, edited by Thomas R. Blanton IV and Raymond Pickett, 125–53. Minneapolis: Fortress, 2017.

West, Gerald O. "Biblical Hermeneutics in Africa." In *African Theology on the Way: Current Conversations*, edited by Diane B. Stinton, 21–31. SPCK International Study Guide 46. London: SPCK, 2010.

Westernmann, William L. *The Slave Systems of Greek and Roman Antiquity*. Memoirs of the American Philosophical Society 40. Philadelphia: American Philosophical Society, 1955.

BIBLIOGRAPHY

Williams, Demetrius K. "No Longer as a Slave." In *Onesimus, Our Brother: Reading Religion, Race, and Culture in Philemon*, edited by Matthew V. Johnson et al., 11–46. Paul in Critical Contexts. Minneapolis: Fortress, 2012.

Wilson, Robert McL. *A Critical and Exegetical Commentary on Colossians and Philemon*. ICC 51. London: T. & T. Clark, 2005.

Witherington, Ben, III. *The Letters to Philemon, the Colossians, and the Ephesians: A Socio-Rhetorical Commentary on the Captivity Epistles*. Grand Rapids: Eerdmans, 2007.

———. *Paul's Narrative Thought World: The Tapestry of Tragedy and Triumph*. Louisville: Westminster John Knox, 1994.

Wright, N. T. *Paul and the Faithfulness of God*. 2 vols. Christian Origins and the Question of God 4. Minneapolis: Fortress, 2013. Kindle.

Wright, Tom. *Paul for Everyone: The Prison Letters; Ephesians, Philippians, Colossians, and Philemon*. 2nd ed. London: SPCK, 2004.

Yarchin, William. *History of Biblical Interpretation: A Reader*. Grand Rapids: Baker Academic, 2011.

Index

Adams, Edward, 116
Aden, John Akare, 142
adonai, 121
Aelia Sentia (lex), 62
aeon, 106
akatshi (leaves), 83
Alter, Robert, 39, 77, 78
amicus domini, 12
ami-de-nous, 87
analepsis, 22
Annotationes in Epistolam ad Philemonem (Grotius), 11
Apostle of the Crucified Lord (Gorman), 72n2
apostolic authority, Paul's renunciation of, 128-29
Apphia, 75, 88, 91
Aquinas, Thomas, 10
Archippus, 15, 75, 76, 79, 88, 91
Aristotle, 51-53
The Art of Biblical Narrative (Alter), 39
The Art of the Novel (James), 25
assembly *(ekklesia)*, 117
Atlantic slave trade, 141-42
Auerbach, Erich, 38
Augustine of Hippo, 1, 8-10
    On Christian Doctrine, 8, 45-46
Augustus, 63

Bales, Kevin, 69
Bantu peoples, 141-42
Bar-Jesus, 85
Barnett, Clive, 32
Barth, Marcus, 14, 88
Barthes, Roland, 20

Battle of Ambuila, 142
Baudouin, King of Belgium, 143-44
The Beginnings of Jewishness (Cohen), 95
Beker, J. Christiaan, 37
Belgium, 143
    Lumumba's assassination, role in, 148
Benedict XVI, Pope, 93, 134
    Berlin Conference, 36n132, 142, 143
Bhabha, Homi, 31
Bieberstein, Sabine, 17, 88
bien-aime, 87
Biville, Frederique, 83-84
Blanke, Helmut, 14, 88
Boka, Simon-Pierre, 139
"bonded" employee, 68
Booth, Wayne, 25
Bourquin, Yvan, 38
Boyarin, Daniel, 124
Bradley, Keith, 59
    demographic test for slave society, 47
    familia urbana and *familia rustica*, 54
    slave revolt analysis, 58
    sources of slavery, 49-50
Bremmer, Jan N., 117
Bremond, Claude, 20
Brogdon, Lewis, 16, 127
brotherhood
    Christian redefinition of, 94-97
    Greco-Roman view of, 96-97
    Jewish view of, 94-96
    Onesimus as brother, 92-102
    Paul's rhetorical use, 91, 93-94
Brueggemann, Walter, 165
Bultmann, Rudolf, 106-7

Index

Cadwallader, Alan, 99–100, 102
Callahan, Allan D., 15–16, 98–102
Cao, Diego, 141
captatio benevolentiae, 155
Carney, James J., 166
Catholic Church, in DRC, 136–38, 157
    religious denominations and, 156
    role of, 137–38, 146, 164
    in struggle for justice and peace, 138
CENCO. *See* Conference Episcopale Nationale du Congo
CENI. *See* Commission Electorale Nationale Independente
Cerfaux, Lucien, 114
charity, 157–58
Chatman, Seymour, 23–24, 25
child soldiers, 152
Chinnappa, Valan, 43
Christology
    and ethics, 121–22
    motif in Philemon, 121–23
Chrysostom, John, 1, 5, 6, 9
    exegesis, apologetic nature of, 2
    fugitivus hypothesis, 44
    interpretation of Letter to Philemon, 2–4
    sermonic musings, 15
Church
    Catholic. *See* Catholic Church
    household church, 80, 81, 98, 116–18, 120, 122, 135, 138, 155
    revivalist churches, 135–36
Church, Frank, 82
The Church in the Theology of St. Paul (Cerfaux), 114
Cicero, 61–62, 83
    on Jews and Syrians, 67
    on manumission timeframe, 61
Codex Claromontanus, 100
Cohen, Shaye J. D., 95–96
colonization, 139–47
    Leopold II and Belgian government, 143
    Lumumba's rejection of, 145–46
    and national anthem, 140–41
    oppression and exploitation, 145–46

coltan, 151
Coming to Terms: The Rhetoric of Narrative in Fiction and Film (Chatman), 23–24
Commission Electorale Nationale Independente (CENI), 156
composition (artistic arrangement), 20
conceived space, 76–79
Conference Episcopale Nationale du Congo (CENCO), 137
Congo. *See* Democratic Republic of the Congo
Congo Free State, 143
Congolese Christians, 133–38, 170–71
    authentic love, 157
    Catholic bishops, 165–68
    koinōnia of faith and, 138, 155, 157
Congolese elite, 147
Congolese people, 151–65
    destined to create, 153
    etat d'ame of, 139–40
    resisted foreign powers, 142
    solidarity awareness, 160
    victims of atrocities, 168
    work ethics, 154
    See also Democratic Republic of the Congo (DRC)
Conrad, Joseph, 143
conversion
    to Judaism, 95
    of Sergius Paulus, 85
    theology of, 95–96
Corinthians, 1

Davies, W. D., 106
debout, 160
"Debout Congolais" (Arise Congolese), 139–41, 153
debt bondage, 48, 69. *See also* slavery
de Certeau, Michel, 25
De Doctrina Christiana (Augustine), 8, 45–46
dehumanization, 133–34, 138
    injustice, 42
    modern forms of, 66–70
    other forms of, 69–70

Index

Democratic Republic of the Congo
(DRC), 19, 46, 131, 138–52
    Congolese quid, 153–54
    cultural and christian values, 154–59
    education system in, 164
    national anthem of, 138–41
    natural resources of, 151
    religious leaders in, role of, 165
    revivalist churches in, 135
    slavery in, 67, 69–70
    See also Congolese Christians; Congolese people
de Saussure, Ferdinand, 20
Deus Caritas Est (Pope Benedict XVI), 134
Devereaux, Constance, 25
de Vos, Craig, 16
Dibelius, Martin, 106
Digest (Callistratus), 60
dignity, 81–82
    denial of, 152
    God-given, 138
    of Onesimus, 81, 93, 100–102
Diogenes the Cynic, 53
disposition (logical arrangement), 20
Djewiro, Etiti Yomo, 140, 140
Djomo, Nicolas, 137, 165–67, 168
Dodd, Charles H., 106
dramatis personae, 79, 80
Draper, Jonathan A., 132–33
DRC. *See* Democratic Republic of the Congo
Dunn, James D. G., 104, 105–6, 113, 122

The Earliest Christian Meeting Places (Adams), 116–17
ecumenism, spontaneous, 136–37
eglises de reveil (revivalist churches), 135
Egypt
    Ethiopian slaves in, 68
    runaway slaves in, 59
    wanted posters, 60
ekklesia (assembly), 117
emotional space, 37
enslavement. *See* slavery
Epaphras, 76, 79, 90
Ephesians, 5
Ephesus, 74

eschatology
    Furnish's use of, 108, 110
    Hays on new creation and, 110
    and identity of believers, 113–14
ethics of *koinōnia*, 103, 121, 168–71
    Letter to Philemon and, 123–31
    narrative, 112
    Onesimus' new identity and, 130
evangelization, 12, 87, 146
    authentic, 136–37
    Onesimus and, 90
    statistics on, 135
    work of, assessment of, 133–34, 138, 171
    work of, Congolese Christians and, 133–34
exclusionary *koinōnia*, 127
exodus narrative, 77
exordium, 82–83

faith, 94, 103, 104
    eschatological community of, 118
    interrelationship with praxis, 106
    justification by, 113
    koinōnia of. *See koinōnia* of faith
Falx, Marcus Sidonius, 57, 63, 65
familia, 55–56, 62, 65
familia Caesaris, 55
familia urbana, 54
Fides et Ratio (Pope John Paul II), 153
Fitzgerald, John, 7, 8
Fitzmyer, Joseph A., 90, 101
Fludernik, Monika, 20, 22, 23, 25
Focant, Camille, 87
Foucault, Michel, 26–27
Francis (Pope), 159
    on fraternity and social friendship, 155
    on prophetic ministry, 156
    on social and political charity, 157–58
fratres, 97
freed slaves, 64–66
Friedl, Alfred, 5, 6
Friedman, Susan, 25–26
frui, 8
Fufia Canini (lex), 62
fugitivus (a runaway slave), 4, 12, 15, 18, 44

Index

Furnish, Victor Paul, 107–10
  motif model, 112–13
  on sanctification, 109
  Theology and Ethics in Paul, 107, 113

Gadamer, Hans-Georg, 132–33
Galatians, 1, 4, 41, 43, 44
Garnsey, Peter, 48, 52–53
Genette, Gérard, 20, 21–23, 25
  Narrative Discourse, 21, 22
Gentiles, 77, 85–86, 95–96
  audience, 97
  exclusion of, 95
  name changes, 85
  new people of God and, 92
gentilism, 135
Gignac, Alain, 85, 87
Golden Ass (Apuleius), 55
Goldingay, John, 124
Gorman, Michael J., 71, 129
  Apostle of the Crucified Lord, 72n2
Greco-Roman worldview
  brotherhood in, 96–97
  slavery in, 77, 78
Griffin, Martin, 25, 75
Grotius, Hugo, 11, 13

Halakhah deals, 105n6
Hanson, John H., 142
Hays, Richard B., 41, 42
  The Moral Vision of the New Testament, 109–10
Heidegger, Martin, 26, 107
Heil, John Paul, 90
Herman, David, 20
Heschel, Rabbi Abraham Joshua, 105n6
Hess, Remi, 28–29
Ho, Alex, 108
Holy Spirit, 5, 85, 115
household church, 80, 81, 98, 116–18, 120, 122, 135, 138, 155
Houston, Joshua, 92
Hunt, Peter, 55–56, 60, 62, 63

impulsore chresto, 130
inclusio, 86, 89–91

Jacob, Louis, 95
James, Henry, 20–21
Jameson, Fredric, 33
Jansen, John, 125
Jerome, 1, 2
  interpretation of Letter to Philemon, 4–6
  philological skills of, 5–6
Jesus Christ
  grace and peace from, 92
  as prisoner's master, 85–86, 89–91
  in rhetorical *inclusio*, 89–91
  shared identity in, 93–94
Jews/Jewish, 67, 92, 94–95
  slave legislation, 78–79
  theology, 77
  understanding of slavery, 78–79
John Paul II (Pope), 153
  on family and communion, 161
  Fides et Ratio, 153
  on human dignity, 155–56
  on self-knowledge, 153
Johnson, Mark, 34
Johnson Hodge, Caroline, 97
Judaism, 95, 105n6

Kabila, Joseph, 138, 151
Kabila, Laurent-Désiré, 149–51
Ka Mana, Godefroid, 153, 160
Kamuina Nsapu, 159
Kasavubu, Joseph, 148
Kimpa Vita, 142
kinship language, 93–102
Knox, John, 11
  fugitivus hypothesis, challenged, 15–16
  Philemon among the Letters of Paul, 76
koinōnia, 16, 17, 19, 129, 135, 138
  defined, 123–24
  ethics of, 103, 112, 123–31, 168–71
  exclusionary, 127
  inclusive, 127
  theology of, 103
koinōnia of faith, 131, 155, 170
  Djomo's, 167
  effective, 103, 126, 130, 133, 138, 157, 164, 167, 168
  in Jesus, 122–23, 130

Index

Mukwege's, 168
Paul's prayer for effectiveness, 127
Philemon's, 103, 122–23, 126, 127, 130, 138, 157
koinōnia-space, 44, 45, 53, 134, 158
   as communion of faith, 155
   construction of, 155, 170
   in DRC, 160–65
   as foundation for democracy, 158

Lakoff, George, 34
Lampe, Peter, 12
Laodicea, 76
La production de l'espace (Lefebvre), 28–31
Lefebvre, Henri, 27–30, 73, 76, 79, 169
Leibniz, Gottfried, 34
Leopold II, King, 69, 142–44
Letter to Philemon
   acts outlined by Gorman, 72–73
   Augustine's commentary, 8–10
   Chrysostom's interpretation, 2–4
   conceived space, 76–79
   ethic of *koinōnia* and, 123–31
   formalist narrative theory, 20–24
   historical analysis of, 11–13
   indicative and imperative in, 112–23
   Jerome's interpretation, 4–6
   kinship language, 93–102
   lived space, 79–82
   narrative criticism and, 40–44
   narrative theory, 19–26
   perceived space, 74–76
   personal names and their qualification, 83–89
   pragmatic approach to, 13–19
   pragmatic or contextual narratology, 24–26
   repetition, 89–93
   rhetoric in. *See* rhetoric, in Letter to Philemon
   spatial theory, 26–37
   as story, 71–73
   Theodore of Mopsuestia's interpretation, 7–8
   trialectics of spatiality in, 73–82
lex Fufia Canini, 62

lictor, 63–64
Lightfoot, John Barber, 14
lived space, 79–82
Lohse, Edward, 86
Lola, Nicolas Djomo, 165
Longenecker, Bruce W., 43
Lotman, Jurij, 35
Lumumba, Patrice
   betrayal and assassination, 148
   denunciation of colonialism, 146
   independence speech, 144–46
   on self-knowledge, 154
l'Universite Notre Dame de Tshumbe (UNITSHU), 166
Lutete, Ngongo, 42
Luther, Martin, 10
Lutumba, Joseph, 139

Malula, Joseph, 137
Malu Malu, Apollinaire, 137
manumission, 61–66
   age limits, 62
   frequency of, 61
   legal texts, 62
   owners granted, 63
   as social achievement, 63–64
Marchal, Joseph, 17–18, 99–100, 102
Marguerat, Daniel, 38, 39
Mark as Story: An Introduction to the Narrative of a Gospel (Rhoads and Michie), 39
Marx, Karl, 31
Mashiach, 122
metalepsis, 22
métro-boulot-dodo (subway-work-sleep), 27
Michie, Donald, 39
Mimesis: The Representation of Reality in Western Literature (Auerbach), 38
Mobutu Sese Seko, 137
   authenticity campaign, 148
   coup and dictatorship, 148–49
   on failures of educated elite, 163
   repression and resistance, 149
Monsengwo, Laurent, 137–38
The Moral Vision of the New Testament (Hays), 109–10

Index

Moretti, Frank, 25
Mosengwo, Laurent, 137
Moulin, St., 136
Mukwege, Denis, 165, 167–68
Mukwege Foundation, 167, 168
Munga: une ethique en un milieu africain, Gentilisme et Christianisme (Nyeme), 134
Museveni, Youweri, 154

Narrative Criticism of the New Testament: An Introduction (Resseguie), 40
Narrative Discourse (Genette), 21, 22
natural slavery, 51–52
Ndaywel, Isidore, 147, 163
New Testament and the People of God (Wright), 42
Newton, Isaac, 34
New World slavery, 49, 67–69
Ngoma-Binda, Phambu, 161
Ngongo Lutete, 142
Nietzsche, Friedrich, 26
Nordling, John, 67, 68
Nyeme, Jean Adalbert, 134

obsequium (social respect), 65
Odyssey (Homer), 38
Okitafumba Lokola, Raphael, 166
Okito (heir), 83
On Christian Doctrine (Augustine), 8
Onesimus, 4, 46, 80–82, 127
    as brother, 92–102
    new identity, 130
    spiritual transformation, 90
    usefulness to Philemon, 80–82
Osiek, Carolyn, 130
Ozturk, Ilhan, 162

paidagōgos, 62
Parsons, Michael, 107
Patterson, Orlando, 51, 63, 80
    definition of slavery, 48–49
    on slavery as power relation, 66
Paul (apostle), 46, 67, 79–80, 85–86
    view of slavery, 53
    See also Letter to Philemon

Paul's Narrative Thought World (Witherington), 42
Paulus, Sergius, 85
Paul VI (Pope), 164–65
peace
    Hebrew background in *shalom*, 119
    Pauline use of, 119–20
perceived space, 74–76
Petersen, Norman R., 13, 42, 81
    on narrative analysis, 40
    Rediscovering Paul, 41
Philemon. *See* Letter to Philemon
Philemon among the Letters of Paul (Knox), 76
Philippians, 126, 129
pietas, 95–96
pilleus, 64
Plato, 52
Politics (Aristotle), 51–52
Postmodern Geographies (Soja), 30
Powell, Mark Allan, 40
The Power of Women (Mukwege), 168
Protestant Reformation, 2, 10

qahal (congregation), 114

rape, 151
Rediscovering Paul (Petersen), 13, 41
Resseguie, James L., 40
revivalist churches, 135–36
rhetoric, in Letter to Philemon, 82–102
    kinship language, 93–102
    personal names and their qualification, 83–89
    repetition, 89–93
The Rhetoric of Fiction (Booth), 25
Rhoads, David, 39
Ricoeur, Paul, 24, 25, 41, 42
Roman Empire, 46, 102, 130
    economic reliance on slaves, 48
    manumission in, 61–62
    as slave society, 47–48
Roman slavery, 46–53
    manumission, 61–66
    master-slave relationship, 54–57
    modern forms of dehumanization and, 66–70

Index

natural slavery, 51–52
    resistance and agency, 57–61
    slave labor, 54–57
Romeo and Juliet (Shakespeare), 83
Rubenstein, Mary Jane, 34
rustici, 54
Rwanda
    claims on Kivu, 151
    intervention in Congo, 149–52

Sabinus, Calvinus, 68
Said, Edward, 31
Saint Moulin, Léon de, 134–36
Sampley, J. Paul, 104–5
sanctification, 108, 109
Schussler Fiorenza, Elisabeth, 133
Scramble for Africa, 36–37
Serapias, Aurelius, 59
shalom, 119
slavery, 49–50, 77–78, 130–31, 152
    Atlantic trade, 141–42
    Belgian continuation of exploitation, 144–46
    Congo Free State and, 143
    definition, 48
    dehumanizing evil of, 131
    kinless, 48
    labor, 54–57
    natural, 51–52
    New World, 49, 67–69
    Roman (*See* Roman slavery)
    violence and, 67
Slavery and Social Death (Patterson), 51
Slavery and Society at Rome (Bradley), 47, 55
Sleeman, Matthew, 32
Soards, Marion, 90
Soja, Edward, 30–33, 73, 79, 169
    Postmodern Geographies, 30
    Thirdspace, 30–32
space, 25–37
    conceived, 76–79
    emotional, 37
    koinōnia-space. See *koinōnia*-space
    Lefebvre's multidimensional approach, 30–31
    Lefebvre's triplicity of, 29

    lived, 79–82
    narrative, 35
    perceived, 74–76
Spartacus, 58
Spivak, Gayatri, 31
Standard Cross-Cultural Sample, 48–49
Stoicism, 52–53
Story and Discourse (Chatman), 23
Syrians, 67

Theodore of Mopsuestia, 1, 7–8
theology, 104–12
    Christian, 53
    coherent structure of, 104–12
    of conversion and inclusion, 95–96
    Jewish, 77–78
    motif in Philemon, 118–21
Theology and Ethics in Paul (Furnish), 107, 113
thirdspace, 19, 98
Thirdspace (Soja), 31–32
Timothy, 79, 86–87, 88, 91, 94
Todorov, Tzvetan, 20
Trefon, Theodore, 135
Treggiari, Susan, 66
trialectics of spatiality in, 73–82
Truth and Method (Gadamer), 132
Tshisekedi, Félix, 147, 151
Turner, Thomas, 143
Tychicus, 76

Uganda, 149–52, 154
United Nations Children's Fund (UNICEF), 162
UNITSHU. *See* l'Universite Notre Dame de Tshumbe
urbani, 54
uti, 8

Van Dyke, Robert, 16–17
Van Reybrouck, David, 141–42, 143, 150, 151
Verboven, Koenraad, 66
vernae, 49–50
voluntarium, 6
vorgeschichte, 12
Vulgate, 4, 6

Index

Wall, Robert W., 85
Walo, Rebecca, 166
wanted poster, 60
Weissenrieder, Annette, 117–18
West, Cornel, 31
West, Gerald O., 132–33

Westermann, William, 67
What Is Narrative Criticism? (Powell), 40
Wirkungsgeschichte (reception history), 17
Witherington, Ben, III, 13–14, 40, 42
Wright, N. T., 14, 42, 104

www.ingramcontent.com/pod-product-compliance
Lightning Source LLC
Chambersburg PA
CBHW031359230426
43670CB00006B/594